Measuring Sustainable Development and Green Investments in Contemporary Economies

Mihai Mieila
Valahia University of Târgoviște, Romania

A volume in the Advances in Finance, Accounting, and Economics (AFAE) Book Series

IGI Global
DISSEMINATOR OF KNOWLEDGE

www.igi-global.com

Published in the United States of America by
IGI Global
Business Science Reference (an imprint of IGI Global)
701 E. Chocolate Avenue
Hershey PA 17033
Tel: 717-533-8845
Fax: 717-533-8661
E-mail: cust@igi-global.com
Web site: http://www.igi-global.com

Library of Congress Cataloging-in-Publication Data

Names: Mieila, Mihai, 1975- editor.
Title: Measuring sustainable development and green investments in contemporary economies / Mihai Mieila, editor.
Description: Hershey : Business Science Reference, [2017]
Identifiers: LCCN 2016053743| ISBN 9781522520818 (hardcover) | ISBN 9781522520825 (ebook)
Subjects: LCSH: Sustainable development. | Economic development--Environmental aspects. | Microfinance.
Classification: LCC HC79.E5 M426 2017 | DDC 338.9/27--dc23 LC record available at https://lccn.loc.gov/2016053743

This book is published in the IGI Global book series Advances in Finance, Accounting, and Economics (AFAE) (ISSN: 2327-5677; eISSN: 2327-5685)

British Cataloguing in Publication Data
A Cataloguing in Publication record for this book is available from the British Library.

Advances in Finance, Accounting, and Economics (AFAE) Book Series

ISSN:2327-5677
EISSN:2327-5685

Mission

In our changing economic and business environment, it is important to consider the financial changes occurring internationally as well as within individual organizations and business environments. Understanding these changes as well as the factors that influence them is crucial in preparing for our financial future and ensuring economic sustainability and growth.

The **Advances in Finance, Accounting, and Economics (AFAE)** book series aims to publish comprehensive and informative titles in all areas of economics and economic theory, finance, and accounting to assist in advancing the available knowledge and providing for further research development in these dynamic fields.

Coverage

- Economic Theory
- Internet Banking
- International Economics
- Economics of Innovation and Knowledge
- Fiscal Policy
- Finance
- Applied Accounting
- E-Accounting
- Public Finance
- Bankruptcy

The Advances in Finance, Accounting, and Economics (AFAE) Book Series (ISSN 2327-5677) is published by IGI Global, 701 E. Chocolate Avenue, Hershey, PA 17033-1240, USA, www.igi-global.com. This series is composed of titles available for purchase individually; each title is edited to be contextually exclusive from any other title within the series. For pricing and ordering information please visit http://www.igi-global.com/book-series/advances-finance-accounting-economics/73685. Postmaster: Send all address changes to above address.

Titles in this Series

For a list of additional titles in this series, please visit: www.igi-global.com

Applied Behavioral Economics Research and Trends
Rodica Ianole (University of Bucharest, Romania)
Business Science Reference • copyright 2017 • 255pp • H/C (ISBN: 9781522518266) • US $160.00 (our price)

Value Relevance of Accounting Information in Capital Markets
Marianne Ojo (George Mason University, USA) and Jeanette Van Akkeren (QUT School of Accountancy, Australia)
Business Science Reference • copyright 2017 • 323pp • H/C (ISBN: 9781522519003) • US $205.00 (our price)

Handbook of Research on the EU's Role and Representation in the G20 Political and Economic Climate
Abdulkadir Isik (Namik Kemal University, Turkey)
Business Science Reference • copyright 2017 • 429pp • H/C (ISBN: 9781522508564) • US $310.00 (our price)

Examining the Role of National Promotional Banks in the European Economy Emerging Research and Opportunities
Iustina Alina Boitan (Bucharest University of Economic Studies, Romania)
Business Science Reference • copyright 2017 • 184pp • H/C (ISBN: 9781522518457) • US $120.00 (our price)

Tools and Techniques for Economic Decision Analysis
Jelena Stanković (University of Niš, Serbia) Pavlos Delias (Eastern Macedonia and Thrace Institute of Technology, Greece) Srđan Marinković (University of Niš, Serbia) and Sylvie Rochhia (Université Côte d'Azur, CNRS, GREDEG, France)
Business Science Reference • copyright 2017 • 305pp • H/C (ISBN: 9781522509592) • US $205.00 (our price)

Corporate Espionage, Geopolitics, and Diplomacy Issues in International Business
Bryan Christiansen (PryMarke, LLC, USA) and Fatmanur Kasarcı (PryMarke Business Academy, Turkey)
Business Science Reference • copyright 2017 • 374pp • H/C (ISBN: 9781522510314) • US $210.00 (our price)

Table of Contents

Detailed Table of Contents

A vital issue that must be considered by all functional areas in recent times is green safety and sustainable ecological balance. To be part of this environment-friendly investment, even the banking sectors of the most environmentally affected countries in the world invest voluntarily in social and environmental activities that targets socially-responsive business and ethics in the form of green banking. Green banking mainly involves the environmental and social responsibility of banks in terms of the contribution they make towards ensuring sustainability of the environment and ecological system, through the wide range of financial products and services that they offer. This chapter will primarily focus on the present status of the banks in complying with the green banking policy to save the environment as well as to increase financial sustainability from the perspective of a developing country like Bangladesh.

The appearance of the concept of sustainable development, although a sort of universal remedy at its beginnings, is becoming increasingly frequently the object of tensions both as objectives but especially as content. Regarding its objectives, the debate is organized around a logic based on the theory of the stakeholders but also on the competing logic that mobilizes an ethics of responsibility as teleological principle. Consequently, the meanings and implicitly the programmes of sustainable development are also the object of certain controversies and remain susceptible of being solved by a process of normalization of their contents. However, this dynamics of normalization itself is the bearer of certain "perverse effects", already noticed in the accountancy standards domain and, under these circumstances, this dynamics of normalization cannot pretend to be the solution for regulating these controversies. The problem are mainly the weak doctrinal points characterizing Sustainable Development today, obviously, by comparison to what it wanted to be.

Microfinance institutions have been effective rural banking channels that extended financial services to low-income individuals, particularly women in developing country settings. Since its inception, microfinance has evolved as an economic development approach and has grown to enormous scale in Bangladesh, with a reported approximate 23 million borrowers in a country of roughly 150 million people. These numbers reveal the highest population saturation of microfinance in any country. However, with the maturity of the microfinance market in recent years, competition has subsequently increased among various financial and non-financial institutions. Against this backdrop of intense competition, this chapter aims to focus on the current institutions of Bangladesh that has made the microfinance service almost a sole option for the downtrodden segment of the low-income society. In particular, various approaches of microfinance and its operational structure by these institutions including the challenges and attributions of a dynamic micro credit concept will be highlighted.

This chapter aimed to investigate green performance strategies in the Romanian economy. In the first part, authors exposed specific definitions and concepts related to the green economy, as they appear in the literature in the field. The European context and the main ways of implementation of the green economy are presented as they result from the objectives of The Agenda 2020 UE and The Agenda 2030 UNO. Green Performance in Romania during 2010-2014 is assessed by analyzing the environmental protection expenditures, environmental taxes, greenhouse gasses emissions, green jobs roles, and Environmental Performance Index. The sustainable economic growth effects are materializing in a major growth of the ecological productivity, an increased amount of energy derived from renewable sources, emissions reduction, improved air and water quality, widened access to the benefits of civilization - education, water sanitation. Thus, this green growth "can fight" against climate change. Also, green growth provides opportunities for creating new jobs requiring new skills.

Nearly 250 million years ago, the Earth was shaken by the amplest extinction known so far, which led to the extinction of up to 96% of all the marine species, 70% of the vertebrate species, and almost all the insects. This extinction affected the whole range of biodiversity so much. Nature took almost 10 million years to recover after this event. Life was really in danger on our planet at that moment, due to the dismal conditions that were created, and the current research shows that these dire conditions continued to occur, in the natural environment, after that, triggering numerous outbreaks that occurred for five to six million years following the initial crisis, triggered by the carbon rise and the repeated shortages of oxygen, the increased warming and other such adverse effects, which, once initiated, were uncontrollable and had disastrous effects. When life returned to normal and, gradually, after several million years, a new beginning was possible, the significant elements that caused the disaster - global warming, acid rain - sound strangely familiar to us today.

We have presented the forest as an ecosystem, the socio-economic development of the forest ecosystems in the rural area and the sustainable management of the forest as an ecosystem. The debate on the public assets of the forests and on climate change will nourish the discussions related to the future form of the Common Agricultural Policy at a moment when the European Union is preparing its new forest strategy. A new sustainable rural development policy will need to rely on a strong will, based on the support of the States for the most disinherited rural areas in point of location, accessibility, economic development and services for the population. "The rural world" represents an opportunity for our country (until 2020); we only need to want to take advantage of these resources for a more sustainable development.

Green investments are the perfect tool to generate complex self-regenerating systems in order to achieve a sustainable development. Even if the burden of transition from high polluting economy to a green economy is high, the cost should be split among all that have interest in achieving this goal. The switch to green is an international current that will ultimately force the change if it is not made willingly. All parties have an interest to promote change before the change gets them on the wrong foot. In this regard, the chapter aims to emphasizing the potential benefits of the transition to a green economy in terms of reducing poverty, enhancing food security, nutrition and health on a sustainable basis while promoting ecosystem stability. Thus, increased green investments throughout the food system are imperatively needed so that changing the way food is obtained could become a powerful force for sustainable development.

This chapter discusses sustainable development (SD) planning in manufacturing facilities. The industrial sector uses half of the world's energy, and manufacturing, as the core of this sector, contributes significantly to energy consumption and environmental footprints. In this chapter, in the first step, energy consumption, as one of the main factors influencing SD in manufacturing, is analyzed from different perspectives, and its impact on SD is studied. Thereafter, several energy-aware operations management approaches are proposed. These approaches integrate energy consumption into classic production planning and scheduling decisions. In the second step, a generic sustainability-based decision-making framework is proposed for maintenance strategy selection problem, considering three pillars of sustainability. For this purpose, various indicators are proposed for each sustainability factor that has an impact on maintenance planning decisions. The maintenance strategy alternatives are evaluated for each indicator and the best alternative is selected using a decision-making method.

Preface

Measuring green economics and investments represents a major topic in analyzing the current economic evolution, taking into account that this relies on a specific generation of economic development pattern. Such a research subject is developed and determinant by numerous factors, including governments and entrepreneurs which use production factors in order to achieve competitive advantage in competitive markets. The problems still remain: How is green economic development measured? How should an economy be considered "green"?

The international economy is in a massive change and it is booming. Over the last period numerous specialists have developed some popular alternative in understanding green economics but less telling how it should be measured. However, the research on measuring green economics and investments has to represent a major initiative, in order to take into account the wider economic and social contexts within they operate in the society. The book addresses the specific subject of measuring green economics and is intended to bring answers to such concerns.

This book project aims to fulfill some major aspects regarding the measuring of sustainable economics and investments taking into consideration the current status of world development. Measuring the green economics and investments is a quite difficult task considering that practices differ in various countries and continents.

The need for a book with the main research topic measuring the green economics is quite major, taking into consideration the recent evolutions in the field. The book will present some of the most controversial aspects in measuring green economics and investments being at the same time a basic work this domain. Also there will be developed some of the newest approaches regarding the measuring green economics practices, as specific tools in understanding the current evolution of society.

As a short definition of the subject area, the main subject addresses a very contemporary aspect as the green economies and investments measurement represents actual paradigms in defining a functional pattern towards development.

The main aims of the book will be addressed to the research areas concerning the measuring of sustainable development, structural investments and the economic structures in the global economies. Thus, among the book chapters' topics are intended but not limited to the following aspects:

- Green economic structures,
- Economic paradigms,
- Business management strategies,
- Business econometrics,
- Investments models and paradigms,
- Green investments strategies and approaches,
- Business modeling,
- Investments patterns and econometrics,
- Consumptions patterns.

The general objective of the book is to extend the research area concerning the measuring of sustainable development by adding new perspectives in the field, by taking into consideration the newest trends and practical approaches. Also the intention is to design a competitive framework, both theoretical and practical by mobilizing contributors with highly expertise regarding the subject of measuring of sustainable development and green investments. The special objectives desired for the book are mainly referred to:

- To create a reference piece for academia, practitioners, students, and other institutions regarding the subject of measuring of sustainable development and green investments;
- To highlight the newest findings in the field;
- To design a research publishing project for dissemination the research information to a larger audience;
- To provide both a theoretical and practical research framework.

The book is intended to become a reference in field of measuring of sustainable development and green investments taking into consideration the experience and the expected contributors to this book project.

The book is addressed to a wide range of public, starting with professionals and researchers working in the field of measuring sustainable development and green investments, continuing with professors, students and academia members and not last, to the practitioners and governmental authorities. Since the contributions contain theoretical aspects and numerous study cases, the target audience is intended to be quite large. The book will address to measuring sustainable development and green investments aspects which represents a hot point for developing countries and economies in transition.

The results will be shared through the international network of research institutions, universities, academia and researches in spheres as: green economics and investments, green development strategies, economic models and patterns, and business theory. The book is planned to be developed as a reference and support in understanding and teaching aspects concerning the measurement of sustainable development and green investments.

I hope this book will provide useful insights regarding the measuring of sustainable development and green investments in contemporary economies.

Mihai Mieila
Valahia University of Târgoviște, Romania

Chapter 1
Green Investments and Returns:
A Developing Country Perspective

Nabila Nisha
North South University, Bangladesh

ABSTRACT

A vital issue that must be considered by all functional areas in recent times is green safety and sustainable ecological balance. To be part of this environment-friendly investment, even the banking sectors of the most environmentally affected countries in the world invest voluntarily in social and environmental activities that targets socially-responsive business and ethics in the form of green banking. Green banking mainly involves the environmental and social responsibility of banks in terms of the contribution they make towards ensuring sustainability of the environment and ecological system, through the wide range of financial products and services that they offer. This chapter will primarily focus on the present status of the banks in complying with the green banking policy to save the environment as well as to increase financial sustainability from the perspective of a developing country like Bangladesh.

DOI: 10.4018/978-1-5225-2081-8.ch001

INTRODUCTION

Global warming or the 'Green House Effect' has made many organizations environmentally conscious. As a result, green investments today are at the forefront of a significant number of business operations across the world. Green investments generally call for companies to finance green technology and pollution reducing projects that can lessen the impact of their operations on the environment, thereby leading towards an overall sustainability. In line with this global development and as a response to environmental degradation, financial sectors of many developed and developing countries have adopted green banking policies to address this issue of sustainable business practices. Green banking involves the environmental and social responsibility of banks in terms of the contribution they make towards ensuring sustainability of the environment and ecological system, through their in-house operations and the wide range of financial products and services that they offer. This chapter sheds some light into the present status of the banks in complying with the green banking policy to save the environment as well as to increase financial sustainability from the perspective of a developing country. To pursue this purpose, conceptual research models and a survey questionnaire based on the models were developed to study the general perception of bankers regarding environmental safety and the concept of green banking, along with the current range of green products and services being offered in Bangladesh. Responses from the survey were also used to examine bankers' attitude towards the adoption of green banking initiatives in a developing country like Bangladesh. Findings of this chapter will provide further insights into understanding the environmental responsibility and the environmental performance through the perception and attitude of bankers. Moreover, this study can assist various commercial banks to take into account varied perspectives of bankers while considering the idea of investing in green banking or other forms of green investments in order to aid the sustainable development of all financial products and services in Bangladesh.

BACKGROUND

In recent years, the eminent problem of global warming has finally shifted the attention of business practices of all functional areas to climate change, resource efficiency and environmentally conscious issues. As such, initiatives related to green safety and sustainable ecological balance is growing in support. To be part of this environment-friendly investment, most of the companies today focus more upon socially-responsible approaches rather than the traditional profit maximization (The Financial Express, 15 July, 2015). In other words, business practices has moved away from the 'profit, profit and profit' motive to the objective of 'planet, people and profit'. A recent report by OECD claimed such socially-responsible approaches as green investments or investments that are broadly related to the sustainability of the environment (Inderst, Kaminker & Stewart, 2012).

Green investments can be made by companies to their underlying technology, projects or ventures as well as their financial products and services (Croce, Kaminker & Stewart, 2011). For instance, any investments in renewable energy, recycling and waste management, water management, energy efficiency or environmental technologies are various ways of appearing 'green' in the market (The Daily Observer, May 26, 2015). Besides, going paperless to save the environment is another approach to define 'greenness' for specific goods and services.

Although green investments are a global initiative, these eco-friendly policies play a special role particularly for those developing countries which are more vulnerable to climate changes and where natural calamities are a common phenomenon (The Financial Express, 29 July, 2013). One such example is that of Bangladesh, which is a low carbon emitting country and has historically suffered huge losses due to changes in climate patterns. As a result of these adverse effects and to initiate a progressive step worldwide, the central bank of the country, Bangladesh Bank, has shown a profound commitment towards the vision of green investments and has opted towards congenial business operations that are sustainable towards the environment (Ahmad, Zayed & Harun, 2013). Prominent examples of green investments in Bangladesh include the use of natural non-toxic materials and recycled wastes in the ceramics sector; environment-friendly buildings and land projects using the highest standards of green technology, effective wastage management and efficient energy systems, organic compounds for building materials, and eco-friendly paints by the real estate sector; tree planting initiatives, the use of renewable energy and installation of eco-friendly solar panels, introduction of environment-friendly public transports, etc (The Financial Express, 1 August, 2015). Moreover, Bangladesh Bank is also going to commence a new Export Development Fund worth about US$ 500 million to support environment-friendly industrial and development projects in the country, as a global response to save the environment (The Financial Express, 15 February, 2015).

Environmental degradation has become such a pressing issue today that even the financial sectors need to address this universal issue. This is because financial institutions, particularly banks, play a vital role in the economic system of a country and generally affects all types of business practices through their financing activities. Thus, banks should contribute to the saving of the environment by considering environmental aspects as part of their lending and investing principles, which would then divert industries to invest in environmental management and the use of appropriate green technologies (Masukujjaman & Aktar, 2013). In fact, banks these days are quite pro-active in terms of green investments on the global front. Adoption of eco-friendly banking practices and in-house operations, broadly known as green banking, is a prime example of green investments by the banking sector (The Daily Observer, May 26, 2015).

Green banking mainly focuses on two aspects: green revolution of internal operations through the consumption of renewable energy, digitalization and other measures that can reduce the emission of carbon mark from the banking activities and the use of environment-friendly financing like sustainable banking, ethical banking, green mortgages, green loans, green credit cards, mobile banking, online banking, etc. (Inderst et al., 2012). Adoption of such green banking initiatives can be found in many developed economies across the world. For example, HSBC has developed cheaper air and road travel incentives as a green choice for environmentalists and this has been aimed at saving paper by receiving no paper statements and doing no paper marketing. The UK Green Investment Bank, on the other hand, finances green projects on commercial terms and helps fund the creation of new energy and waste infrastructure across the country, thereby reducing a substantial amount of greenhouse gas emissions (Hossain, Ahmed & Nisha, 2015). Hang Seng Bank from Hong Kong introduced an integrated system that reduces the use of papers to save the environment and provides a comprehensive range of banking and general insurance products and services that can be availed either through mobiles or internet. Additionally, banks worldwide use energy-wise Green Machines, which source power from clean, emission-free methods such as wind power and invests hugely for local environment and wildlife projects in their community (Hossain et al., 2015). Even the introduction of green channel counters and green finance portfolios by the State Bank of India and Bank of Indonesia are different forms of green banking initiatives that can be observed from the global front.

The banking sector of Bangladesh is also equally contributing to green investments and has successfully adopted various forms of green banking policies that is being applied by the central bank as well as the leading commercial banks of the country. It thus becomes important to gain insights into the green banking activities that is being adopted in Bangladesh both for in-house operations and financing activities of the banks. In particular, outlooks of bankers with regard to such initiatives of green investments by the financial sector need to be examined in order to understand and assess their social responsiveness in the context of Bangladesh.

ISSUES, CONTROVERSIES AND PROBLEMS

The banking industry is an integral component of the financial system of Bangladesh and plays a crucial role in the economic development of the country. Over the last 30 years, there has been a steady growth in this sector, as several private and foreign banks entered the country and led to the development of the country's financial architecture. Currently, this industry consists of four state-owned banks, four specialized banks, thirty-one private commercial banks, eight Islami Shariah based private commercial banks, and nine foreign commercial banks (Hossain et al., 2015). All these scheduled banks are solely monitored and regulated by the central bank of the country - Bangladesh Bank, which formulates and implements policies and guidelines related to various financing and banking issues.

One such guideline issued by Bangladesh Bank during 2011 is related to environmental risk management and green banking. The guidelines of this Green Banking Policy aimed to ensure environment-friendly business practices by banks and financial institutions by incorporating environmental risks into Core Risk Management (CRM), thereby promoting sustainable financial and economic growth across the entire country. This step by Bangladesh Bank is a profound commitment towards the vision of green world through green initiatives in Bangladesh. In fact, it is probably the only central bank which has issued such an indicative guideline for green banking in the South-Asian continent.

Under this Green Banking Policy, Bangladesh Bank initially selected ten commercial banks in Bangladesh for implementing green banking practices on the basis of their CAMELS rating and Risk Based Capital Adequacy (RBCA) measurement (The Daily Observer, May 26, 2015). The central bank authority then instructed these banks to consider the following major activities under green banking: Green Banking Unit, Green Banking Policy, Green Banking Budget, Online banking, Mobile and Internet banking, Allotment of funds in green financing and Environment risk rating. Over time, all the scheduled banks of Bangladesh initiated their own Green Banking Policy Guidelines approved by their respective Board of Directors as well as have Green Banking Unit (GBU) for pursuing Green Banking activities. They even have their own Green Office Guide for conducting various in-house green activities today. For instance, a glance at the current major green house activities of banks in Bangladesh reveal the use of

e-statement for customers instead of paper statement, making online communications, using more daylight instead of electric lights or using energy saving bulbs such as LED lights, video/audio conferencing instead of physical travel, sharing electronic files, voice mail, and e-mail instead of paper memos, using papers on both sides, common use of table stationeries instead of individual use and efficient use of printer cartridges, photocopy toner, office stationary, etc. Additionally, Bangladesh Bank introduced a number of refinance lending for renewable energy generation, effluent treatment plants and energy efficient kilns for manufacturing bricks. A revolving refinancing fund has also been placed in the areas of solar irrigation pumps, solar home systems, biogas plants, effluent treatment plants, brick kiln and solar photo voltaic module assembling plants, etc – with the sole aim of promoting green investments in Bangladesh.

However, amidst all these green investments and green banking developments in the country, banks have been facing major challenges in the implementation of this Green Banking Policy. The foremost challenge has essentially been the 'mandated' implementation of green banking initiatives by the banks. Since it has been made mandatory by the central bank, despite having inhibitions about it, all scheduled banks of Bangladesh had to implement various methods of green banking within their operational structures for both their banking transactions and in-house activities. The lack of the option of voluntariness in this regard has met with certain resistance from the top management as well as the operational staff of the banks. Change in the working environment and the alternate provision of banking services under green banking resulted in problems like coordination among all concerned authorities for green banking, proper awareness and effective implementation, immediate concentration on lending policies and procedures of the banking sector, high costs of implementation, conflict among management and bankers, etc. As such, it becomes imperative to examine the thought process of bankers towards the concept and implementation of the Green Banking Policy, since they are the ones who are at the forefront of execution of the green banking initiatives in the banking sector.

With regard to green banking, a limited number of studies have been conducted in the context of Bangladesh. For instance, Masukujjaman and Aktar (2013) highlighted the green banking road map in Bangladesh, the status of its implementation and also explored the activities of commercial banks in comparison with global green banking initiatives. The study concluded that Bangladesh is far behind their counterparts from the developed countries, but as of now, most of the banks are in a transition to green banking in the country. Ullah (2013) then conducted a comparative analysis among different types of banks operating in Bangladesh and tried to conclude whether the banks have properly adopted the Green Banking Policy guided by the Bangladesh Bank. Findings by Ullah (2013) claimed that only public and foreign commercial banks have invested in green banking projects whereas the initiatives of state-owned commercial banks or state-owned specialized development banks are nothing remarkable to be reported. Next, Ahmad et al. (2013) explored the green banking activities of all commercial banks in Bangladesh and attempted to determine the reasons behind adopting green banking from the perspective of bank employees. Six factors namely economic factor, policy guideline, loan demand, stakeholder pressure, environmental interest and legal factor were found to be the major influencers regarding the adoption of green banking by the commercial banks. Shakil, Azam and Raju (2014) also did an evaluation of green banking practices among the scheduled banks of Bangladesh and found that while some banks has taken certain green banking initiatives, there are still a good number of banks which are in the first phase of the Green Banking policy guideline set by Bangladesh Bank. Findings by Shakil et al. (2014) further stated that it is due to large initial cost and lack of governmental and technical support, that green banking practices is not implemented on a large scale in Bangladesh.

Furthermore, there are a number of local studies which were conducted related to various aspects of green banking practices in Bangladesh. While Masum (2015) highlighted the need for green banking in Bangladesh, Hossain and Ahmed (2015) outlined the phases of implementation under the Green Banking Policy guidelines set by the Bangladesh Bank. Next, Hossain et al. (2015) explored consumer attitudes and perceptions towards green banking in Bangladesh and Hossain, Rahim & Hussain (2015) analyzed the future of green banking for the country. With respect to promoting a greener economy, studies by Nisha, Idrish & Hossain (2015) did an empirical analysis to understand the factors behind consumer acceptance and use of mobile banking services in Bangladesh. In addition, Hossain, Jilani & Haque (2015) evaluated the option of Islamic finance as a greener alternative for the banking sector of Bangladesh. Overall, if a conclusion is drawn from these past studies, it can be observed that only one significant research of Ahmad et al. (2013) considered the perspective of bank employees towards the concept of green banking. In view of everything, this is a crucial aspect that needs to be further studied.

As such, this study focuses on the examination of the perception of bankers towards environmental issues and green investments, thereby highlighting their attitude for green banking initiatives, its products and services and the future potential of such practices in the context of Bangladesh. The method of Structural Equation Modeling (SEM) was mainly applied to investigate the underlying relationships related to the perceptions and attitudes of bankers towards green banking practices in the country. SEM has the ability to isolate observational error from measurement of latent variables like the proposed constructs in this study. Thus, the use of SEM for evaluating the perceptions and attitudes of bank employees is the unique contribution of this chapter, since to the best of the author's knowledge SEM has not been used for any green banking research in the context of the bankers in Bangladesh.

RESEARCH MODEL AND HYPOTHESES

This chapter seeks to explore the extent to which bankers' perceptions about the environment, particularly the environment of Bangladesh, as well as their general perception about green investments influence their attitudes towards green banking approaches. Moreover, this research claims that the attitude of bankers will ultimately shape their reasons for using green banking and its related products and services and will also determine the future potential of such green banking initiatives from the bankers' perspectives.

In order to quantify these relationships, two research models were developed. The first model explored the relationship of factors such as bankers' general perceptions of environment and green investments with their attitude towards various forms of green banking initiatives currently being undertaken in Bangladesh. The second proposed model, on the other hand, investigated the extent to which the bankers' attitude towards green banking influenced their reasons for using green banking, its related products and services as well as their perceptions about the future potential of green banking approaches in Bangladesh.

Next, a three-part methodology was utilized to understand these relationships conceptualized in the two research models. This methodology consisted of a survey instrument development, an Exploratory Factor Analysis (EFA), a Confirmatory Factor Analysis (CFA) and Structural Equation Modeling (SEM) to further confirm correlations and inferred causal relationships among the factors of the two models. Surveys were conducted using focus groups and walk-through assessments of selected commercial banks from where the bankers' perspectives were obtained. Once the survey instruments were created, industry experts like bank officials and managers were requested to review the questionnaire before the survey data were collected in person.

The responses from the questionnaires were then analyzed using SPSS Statistics Base and through their descriptive statistics, outliers were identified that might have resulted from possible data entry errors. The survey data was split into two parts following the outlier identification and an exploratory factor analysis was run on one dataset to determine the underlying factor structures. Finally, using the results of the exploratory factor analysis, the user-friendly interface of SPSS Amos was used to run a confirmatory factor analysis, using the second dataset to examine the reliability and validity of the measurement models without identifying the directional relationship among the factors. The two hypothesized models were then drawn to examine the underlying directional relationships among bankers' perception and attitude towards the green banking activities of the Bangladesh banking sector. See Figure 1 and Figure 2.

The hypothesized models and the proposed hypotheses are given below:

H1: General perception about the environment significantly affects the attitude of bankers towards green banking.

H2: Perception about green investments significantly affects the attitude of bankers towards green banking.

Figure 1. Proposed research structure 1

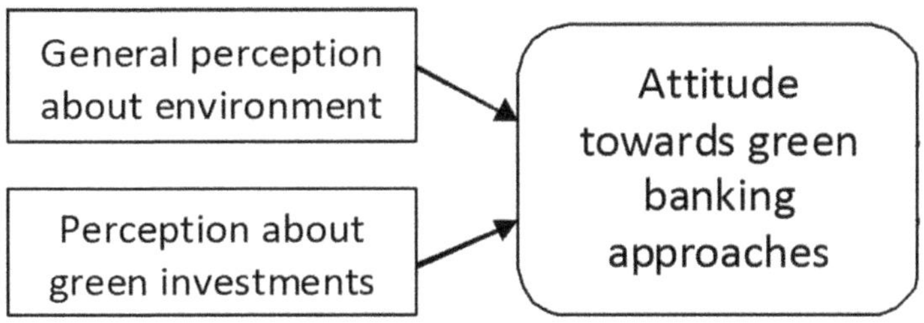

Figure 2. Proposed research structure 2

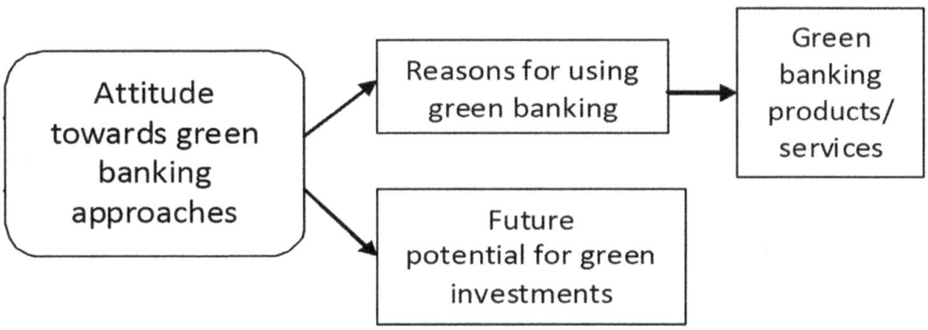

H3: Attitude of bankers towards green banking approaches significantly affects their reasons for using green banking.

H4: Attitude of bankers towards green banking approaches significantly affects the future potential of green banking initiatives.

H5: Reasons by bankers for using green banking significantly affect the concept of green banking products and services.

RESEARCH METHOD

To investigate the two research models, methods and techniques employed for data collection involved a primary research. The primary research involved gathering of data by conducting survey of a representative convenience sample of 800 bankers from selected commercial banks operating in the capital city of Bangladesh - Dhaka. The bank representatives were particularly surveyed and interviewed regarding the green banking initiatives employed by their banks. The survey required developing and circulating questionnaires for the bankers by presenting the information in quantifiable terms, in order to gauge the impact of their perception of environment and green investments upon their attitudes towards green banking initiatives and how this attitude was influencing their reasons for using, offerings and future potential of green banking products and services.

As such, the questionnaire was designed to enable the respondents to rate, on a Likert scale of 1 to 5, the extent to which they are aware of and care about environmental changes, the extent to which they think that the environment of Bangladesh is adversely affected due to climatic changes and whether they believe that Bangladesh needs to take precautionary measures regarding environmental issues in the form of green investments. This questionnaire also sought to find out the respondents' attitude towards green banking initiatives, in terms of their interest and support for such practices, their reasons for using green banking, their perception of future potential of green banking in Bangladesh as well as their perception about the different types of green banking products and services that commercial banks currently operating in Bangladesh offer. After a three-week survey, 733 completed and usable responses were finally obtained from the survey.

The two conceptual research models were then tested using the structural equation modeling (SEM) facilitates of SmartPLS (version 2.0). Through partial least squares (PLS) method, first the measurement models were examined to assess the reliability and validity of all variables and then, the structural models were analyzed to examine the relationships hypothesized in the two research models.

MEASUREMENT MODEL ANALYSIS

Results from the measurement models are presented in Table 1 and Table 2 and it includes information about the reliability, validity, correlations and factor loadings. The composite reliabilities of the constructs ranged between 0.700 and 1.000, which exceeds the 0.7 recommended cut-off values (Nunnally & Bernstein, 1994). The average variance extracted (AVE) was greater than 0.5 in all cases and greater than each square correlations, which indicates that all the three models have both convergent validity and discriminant validity (Fornell & Larcker, 1981). Moreover, the internal consistency reliabilities (ICRs) of multi-item scales modeled with reflective indicators was 0.75 or greater, suggesting adequate reliability. The pattern of loadings and cross-loadings also supported internal consistency and discriminant validity, with some exceptions: two items from each construct of general perception about environment and perception about green investments from research model 1; and, one item from each construct of reasons for using green banking and future potential

Table 1. Factor loadings, composite reliability and AVEs

Research Model 1				
Constructs	**Items**	**Factor Loadings**	**Composite Reliability**	**AVE**
General perception about environment (GEP)	GLOBWAR	0.865	0.899	0.786
	CLIMCHANGE	0.836		
	ENVCARE	0.700		
	ENVSUST	0.848		
	BDENVVUL	0.924		
	BDCALAMITY	1.000		
Perception about green investments (PGI)	GIAWARE	0.700	0.707	0.608
	GITYPES	0.714		
Attitude of bankers towards green banking (AGB)	GBACT	0.903	0.829	0.695
	SPREADGB	0.758		
	GBMANDATES	0.882		
Research Model 2				
Constructs	**Items**	**Factor Loadings**	**Composite Reliability**	**AVE**
Attitude of bankers towards green banking (AGB)	GBACT	0.865	0.825	0.706
	SPREADGB	0.809		
	GBMANDATES	0.789		
Reasons for using green banking (RGB)	SOCIALRES	0.782	0.778	0.699
	ENVCON	0.814		
	RISKMIN	0.674		
	IMAGEIMPRO	0.733		
	GOVPRE	0.609		
	STKPRE	0.887		
	CBPRE	0.846		
	SUSTDEVRES	0.753		
Future potential for green banking initiatives (FP)	GBFUTUREOV	0.767	0.804	0.673
	GBINFUTURE	0.870		
	GBPOLDEV	0.740		

continued on following page

Table 1. Continued

Research Model 1				
Constructs	**Items**	**Factor Loadings**	**Composite Reliability**	**AVE**
Green banking products/ services (GBP)	EBSERVICE	0.845	0.754	0.607
	MOBBSERV	0.706		
	OFFAUTO	0.772	0.829	0.709
	ECOMM	0.908		
	PLESSTRANS	0.810	0.808	0.784
	GFINPROJ	0.767		
	GENSOURCE	0.713		

Table 1 Notes

1. GLOBWAR (global warming), CLIMCHANGE (climate changes), ENVCARE (environmental care), ENVSUST (environmental sustainability), BDENVVUL (Bangladesh environmental vulnerability), BDCALAMITY (Bangladesh natural calamities).
2. GIAWARE (green investments awareness), GITYPES (types of green investments).
3. GBACT (green banking act), SPREADGB (spread of green banking initiatives), GBMANDATES (mandates for green banking policy).
4. SOCIALRES (social responsibility), ENVCON (conservation of environment), RISKMIN (risk minimization), IMAGEIMPRO (improve industry image), GOVPRE (pressure from the government), STKPRE (pressure from the stakeholders like customers or employees), CBPRE (pressure from the central bank), SUSTDEVRES (sustainable development of resources).
5. GBFUTUREOV (overall future for green banking), GBINFUTURE (future initiatives of green banking), GBPOLDEV (policy developments for green banking).
6. EBSERVICE (electronic banking service), MOBBSERV (mobile banking service), OFFAUTO (office automation), ECOMM (electronic means of communications), PLESSTRANS (paperless transactions), GFINPROJ (green financing projects), GENSOURCE (green energy sources).

Table 2. Measurement models estimations

	ICRs	GEP	PGI	AGB	RGB	FP	GBP
GEP	0.843	**0.866**					
PGI	0.851	0.413	**0.887**				
AGB	0.809	0.354	0.368	**0.836**			
RGB	0.887	0.423	0.338	0.310	**0.734**		
FP	0.894	0.316	0.578	0.244	0.524	**0.847**	
GBP	0.835	0.285	0.033	0.133	0.562	0.441	**0.788**

Table 2 Notes

1. GEP (general perception about environment), PGI (perception about green investments), AGB (attitude of bankers towards green banking), RGB (reasons for using green banking), FP (future potential for green banking initiatives), GBP (green banking products/services).
2. Diagonal elements represent the AVEs, while off-diagonal elements represent the square correlations.

of green banking and two items from green banking products and services under research model 2 were deleted, due to their low loadings and high cross-loadings.

STRUCTURAL MODEL ANALYSIS

The path coefficients and significance levels in the structural models are presented in Figure 3 and Figure 4. The construct of general perception about environment (0.192, $p<0.05$) from research model 1 displayed a significant path towards the attitude of bankers for green banking approaches while the perception of green investments (0.122, $p>0.05$) showed an insignificant path in shaping the attitude of bankers.

On the other hand, the construct of attitude of bankers for green banking approaches in research model 2 reported a significant and positive path towards reasons for using green banking initiatives (0.407, $p<0.05$) and future potential for green banking (0.380, $p<0.05$). However, the same behavioral path was not seen regarding green banking products and services (0.296, $p>0.05$), which were found to be insignificant in the model.

Therefore, all hypotheses with the exception of H2 from research model 1 and H5 from research model 2, are supported. As such, it can be stated that the hypothesized relationships between environment and the attitude of bankers towards green banking, along with the reasons for using green banking and its future potential being shaped by the bankers' attitude have been rightly proved.

Figure 3. Results of structural equation modeling 1

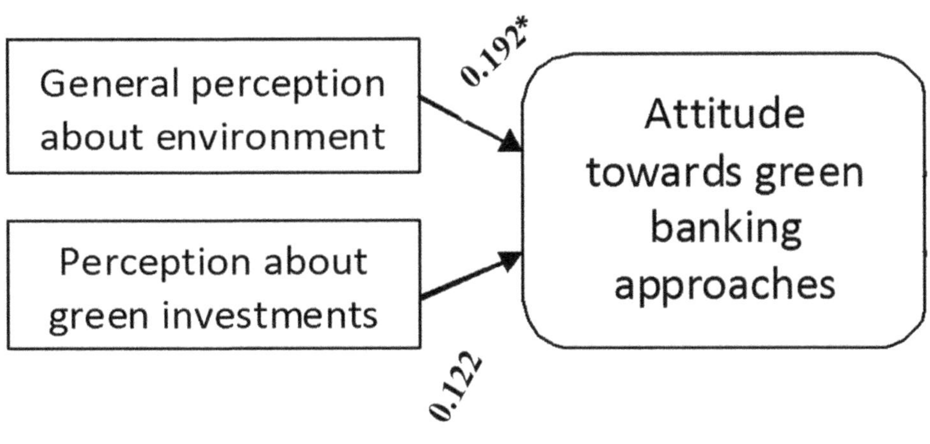

Figure 4. Results of structural equation modeling 2

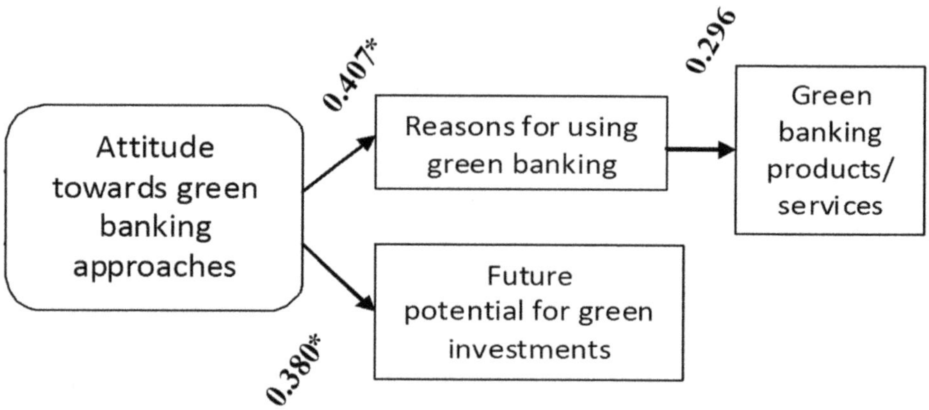

SOLUTIONS AND RECOMMENDATIONS

This study has revealed quite a few understandings towards the perception and attitude of bankers regarding the concept of green banking, its related products and services and its future potential in Bangladesh. Findings of the study show that bankers are quite well-informed about the general conditions of the world environment and they have clear ideas about global warming and the impact that climate changes can have upon the environment. Moreover, a good number of bankers displayed interest and agreement regarding the care and sustainability of the environment that is being promoted today worldwide. Most of the bankers were even found to be aware of the vulnerability of environmental conditions in Bangladesh and how this degradation was inviting natural calamities to the country. As such, it can be deduced from the survey results that bankers in Bangladesh are clearly in favor of saving the environment.

However, most of the bankers did not know that a broad term used to refer to methods of environmental sustainability is actually the green investments. Some of them could identify ways to care for the environment or sustain resources like saving power, gas or water, reduced use of papers or controlling pollution, but a majority of the bankers did not have vivid ideas as to what can be varied ways of green technologies or green investments. As such, the central bank of Bangladesh in association with the government can fund documentaries wherein facts about global warming and different types of green investments can be displayed to create awareness and to educate the bankers as well as the general people of the country. This will help to change the perception of people towards green investments and bankers can get more ideas regarding the use of green financing like green bonds or green asset classes in their institutions. Survey results at this point give an impression that bankers actually opted for the use of green banking as part of their in-house activities and external functions only because the central bank of Bangladesh mandated the use and application of the Green Banking Policy. This implies that although bankers did care for the environment and were interested to sustain resources, they did not have adequate knowledge regarding the overall concept of green investments.

To further analyze the situation and attitude of bankers, the survey then probed onto the reasons as to why bankers accepted the use of green banking in their institutions. Results indicated that a majority of the bankers agreed that green banking techniques were being applied into their institutions to comply with the mandated policy of the central bank. To add more, some bankers feel that rather than being socially responsible or caring for the environment, employment of green banking in some selected banks of Bangladesh is just an act of image resurrection and a result of stakeholder pressure. For instance, some bankers claimed that using green banking helps to attract international customers to the bank to a large extent since being socially responsible is a concern for many of the clients today. Nonetheless, at least green banking techniques are being used and that is a major takeaway for a developing country like Bangladesh. Bankers, however, claimed that the reasons why green banking are being used in their banks did not have anything to do with the products and services that are currently being offered under green banking in the country. For example, survey results reported that electronic communication and office automation have been willingly accepted by bankers as part of in-house green banking approaches. This is because bankers feel such techniques made work life easier and convenient for them and if in the process, it helps to save the environment as well then it is an added advantage for the banking sector. On the other hand, most of the bankers stated that electronic banking, mobile banking or the use of ATMs and credit/debit cards might be methods of green banking but it has been mostly accepted by both customers and the bankers because banking transactions become a lot easier with such services. At this point, it can be deduced that the attitude of bankers towards green banking products and services is quite positive and the reasons for using green banking in their institutions did not define their attitude towards the use of its related products and services.

Moreover, bankers evidently came up with various ideas regarding the future potential of green banking in the banking sector as well as other industries of Bangladesh. For instance, some bankers feel that the commercial banks should provide more loans at lower interest rates to eco-friendly industries or pro-environmental projects undertaken by any industry. This will help to spread the concept of green banking to other sectors of the country. Banks can also encourage borrowing facilities to those industries which plan to fund the implementation of solar energy programmes, green plantations, micro and macro level hydro projects, bio-mass electricity or bio-gas projects for the country. A majority of the bankers further stated that both the central bank and commercial bank authorities can impose restrictions on establishment of any industry or projects without using the green banking methodologies. Survey results thus indicated that the attitude of bankers in Bangladesh mostly is in favor of creating awareness and spreading green banking approaches, not only in the financial sector but to other major industry settings of the country as well.

Findings of this chapter are mostly in line with the results reported by Ahmad et al. (2013) and Ullah (2013). Ahmad et al. (2013) claimed that policy guidelines by the central bank and stakeholder pressure are two major influencing factors for the commercial banks of Bangladesh to adopt green banking; while, Ullah (2013) stated through a comparative analysis of the country's commercial banks that brand image is a prime reason why the financial sector opts for green banking approaches in Bangladesh. Overall, it can be concluded that acceptance of green banking in both internal and external activities of banks in Bangladesh may have been acts of image improvement, pressure from central bank and stakeholders or just another progressive step to match with the developed economies. However, since every step counts, green banking approaches in Bangladesh can be treated as another small contribution to green investments, environmental care and sustainability and a better global environment from this side of the world.

All these recent developments in green banking initiatives by the banking sector of Bangladesh like online services, internet or mobile banking, office automation or electronic communications, conveys much significance. Already through various in-house green banking methods, banks are attempting to reduce the use of paper inside their offices and in their transactional activities, but since the present era is that of computers, more automation can be achieved by the banks. For instance, all communications regarding loan applications, credit proposals and their approvals can be conveniently done through electronic means which not only eliminates the use of paper but also saves time. Even the issuance of circulars from the central bank or from other commercial or foreign banks can be easily converted into electronic circulars, which can be reproduced and circulated through emails to all other urban and rural branches of the banks. Communications between different departments, branches and head office of the bank can also be efficiently done through this electronic means of circulation which will clearly eliminate the use of papers and save the environment. It is therefore imperative that the government of Bangladesh mandates the use of electronic means for all intra-bank, inter-bank and central bank communications. Such a step by the government will further their vision of a 'Digital Bangladesh' in the country as well (Islam & Khair, 2012).

Banks nowadays widely encourage the use of internet banking, mobile banking and the use of electronic bank statements in Bangladesh. However, papers like deposit slips or cheque books are still in use. Introduction of bank cards with secured chip and pin numbers can replace the use of such documents for banking transactions. A major challenge in such an initiative might be the unavailability of proper technological infrastructure and resources, but government support in the form of financial assistance to improve the facilitating conditions of the country can aid the banking sector to introduce such socially responsive business practices. Additionally, banks can establish an online resource center to eliminate the use of any hard copy for bank manuals, reference books, client circulars, etc.

Implementation of all green banking initiatives is a long-term project and like everywhere in the world, any such environmental-friendly measures are expensive (The Financial Express, 29 July, 2013). However, to safeguard the environment from the impacts of global warming and climatic changes, it is necessary to implement various forms of green investments and green technologies to mitigate any environmental hazards. In the context of Bangladesh, a positive perception for the environment and an equally positive attitude of bankers towards the use and future potential of green banking approaches for in-house and external activities of the banking sector, clearly paves the way of implementing other forms of green investments in the country. The government and the central bank of Bangladesh should thus be more forthcoming in this regard by making budgetary allocations to promote green industries and by providing more financing facility for extensively implementing green investments in the financial sector, ultimately encouraging other industries of the country to participate as well.

FUTURE RESEARCH DIRECTIONS

The present study is solely based upon the green banking initiatives of some selected commercial banks of Bangladesh. Future research can examine the forms of green banking activities adopted by the central bank or the nationalized banks of the country. A similar research can also be conducted for a different developing country to do a more in-depth analysis of green investment approaches. Moreover, this study has mainly emphasized on the assessment of the perceptions and attitudes of bankers towards green banking. A longitudinal study can be adopted in future works to examine a different research model in order to examine the factors that can influence the adoption of green banking from the perspective of customers. This will provide a better insight into the perceptions of users and can help to enhance the understanding of individual users' intention to adopt green banking services in the context of Bangladesh.

CONCLUSION

The primary objective of this chapter is to provide a conceptual model that determines the perception of bankers towards environment, green investments and their attitude towards green banking that defines the reasons for using its related products/services and the future potential of such initiatives. Lack of studies in the area of bankers' perceptions and attitudes towards environmental safety and the concept of green banking is a major reason why such study is required to obtain a clear picture of the present status of commercial banks and their role in the adoption of green banking practices, particularly in developing countries. Thus, the findings of the current study are expected to make a significant contribution to the emerging literature on green banking studies by going beyond comparative analysis of banks and employing variables to assess the perception and attitude of bankers, who are mainly the people involved in the implementation and execution of green baking approaches. Results reveal that the perception of bankers towards environmental protection, care and sustainability was quite positive, but despite their agreement about environmental safety the bankers displayed limited knowledge about the concept and related methods of green investments. A more deterministic role that defines the attitude of bankers towards green banking has been mainly identified as image improvement and/or pressure from the central bank and stakeholders of the banking sector. In contrast, since green banking initiatives has made banking transactions easier to avail and working conditions more convenient for the bankers, no matter whatever the reason is for the individual banks to adopt green banking practices, bankers mostly are in favor of such initiatives and its related products/services. A significant number of bankers also gave a lot of insights regarding the future potential of green banking practices for the commercial banks of Bangladesh. Since the findings of this research are perceptual in nature, the attitude of bankers can be further influenced by appropriate documentaries to create awareness regarding global warming, environmental safety issues and green investments. Moreover, the intervention of government through budgetary allocations for green banking and increased involvement of the central bank to promote financing facilities for green initiatives can enable a more positive, supportive and encouraging attitude of bankers towards green banking practices in Bangladesh.

REFERENCES

Ahmad, F., Zayed, N. M., & Harun, M. A. (2013). Factors behind the adoption of green banking by Bangladeshi commercial banks. *ASA University Review*, *7*(2), 241–255.

Croce, R. D., Kaminker, C., & Stewart, F. (2011). *The role of pension funds in financing green growth initiatives*. OECD Working Papers on Finance, Insurance and Private Pensions, No.10, OECD Publishing.

Fornell, C., & Larcker, D. F. (1981). Evaluating structural equation models with unobservable variables and measurement error. *JMR, Journal of Marketing Research*, *18*(1), 39–50. doi:10.2307/3151312

Gani, M. O. (2013, July 29). Green banking: Concept and policy guidelines. *The Financial Express*.

Hossain, M. Z., & Ahmed, M. (2015). Green banking in Bangladesh. In Green Banking in Bangladesh and Beyond, (pp. 17-47). Zaman Printing and Packaging.

Hossain, M. Z., Ahmed, M., & Nisha, N. (2015). Consumer attitudes and perception towards green banking in Bangladesh. In Green Banking in Bangladesh and Beyond, (pp. 48-76). Zaman Printing and Packaging.

Hossain, M. Z., Jilani, S. N., & Haque, H. (2015). Islamic finance as a greener alternative. In Green Banking in Bangladesh and Beyond, (pp. 201-217). Zaman Printing and Packaging.

Hossain, M. Z., Rahim, M. A., & Hussain, T. (2015). The future of green banking in Bangladesh. In Green Banking in Bangladesh and Beyond, (pp. 77-88). Zaman Printing and Packaging.

Inderst, G., Kaminker, C., & Stewart, F. (2012). *Defining and measuring green investments: Implications for institutional investors' asset allocations*. OECD Working Papers on Finance, Insurance and Private Pensions, No.24, OECD Publishing.

Islam, M. J., & Khair, R. (2012). Preparation of e-Government in Bangladesh: An exploratory analysis. *JU Journal of Information Technology*, *1*, 19–26.

Islam, M. T. (2015, May 26). Green banking and its present scenario in Bangladesh. *The Daily Observer*.

Masukujjaman, M., & Aktar, S. (2013). Green banking in Bangladesh: A commitment towards the global initiatives. *Journal of Business and Technology*, *8*(1&2), 17–40.

Masum, M. (2015). The need for Green banking in Bangladesh. In Green Banking in Bangladesh and Beyond, (pp. 3-16). Zaman Printing and Packaging.

Nisha, N., Idrish, S., & Hossain, M. Z. (2015). Consumer acceptance and use of mobile banking services in Bangladesh. In Green Banking in Bangladesh and Beyond, (pp. 155-182). Zaman Printing and Packaging.

Nunnally, J. C., & Bernstein, I. H. (1994). *Psychometric Theory*. New York: McGraw-Hill.

Roy, J. K. (2015a, August 1). Green stocks: Green investment, green return. *The Financial Express*.

Roy, J. K. (2015b, July 15). Promoting green businesses in Bangladesh. *The Financial Express*.

Shakil, M. H., Azam, M. K. G., & Raju, M. S. H. (2014). An evaluation of green banking practices in Bangladesh. *European Journal of Business and Management*, *6*(31), 8–16.

The Financial Express (2015, February 15). BB to create $500m fund for green industries. *The Financial Express*.

Ullah, M. M. (2013). Green banking in Bangladesh – A comparative analysis. *World Review of Business Research*, *3*(4), 74–83.

ADDITIONAL READING

Bahl, S. (2012). Green banking - The new strategic imperative. *Asian Journal of Research in Business Economics and Management*, *2*(2), 176–185.

Bahl, S. (2012). The role of green banking in sustainable growth. *International Journal of Marketing. Financial Services and Management Research*, *1*(2), 27–35.

Bihari, S. C. (2010). Green banking towards socially responsible banking in India. *International Journal of Business Insights & Transformation*, *4*(1), 82–87.

Biswas, N. (2011). Sustainable green banking approach: The need of the hour. *Business Spectrum*, *1*(1), 32–38.

Dash, R.N. (2008). Sustainable 'Green' Banking: The Story of Triodos Bank. *Cab Calling*, 26-29.

Goyal, K. A., & Joshi, V. (2011). A study of social and ethical issues in banking industry. *International Journal of Economics and Research*, *2*(5), 49–57.

Kaeufer, K. (2010). *Banking as a Vehicle for Socio-economic Development and Change: Case Studies of Socially Responsible and Green Banks*. Cambridge, MA: Presencing Institute.

Sahoo, P., & Nayak, B. P. (2008). *Green banking in India*. Institute of Economic Growth.

KEY TERMS AND DEFINITIONS

Commercial Bank: A financial institution that accepts deposits and provides loans to the general public. It also provides basic banking services to industries and can fund industry-specific projects as well.

Environmental-Friendly: Any practice that reduces any harmful impact on the environment.

Global Warming: Rapid change in the eco-system that brings about a change in the climate and which can have a direct impact on biodiversity, agriculture, forestry, dry land, water resources and human health.

Green Banking Unit: An operational unit in an organization which consists of employees from various departments and the main function of this unit is to design, evaluate and administer activities related to green banking initiatives of that organization.

Green Banking: An approach that promotes environmental-friendly practices and reduces carbon footprint from banking practices. This can be achieved in many ways such as reduced use of paper through the use of online banking instead of branch banking.

Green Finance: Any financial instruments, investments or projects that are climate change specific and primarily related to renewable energy, environmental technology or sustainability related markets.

Green Investments: Investments that focus their attention to climate change, resource efficiency and the safeguarding of the environment as a whole.

Social Responsibility: Any act or practice that works for the overall benefit of the society and focuses more on the improvement of the economy and eco-system rather than just the maximization of profits.

Sustainable Development: Any practice that has a sole aim to preserve natural resources for the betterment of the environment and eco-system.

Chapter 2
The Management of the Socio-Economic System: The Natural Capital Relation as a Foundation of Sustainable Development

Constanta Popescu
Valahia University of Targoviste, Romania

Constantin Popescu
Valahia University of Targoviste, Romania

Ana Lucia Ristea
Valahia University of Targoviste, Romania

ABSTRACT

The appearance of the concept of sustainable development, although a sort of universal remedy at its beginnings, is becoming increasingly frequently the object of tensions both as objectives but especially as content. Regarding its objectives, the debate is organized around a logic based on the theory of the stakeholders but also on the competing logic that mobilizes an ethics of responsibility as teleological principle. Consequently, the meanings and implicitly the programmes of sustainable development are also the object of certain controversies and remain susceptible of being solved by a process of normalization of their contents. However, this dynamics of normalization itself is the bearer of certain "perverse effects", already noticed in the accountancy standards domain and, under these circumstances, this dynamics of normalization cannot pretend to be the solution for regulating these controversies. The problem are mainly the weak doctrinal points characterizing Sustainable Development today, obviously, by comparison to what it wanted to be.

DOI: 10.4018/978-1-5225-2081-8.ch002

INTRODUCTION: THE RELATION BETWEEN THE NATURAL CAPITAL (NC) AND THE SOCIO-ECONOMIC SYSTEM (SES)

The identification and description of the natural or seminatural environment dominated or created by the human species have changed and evolved from the conceptual model that used to define the environment as a set of factors (air, water, soil, flora, fauna, human settlements), to the recent model, which considers that the environment has a hierarchic spatio-temporal organization, namely, in other words, the environment is a functional hierarchy of systems.

Consequently, ecological systems become:

- Organized units, elements of the hierarchy;
- Self-regulable systems, able to maintain themselves;
- Systems supporting life;
- Systems with a co-linear dynamics, and different carrying and productive capacities, depending on their disturbance degree.

The ecological hierarchy contains two main hierarchic lines of ecological systems highlighting a dichotomy in their spatio-temporal development and representing the central element of the so-called "ecological crisis".

Schematically, here are the 2 lines:

1. Natural and seminatural systems, maintaining themselves and providing a large array of resources and services
2. Ecological systems dominated by man, which depend to different extents on auxiliary energy and matter inputs (e.g.: agrosystems, intensive fisheries, etc.) and man-made systems (urban ecosystems, farms, industrial complexes) which are totally dependent on auxiliary energy and matter inputs coming from the first category – natural and seminatural systems (Allan, D., 1994).

Natural and seminatural ecological systems assure:

1. Renewable resources
2. Series of services beneficial to the social-human system

The most important services assured by the natural and seminatural ecological systems are:

- Control of the climatic composition of the atmosphere, of the radiant energy flow and implicitly climate control

- Control of the water circuit, playing the role of watershed and therefore reducing the risks of floods and droughts
- Main storage lakes
- Pedogenesis as one of the most complex ecological processes, forests being great "plants" creating and settling soils
- Maintaining an inestimable genetic bank from which man has been drawing elements that are fundamental for his civilization: cultivated plants, domesticated animals, products for medicine and industry etc.

It is obvious, however, that natural and seminatural ecological systems, as well as those dominated or created by man are not separate entities, as they are integrated, as components of the Natural Capital and Socio-Economic System, in the ecological hierarchy, constituting simply, ecological systems. Under these conditions, biodiversity acquires at least two great meanings:

1. It is the fundament supporting and feeding SES with resources and services;
2. It is the interface between NC and the structure and metabolism of SES, namely the element permanently in the frontline in the impact areas of SES on NC.

It consequently results that the harmonization of the spatio-temporal relations and energy and matter exchanges between SES and NC is the key element of any socio-economic development strategy meant not to go over the carrying capacity of the environment supporting it.

MANAGING THE RELATIONS BETWEEN SOCIO-ECONOMIC SYSTEM AND NATURAL CAPITAL

Very recent researches have approached the issue of the ecosystem's carrying capacity, a problem preoccupying both demography and human ecology specialists, who would like to be able to estimate using scientific bases the limits of natural development and demographic growth.

The carrying capacity is a feature of each ecological system or category of ecosystems, depending on their development stages and the hierarchic stages they are part of. Consequently, carrying capacity is the concrete expression of the stability domain expressing the ecosystem's ability of changing its structural and functional parameters under the influence of command factors.

An ecosystem's stability domain designates the direction in which it is developing, with the mention that the process is taking place on very large time scales, of over 100 years and that it is reversible, whenever a strong impact is exerted on the system by external factors.

It results, in this context, that the notion of "carrying capacity" actually concerns the operation capacity of large, complex and dynamic systems, such as the ecological systems. At the same time, to each ecological system, one can associate in the domain of goods and services production, a certain productive capacity. This capacity is concretely expressed depending on the fluctuations of the command factors, namely of the trajectory followed by the systems.

The present analysis is substantiating the need that in designing and managing the absolutely necessary socio-economic transition, at least the following parallel of managerial pragmatism ought to be supported:

- The growth or succession of ecological systems in a natural regime and the socio-economic development dominated by economic growth in the socio-economic system, on the one hand;
- Improvement or evolution of the ecological systems and socio-economic development, which ought to focus on increasing the efficiency of the use of energy resources, on the total recycling of raw matter, on the extensive use of informational systems and even the redefinition of the standards related to the quality of life, on the other hand.

Thus, in any socio-economic system, growth needs to be obligatorily recalibrated in the sense of harmonization with the productive and carrying capacity of natural systems, assuring both matter and energy resources, and a series of services, on which the human population's health depends.

Starting from these considerations, one can affirm that the development of the human society supported by economic growth is healthy only if this growth is gradually transformed as the limits of the carrying and productive capacity of the natural capital are gradually reached, by a process of structural and functional improvement.

The process ought not to suppose the increased transfer of matter and energy resources from the natural systems to the socio-economic ones or the accumulation of wastes inside the socio-economic system and of hazardous substances in the troposphere and the hydrosphere.

At least during this stage, when numerous aggressions are noticed on the natural capital, the management of the socio-economic system needs to suppose an alternation of the economic growth with structural and qualitative improvement, which means ecological reconstruction of degraded environments that cannot be rehabilitated in any other way. By ecological reconstruction actions, it will be possible to cover, at least partially, the debt to the environment of the socio-economic system and on this basis, the premises of a new growth will be created.

MANAGING THE RELATION NC-SES

The appearance of the concept of sustainable development, although in the beginning as a universal remedy, is becoming increasingly frequently the object of tensions both in point of its objectives and especially in point of its content.

Regarding the objectives, the debate is organized around a logic based on the theories of the parties concerned, but also on the competitive logic, mobilizing an ethics of responsibility as teleological principle. Consequently, the sustainable development meanings and implicitly programmes also make the object of controversies and remain likely to be solved by a process of normalization of their contents.

However, this normalization dynamics is itself a carrier of "perverse effects", already noticed in the domain of the accounting standards and, under these circumstances, this normalization dynamics cannot claim to be the only solution for the regulation of these controversies.

The problem actually lies mainly in the doctrinal weaknesses characterizing Sustainable Development as a concept today, evidently, by comparison to what it was meant to be.

DEFINITION OF THE GENERAL CONTEXT

In the reports presented at international conferences (Rio 1992, Kyoto 1997, Davos 2001, Johannesburg 2002, Copenhague 2009) and in other much more numerous specialized publications, Sustainable Development has appeared and continues to appear to this day as dominant representative of a new logic of economic and social development. This logic ought to allow the instauration of a just balance between social aspirations, considered as new ones, and an "economic development meeting the needs of each generation, starting with the neediest, without compromising the capacity of the future generations of meeting their own needs" (Brundtland 1987).

The emergence of the concept of Sustainable Development (SD) is from the beginning the subject of some tensions as far as its goals and concept are concerned. These tensions oscillate between a pragmatic approach, based on the stakeholders' theory, and an ethic or moral theory, highlighting a principle of responsibility, largely inspired from Hans Jonas's philosophy (1990). The analysis of these tensions, developed in the first part of this article, helps us understand the context of the debates and especially controversies around the concept of Sustainable Development.

The natural questions around this concept do not stop emerging:

- Is this a new logic that will result either from a better arbitration between short-term concerns (mostly based on economic criteria) and long-term concerns, or from a new definition of performance, extended to the economic aspect, yet relying on social and environmental considerations?
- What are the theoretical bases supporting the codification and development of the SD concept?
- Or does SD simply represent a new concept and a new attempt of justifying and supporting at all costs a sustainable growth or, more importantly, is it an invitation to rethinking the "nature of the firm"?

Between the profoundly contradictory interpretations of the concept and the difficulties encountered in the attempt of defining its dimension from the perspective of the implication in the social aspect, the fundamental elements of economic and social sustainability are hard to impose to be distinguished as recognized and legitimate landmarks on a large scale. It seems that this thing is better defined today by the concept of social responsibility, which has the calling of bringing a more broadly accepted consensus regarding these controversies.

As a new formulation, seemingly with a more broadly accepted mediation potential, it is supposed that the company (the organization), as economic entity, acts on the market and admits that it takes on its responsibility, in various domains such as: accidents, pollution, social troubles caused by managerial decisions, civic and ethic impacts of some strategic decisions, etc.

This is in fact a new modality for the individuals who are behind all that the organization represents of running away from responsibility, invoking precisely the organization's social responsibility and its care for the employees, in front of any regulations and especially of those regarding environmental protection (Myers, N. 1993)

SOCIAL RESPONSIBILITY

This gradual change from one concept to the next will not be without consequences, probably, on the need of "social responsibility", a concept that would have clearly belonged to a separate domain such as business ethics (quite hard to impose even on the theoretical level), which would have previously established principles, springing first of all from the contractual logic among stakeholders, whereas Sustainable Growth is still a very active subject of controversy.

This pre-eminence of the companies' social responsibility as the equivalent of the social dimensions of sustainable development is translated today into a strong tendency of normalization of these dimensions; rating agencies, indicators, audits and the "Stakeholder Report" tend to present sustainability under the form of normative references, all in order to impose it as a standard of reference.

This unstable doctrinal situation, especially of the terms composing the syntagm "sustainable development", does not facilitate the main desideratum for which it has been institutionalized as a leading, namely largely accepted "new paradigm", continuing to permit economic growth. In fact, missing are the norms, dogmas and recommendations able to constitute a real system capable of formulating and developing a "set of doctrines" as a well-structured and legitimate basis to found a renewed thinking and especially new practices.

Doubtlessly, this doctrinal instability needs to be viewed, however, also as a positive thing; it permits and can still pretend that it can influence the objectives, the content and the modalities of government of what Sustainable Growth is actually going to be. In this sense, doctrinal instability itself offers new ways of development for innovating companies and promising research ways for the researchers interested in the increase of this research domain.

SUSTAINABLE DEVELOPMENT FROM ONE TENSION TO THE NEXT

The invention of the syntagm Sustainable Development is often presented as a result of a complex set of multiform pressures, created by groups of actors, with different motivations (Odum, E., 1993). For example, anti-globalization movements and Non-Governmental Organizations stand out as an increasingly stronger presence over the international companies and organizations and institutions operating in the environmental domain. Such organizations (UNEP, UNCTAD, IOM, UNDP, OECD, European Commission) develop actively, especially after the Brundtland Report (WCED 1987), important mechanisms of sensitivization and information among governments and directly involved institutions. (See, for example, the Development Assistance Committee, DAC, OECD, 1996).

Despite the diversity of these approaches, and the variety of their action bases, most of these players seem to agree on the fact that the very syntagm SD as well as the doctrine and evidently the resulting action is the expression of a search of a new development model. This new model seems to be situated at the crossroads of three fundamental principles:

- An economic principle, requiring the rational use of resources, in order to accomplish the desideratum of "maintaining a reasonable living standard, without endangering the future generations' chances.
- An environmental principle, specifying the fact that the civil society needs to protect these resources as the political decision-making top is and will always remain indebted to the economic leaders that have supported them.
- A social principle foreseeing that all people ought to be dealt with correctly.

The very general aspect of these principles, their slightly obligatory character and the absence of a "regulating authority", which would have imposed itself unitarily to all, permanently threaten and generate questions on the intentions lying at the basis of this search of a new development model. The negative aspects of the "old" model are only rarely mentioned (except for the problems brought on the environment by the economic growth at all costs), and it is not clear how our principles of action are to be renewed in the social and especially the economic domain (Popescu, C., 2015).

Consequently, the vague character of the concept, the weakness of the debates around the principle of social equity and the lack of prescriptions, demands or propositions of clear structuring actions can legitimately raise the problem of the real intention of performance of the SD concept.

However, with a series of actors involved in this approach, beyond some pioneering founders, it seems that this attempt to create a new efficiency, different from the economic one, invoking social responsibility and the ecological or environmental calling, has a very small, almost insignificant echo in companies and especially in the big ones. For some operators, the attempt has been advancing better during the last few years, advancing from the logic of "pulling" to that of "pressuring", in the sense that most of the companies characterized as evolving under the pressure of the market situation, of their donors, of the work norms and legislation in the domain, today are beginning to evolve under the mixed integrated market-investor-standard-legislation pressure, namely they are learning to do other kinds of business.

This new commitment to a different kind of business is devoid of challenges for these companies. It brings the need to lead, at least theoretically, to objectives dedicated to SD and, by extension, by means of evaluation criteria, to sustainable performance. Because there is a significant threat floating over the business environment from this perspective and it could "oust from the game" almost half of the companies that have not adopted an environmental management system. Very many authors, both from the academic area, but also even from among the managers, have criticized the excessive burden of the new regulations related to SD and the costs it generates. They recommend the mobilization of the companies around realistic goals, keeping at the same time the financial means they can use to realize the environmental commitments assumed, yet without giving up for good on the market-based instruments, which call for a stakeholder agreement. This tension concerning the SD objectives relies on about two main attractors:

1. The first part of the theory comes from the older, stakeholder theory, which seems to correspond today to the dominant approach in SD matters.
2. The second part stems from references taken from a moral philosophy trying to establish a responsibility principle inspired by moral philosophy and to a lesser extent by the concept of ethics (Myers, N. 1993).

SUSTAINABILITY AND THE STAKEHOLDER THEORY

The sustainable development demands require, in the absence of a supra-national regulation system, a definition of new relations to natural persons, groups and organizations that can affect or can be affected by a company's strategy.

The presence of these stakeholders in the company's strategy threatens to embrace the concept of "Stakeholder Corporation", which would present the company as a constellation of interests, animated by the spirit of cooperation and competitiveness, because surely some of these interests can be at odds.

Theoretically, this approach by stakeholders is part of the agency theory, which presents the firm as a set of contracts based on agency relations, namely relations between principal, initiating actor and agent. These contracts permit the Principal actor, as stakeholder, to monitor and encourage the agent to work in the sense of its interests. These contracts are inherently incomplete, in the sense that the Principal actor, unique or majority shareholder, needs to mobilize control processes and instruments allowing him to exert an adequate corporate government.

This theory has been the object of numerous researches especially regarding the precise nature of these stakeholders and their relations with the firm. Primary stakeholders, hired by contract and involved in the success of the company (shareholders, employees, partners, providers) and secondary stakeholders, who are not directly involved in the functioning of the company (groups of interests, in the domain or having to do with the domain under discussion or opinion vectors, media etc.) ought to maintain the same objectives.

This means integrating conflicting yet legitimate interests, in a common project, based on a capacity of integrating stakeholders, or on their capacity of stimulating the creation of connections generating sustainability and of improving sustainable performance (e.g. the competitive benefits of the social or environmental domain) (Popescu, C., 2011).

However, this approach is, in essence, the problem that leads to a contraction, namely to a restraint, of the activity, when it tries to gather momentum to conceptualize the SD government.

This happens, first, because the organizational structures, namely the functional compartments and the production compartments and the government systems on state level are at this moment mainly meant to serve the internal (or primary) stakeholders.

Secondly, this happens because the external (or secondary) stakeholders do not necessarily feel the need to sign contracts in their relation with the company (organization). In this case, how can stakeholders unwilling to participate fit in?

Moreover, the stakeholder theory relies on arguable hypotheses and contestable and contested axioms. The agency relation actually relies on a partnerial and contractual vision of this interaction between stakeholders and the company, in the sense that it is precisely the conflict of interests that is solved by the contract - the instrument assuring the maximization of the respective interests, on condition that its implementation should be adequately followed and controlled by those responsible.

The moral dimension of these contracts is low, sometimes inexistent, because of the internal ethics codes, on the one hand, which raises the issue of their legitimacy, another key concept, as contestability is possible for these contracts; in fact, they may very well be annulled by their very imperfections. Thus, it is possible that under these moral or ethical aspects of development, the other pole of this tension may emerge, i.e. the one concerning the goals ascribed to Sustainable Development.

According to this second perspective, sustainable development may (or ought to) be taken into account in the economic theory, as a sort of return to morality. This is possible, indeed, namely that beyond the traditional approach of the economy, focusing exclusively on the topic of the "Relations between people and things", we could go back to "the relations among people".

If this aspiration is not just the SD supporters' ambition; it also animates a certain number of individuals or organizations of the civil society, there can appear the sprouts of the emergence or even acceptance of this new perspective holding that "economy is a moral science", based on two pillars:

1. The first is that of social responsibility as exercise of individual freedom, which includes first of all its positive components restoring to us our capacity of behaving as autonomous and responsible individuals and also the freedom and opportunity to participate to the political and social processes affecting our daily life. This notion of responsibility relies on the recognition of the fact that people's life leads to interdependence, which involves mutual obligations concerning the economic, political and social relations that they, people, maintain on mutual bases. Consequently, it is necessary to face the conflicting demands of the diverging principles, and the fact that an economy resulting from large

debates open to participation cannot be reached. In other words, the demand of responsibility calls for freedom of expression of individual principles and freedom of participation, in order to solve social dilemmas, exclusively by opting for work based on dialogue and open debate.

2. The second of these pillars relies on the older idea of the Responsibility Principle, which it proposes as fundament of a real, renewed ethics.

This ethics would rely on the following observation: The action of modern science deeply revolutionized man's relation with nature. Technology is making Nature vulnerable nowadays because of the excessive development of man's power. In this way, man does not become only a leading subsystem but especially someone responsible for his own survival, which becomes threatened by his own action.

RISKS OF THE CONCEPT OF SUSTAINABLE DEVELOPMENT

1. Today, the concept of sustainable development can be taken by the wind toward a Malthusian vision of our society. Why do rich countries, now economically developed, impose on developing countries a limited vision of their development? The first risk would be that such a vision, sprung from the new concept, although not a bad vision and although having even praiseworthy objectives, may also be suspected of also serving to justify the protectionist policies of certain countries that are afraid of competition. This is happening because, often contrary to such a vision, in practice, developed countries do not hesitate to develop their trade with China, despite the risk of devastating ecological footprint supposed by the economic growth of this country, which also derives from such a threat.
2. A second risk is that of misbalanced communication. Namely, either the communication is not followed by actions in the domain of innovation, for example, and the company may grow weak by comparison to its, evidently more innovative, competitors or, on the contrary, the insistence on the communication component can lead to revealing confidential information. In both cases, the organizational coherence and competitiveness would be affected, especially in the context of the Internet revolution.
3. A third risk is that of sliding towards less reliable sustainability models, namely models that would suppose the replacement of the natural capital by a capital of knowledge. Such a model is often adopted and practiced by US agencies, especially, developed mainly on a federal level, and their worldwide branches. This risk consists in the shaping of innovation networks, led from outside Europe, which could destabilize the European institutions and the EU Member

States (research institutes, universities, regulation agencies in the domain of resources etc.).

4. A fourth risk, even more damaging, is that of overemphasizing corporate ethics, at various conferences, in the name of the interest, in fact of the company, of hiding a large-scale lack of morality. In practice, the fluency of the information flows and of the financial flows for globalization is leading to an increase in the uncontrolled foreign investments. This can short-circuit the coordinated European actions in the political and juridical domains, especially, because of the States' cultural bias and administrative rigidities. Generally, the eco-economic theory supports the idea of the need of morals going beyond the framework of the company. On this topic, a modification of the legislation also appears as very necessary.
5. A fifth risk comes from the taking over by the powers controlling the information technology, of the international standardization and regulation procedures. In this way, the richest can impose a model actually leading to a more inequitable distribution of knowledge and consequently of the natural resources. This refers to the so-called open source software, yet the companies or organizations promoting their implementation (including SSLL) can help reduce this risk.
6. A sixth risk results from the fact that evaluation criteria are strongly misbalanced or intertwined, between environment, society and economy, or the implementation of the global models is biased. For example, the environmental bias, often invoked, can in fact mask other deficiencies.
7. The seventh risk is that the tag sustainable development will need to be permanently recovered to be able to support an increasing number of policies or acts that have nothing to do with the notion or have only very superficial connections with it. For instance, sustainable tourism, the application to tourism of the concept of sustainable development tends to be an elite tourism, which, in the name of environmental protection, creates a social barrier by increasing the vacations' price, obviously out of noble, "environmental conservation" considerations, forgetting about the social aspect.
8. Finally, the eighth risk is that the financial analysts motivated to evaluate the company's reports in relation to sustainable development do not have the necessary training in relation to the demands of the concept of sustainable development and do not possess adequate analysis tools (Popescu, C., 2012).

CRITICISM OF THE CONCEPT'S SUPERFICIALITY

The syntagm sustainable development has been criticized both for the lack of clarity surrounding it and for the lack of precision that it emanates. For this reason, the need to review this syntagm appeared quite rapidly both from the sphere of philosophy, which unmasks the fact that sustainable development is on everybody's liking as proposition, theoretical support and political and/or electoral slogan, yet it is so absurd, or rather so vague that it does not manage to say anything.

The term sings rather than says something, because only in art (song) can one conceive the simultaneous existence of two radically different aspects. It cannot say much, because the superficiality of the construction is visible starting from its very title.

If we analyze more attentively the association of the two terms, one can observe that they are even incompatible. Thus, development supposes a process of resuming, permanently to a new level, of extension, resulting in the acquisition of new proportions, significance, force, growth, of the tendency of permanent increase, whereas sustainability rather befriends ecology.

By the association of these terms, practically, as almost total perception, the result has been almost the decoupling of sustainability from nature and ecology, pushing it toward development. This has been possible because while, before, the term sustainable referred to renewable resources, now it has been connected to the term development, and, by this very skillful maneuver, the perception has been changed.

It is very clear for an increasing number of specialists that, when it appeared, the concept was invented in response to the pessimistic vision transmitted by the report The Limits to Growth, of The Club of Rome. And because they wanted to continue the economic growth at all costs, growth has been replaced by development and associated to sustainability so that the new meaning of sustainability passed from the domain of the protection of nature into that of protection of development (Popescu, C., 2014).

This is how the term development was saved, which, also following this report, had somewhat lost some of its content as a concept. For this reason, after the invention of the syntagm, all kind of political actors, themselves defenders of the economic growth, managed to dress their intentions in the concept of sustainable development even though they understood nothing of it. Out of this misunderstanding, the supporters of growth at all costs came to sustain the idea that sustainable development is a development lasting a long time (Myers, N. 1993; Popescu, C., 2015).

CRITICISM OF THE CONCEPT'S CONSEQUENCES

The ecological community considers syntagm that the concept of sustainable development is dangerous, as it can induce measures with unknown and potentially dangerous effects. This concept claims, for instance, that, in economy, just as in ecology, there is an objective interdependence, namely which exists regardless of man's will, and, consequently, isolate actions are impossible. A badly-conceived policy will trigger a multitude of perverse and unwanted side-effects, both ecologically and strictly economically. Many propositions concerning the safeguarding of the environment and the promotion of sustainable development models can actually lead to exactly opposite results. Moreover, they underline the limits of public policies and something that the Public Business School has underlined, i.e. the fact that almost all the communities orient the search of their policies towards their own interests, depending on the pressure and the lobby received, although the information is incomplete and does not really take into account the environmental aspects.

Moreover, profound ecology has built and developed its criticism regretting even the formulation, namely the fact that "sustainable development" is a formula of the domain of magic, addressing the emotions, yet having no concrete or well-defined content. And these last conditions being reunited, they are the very reason why the concept is enjoying such a consensus. Its appeal resides in the impressions and emotions it transmits, and not in the practical benefits of a well-built analysis. Consequently, this syntagm opens the way for dirigistic and draconic measures in its name, yet, unfortunately again, with an unknown and hardly quantifiable efficacy (Popescu C., 2008).

In contrast to these measures, the syntagm is defending the efficiency of private property by encouraging producers and consumers to preserve resources, according to some older principles having to do with harmony and balance and actually supporting the fact that the improvement of environmental quality depends on the market economy and the presence of legitimate and guaranteed property rights. This condition helps effectively maintain and exert individual responsibility and develop stimuli for environmental protection mechanisms. The State can, in this context, create a framework encouraging people to better protect the environment, facilitating, for instance, and even funding, the creation of foundations dedicated to environmental protection.

NEW OBJECTIVES TAKING SHAPE FOR THE NEW DEVELOPMENT TYPE

This dispute for the truth made out of fear gives rise to new imperative demands centered on the need to preserve the future. It is just like the obligation of having an ethics that can communicate with the extreme powers that mankind has today.

This ethics is necessary in everything, because of the threats to nature and the future of mankind precisely due to technical progress and its often devastating potentials, if they are not submitted, as possibilities of exercise, to this principle of responsibility.

Consequently, SD is called to manage well the strong tension developed rapidly between the two poles: that of moral exigency, based on a return to the philosophy of morals, and that of stakeholders, aiming to extend the agency relations to new groups of stakeholders such as the local communities or even their administrations, by the method of partnerships. In this way, they become partners and implicitly stakeholders no longer acting as party in the conflict.

They are united in their incompatibility and under these circumstances the "stakeholder theory" suffers of an acute lack of legitimacy in relation to the new demands imposed by SD.

The approach based on the principle of responsibility is itself obstructed by its own lack of propositions when alternative leadership modalities are discussed, modalities that could assure real freedom in the exercise of an active participation when the community problems are debated.

Today, we are witnessing the appearance of the updated concept of social or societal responsibility, which could constitute a new attractive and unifying pole, generating consensus, even in delicate matters, such as those concerning the environment and the natural resources.

SUSTAINABLE DEVELOPMENT AS A SOLUTION

The publication, in 1987, of the report Our Common Future of the World Commission on Environment and Development, also known under the name of Brundtland Report, after the name of the Norwegian Prime Minister presiding the organism, enunciated and popularized the syntagm sustainable development and created new visions that have gradually replaced the technical-scientific vision on management.

The Report defines sustainability as a resetting or rearranging of all the natural, economic, social, technical, scientific and cultural resources, so that the system resulted may be maintained in a state of spatio-temporal balance.

The definition above clarifies and delineates more clearly several sustainable development aspects which, briefly analyzed, highlight precisely the great sources of conflicts linked to environment in general and especially to forests and forest lands:

- Spatially, sustainable development refers to the entire planet.
- Its trans-generational framework actually connects the sustainability concept to the concept of ethics, bringing into discussion the rights of the future generations.
- Referring to the right to meet their needs, the concept of equity is introduced, regarding the various degrees to which different States affect the environment.

- The comprehension sphere being total, the approach of the social, economic and environmental problems can only be interdisciplinary.
- One cannot ignore the cultural peculiarities of sustainability, such as the customs, traditions and myths, because a culturally inacceptable definition cannot be operative.

Unfortunately, these principles have been considered pretty late, first of all given the scientific and technological optimism, which has promoted and still supports the idea that ecological problems are inevitable side-effects of the scientific and technological progress, and their solution is possible by new technological progresses.

It is necessary to mention that nobody denies the advantages of the scientific and technological progress, yet the use of any resources outside some objective cycles, controlled by the ecological cycles, is damaging and affects the carrying capacity of the natural ecosystems (Popescu, C., 2008).

Multiple examples of overcoming of the carrying capacity of definite ecosystems are eloquent:

- The carbon emission given mainly by the burning of fossil fuels has gone over the carbon lock-in possibilities.
- The cutting of the forests in the large basins of the planet to increase the agricultural area or create specialized cultures (plantations) proved deeply damaging, seriously affecting biodiversity.
- The exploitation of the mineral aggregates from the inner riverbeds by very deep excavations, economically profitable, as well as river course regulations, drainage, damming and other such works have destroyed the lush coppices of the inner rivers in Romania, devoiding the young soils of the contribution of the underground water and of the alluvial deposits stored by periodical flooding.
- Injecting salty water in the oil layers, as technological demand, is deeply damaging for forest ecosystems and for the soils and the underground water.
- The use of the over 600 active pesticide substances, included in several thousand compounds, has considerably increased the cancer risk and seriously affected the fertility of the main mammals, starting with man.
- Food additives, and the technologies based on genetic engineering, combining various DNAs, are environments favoring the appearance of malignant tumors.

From the confluence of ethics with the debates on environmental and forest topics have emerged and are developing today increasingly obviously ecological standards meant to protect the planetary environment, ecological security being invoked increasingly often. Thus, limits have emerged for Sulphur, nitrogen and carbon oxides, radioactivity, and heavy metals concentrations in the air, in the water and in the soil.

The territories of State Unions, as well as those of the States signatory of conventions and agreements are comprised in complex monitoring systems, which suppose the continual supervision of the main environmental factors and components.

Romania avails itself of a network supervising the emissions and overflows in waters, air and soil. At the same time, forest monitoring permits supervising the forests' health state by means of a network of permanent surveys.

The environmental concepts and methodology have evolved along with the development of theoretical ecology from the stage of biological ecology to the present stage of systemic ecology.

SUSTAINABILITY AS A CIVILIZING PROJECT

An operative definition of ecological sustainability calls for an understanding of the fact that sustainable human communities need not grow out of nothing, but need to grow gradually, according to the resilient model of natural ecosystems. Therefore, a sustainable human community needs to be constituted so as to preserve the environment and not destroy it, while evolving technologically, economically, commercially and physically. Thus, the new strategy needs to take into account the thesis according to which sustainable communities need to develop, in the long run, life models of constant interaction with other living systems. Consequently, sustainability does not mean lack of change. Sustainability is a dynamic process of development in common, in harmony with all the components of the environment, integrated in the functional hierarchy of ecosystems, which actually defines the environment.

Since the 1992 summer Conference on Environment and Development organized by the United Nations at Rio de Janeiro, the syntagm Sustainable Development has become an extremely important and circulated concept, especially in the world politics. Yet, leaving aside the fact that, more often than not, politicians but also scientists, increasingly often, invoke the concept because it "looks good", the fulminant increase of its frequency of use cannot be correctly explained except as a hope for a new environmental policy.

This hope needs to take into account an integrated approach of the economic, social and environmental problems, the only one that can take into account the broader context in which these complex environmental issues emerge increasingly often, if we want to find an adequate and acceptable solution, economically and socially.

Actually, it is almost unanimously accepted, in most of the important scientific forums, that in order to attain the desiderata of the new civilizing concept, the most necessary are the economic, social and political changes (Popescu, C., 2011).

As far as the economic domain is concerned, the management of this relation has to begin from the introduction of new forms of administration, taking into account more the factor nature as principal production factor, a factor that has to be taken into account even in the analyses calculating final costs. However, this enterprise will not suppose only the question how can this be done in singular cases, a question that can be answered by political-administrative and/or economic regulations. Ampler and more elaborate research works need to be undertaken to answer the debates and disputes concerning how big the capacity of adaptation of the economy on a global market operating in a decentralized manner can be if the steps to a sustainable development are not established on an international level, in the present context these steps actually having some chances to be even unachievable.

In the social domain, a sustainable management of the relation between SES and NC supposes totally new claims for the principle and practice of equity in distribution, at least for three reasons:

1. Considering the fact that this concept of sustainable development comes from the development policy discourse, what is affected first of all is the distribution of the development chances within the problematic complex north-south or east-west.
2. Secondly, the issue is how well the society might tolerate an ecological modernization that will bring with it not just new chances but also many new problems, if we consider only the analysis of the products' bio-geo-chemical cycles. The question normally arising is how can one guarantee the fact that the possibilities of life, work and consumption will be distributed at least somewhat correctly?
3. To the two issues mentioned previously, one more can be added, namely "intergenerational distribution equity". The interests of the future generations need to be considered within today's distribution of chances, which means that the society needs to take into account the fact that the present is nothing but the past of our future, on whose chances we are deciding now.

These extremely important problems finally refer to the availability of the society, of the economy and of each one of us, of accepting these changes in our production and consumption behavior, and even in our lifestyle.

The most important changes need to occur, however, in the political domain. Even since the formulation of the objectives for a sustainable development, today's political system, programmed in the short run, depending on the success in the elections and oriented towards the increase of the standard of living for the simple reason of allowing the election winners to maintain their power, has certainly been asking for too much.

The implementation of these objectives clearly proves the increased need for change in the domain of politics, because the new value-related orientations and emerging life-styles cannot be regulated on the political or administrative level; they can only be proliferated from a communicative level. Consequently, in the debate on the implementation of the sustainable development concept a consensus has been reached on the fact that only increased citizen participation is the necessary premise for the success of this idea.

This means that both regarding the formulation of the objectives, and regarding their implementation, a totally new "culture of dialogue" is needed, supposing the availability of the people in charge on the political and social level for elaborating objectives and aims, and the steps to their attainment, along with the representative persons, groups and associations committed and responsible.

This topic of sustainability is hard to imagine and specially to impose on today's political world, yet there is no other way, because it has been demonstrated that this sustainability policy asks us all to think, unselfishly, what we could achieve, if our personal interests were to coincide completely with the community's interests. The idea of sustainability leads us, therefore, to a qualitative leap, towards civil participation and finally towards modernizing the definition of the concept of sustainability, which imposes itself therefore as a new, ampler, more complex concept, with a strong civilizing component.

Because the new vision on sustainability no longer concerns only the participation to actions initiated on a political or administrative level, but an aware, responsible participation, a "discussion on the common problems" (according to Aristotle), on the mission of organizing politics.

In other words, one can affirm that the new civilizing project means for the socio-political actors that they need to take on a special responsibility in relation to the political imposition of sustainability, a fact triggering new structural, institutional and financial consequences.

The sustainability that will have to be imposed by political actions is not as simple as it seems if we refer only to the theoretical considerations, but becomes complex and complicated at the same time. On the one hand, intuitively, we understand what this is about, and on this level there are numerous examples. "Even if we want to eat meat, let us not kill the cow, if we want to have milk tomorrow as well, but let us wait to have other milk sources first or let us kill chicken or pigs, raised for meat" as the proverb says. On the other hand, we find it hard to imagine a truly sustainable society because, practically, everything would have to change, including ourselves.

Many things depend on the successful adoption of this concept and on its development, namely on bringing into play its whole array and its entire potential. Sustainability is much more than a simple technocratic project of intelligent resource administration, much more than a simple term of the options of the Club of Rome, of the World Bank, or IMF or UN or FAO. This idea will receive a new impetus understood as a new civilizing project, a new project still deeply rooted in our traditions and especially in our human conscience and which we, men, out of hypocrisy and selfishness, have kept postponing it; maybe sometimes we have even given the impression that we have kept hiding it. Tradition and innovation no longer have to be at opposite poles. A common reservoir of values, ideas and dreams means for us an important cultural resource.

The most often used definition of sustainable development is that given by Lester Brown, the founder of Worldwatch Institute. This definition has been taken over in the report entitled Our Common Future of the Brundtland Commission: "Sustainable development is development that meets the needs of the present without compromising the ability of future generations to meet their own needs", (Lester R. Brown, et. al., 1997).

This definition of sustainable development has indeed been accepted on all levels and is today heralded from all the podiums and by all the organisms, precisely because it sounds good, yet it is almost empty of content, namely it does not say much on the action level. Therefore, the operationalization of the concept of sustainability is a very important mission of the scientific and academic world from everywhere, because, otherwise, the economic top as well as the great finance and its instruments will invent immediately, as actually they have done before, definitions of the kind of: "sustainable development is that development lasting a long time".

If we discuss about sustainability as an ecological, not economic concept, we need to start from the fact that for a functional definition of ecological sustainability one has to start from understanding the reality that sustainable communities need not be started from zero, but we need to gradually transform the existing ones according to the model of the natural ecosystems, which are, in essence, sustainable communities of plants, animals and microorganisms.

As we have seen, we no longer need to prove that the Earth's most important quality lies in its capacity of maintaining life. For this reason, a sustainable human community has to be constituted in such a way that its living structures, technologies and trading, economic and physical structures should maintain nature and life, and not destroy them, as we can see increasingly often, at every step, with the naked eye, today (Lester, R. Brown, et al., 1997).

Sustainable communities develop their models of life in time, in a permanent interaction with other living systems, human and non-human. Consequently, sustainability does not mean that things should not change. It is not a static process, but a dynamic one, of common co-evolution, of all the actors, parties of the whole living kingdom, together with their environment.

Consequently, the debate on sustainable development, in the future, no longer needs to avoid or postpone the aim of reaching a social consensus concerning the new development objectives, other than industrial growth, neglecting natural principles and fantasies such as "technological feasibility", invented by the neo-economic theory, on which the western civilization model, based on economic growth at all costs, relies. This perspective, introducing new objectives, aims to develop an innovative concept for sustainability, able to face the future, a concept cultivating another social development mode, in the sense of a different regulating idea, just as for instance democracy, freedom, justice etc.

Under these circumstances, education for a sustainable development is not just an extension of environmental education, which would include, as extras, social or economic aspects, but will also have to be a strong connective element between political education, global education, environmental education or sanitary education.

Consequently, an idea winning increasingly more ground is the idea that the aim of this UN decennium is to find a common denominator for the multitude of initiatives, from political education to environmental education, from global education to education for peace, subordinating all of these to the larger domain of education for a sustainable development.

IT HAS NEVER BEEN SIMPLER TO BE FAIR

The North is enjoying the products of the south: coffee, cocoa, tea, sugar, rice, bananas and many products of Africa, Asia or Latin America, goods that are naturally part of our daily life. Yet, it is not as natural that the developing countries' producers can live from the fruit of their work. Price evolution and the relation of economic dependence on raw matter push the peasants' families to the brim of poverty. In order for the coffee that we drink to become even cheaper, these peasants have to give up on one thing or the other, again and again, and this is totally unfair.

FAIRTRADE AS ANOTHER WAY?

This idea can be supported according to a very simple algorithm: producers receive for the raw matter fair prices, according to the world market prices. Thus, responsible businesses can be led, and people in the developing countries can assure their existence in the long run, attaining at least the minimum social standards in point of health and education.

Consumers receive, in exchange, tasty and high-quality food. It reaches Europe directly and in a controlled manner, coming from the developing countries carrying the trade mark guaranteeing their origin. In this way, you can enjoy those products with a calm conscience, aware that by making the decision to buy Fairtrade products you personally actively contribute to a juster world!

Fairtrade finally means an efficient means of cooperation, which is sure to do good to all participants to this initiative:

The farmers' families are winners because by Fairtrade they can assure their existence and plan their future. Moreover, the peasants' associations or cooperatives receive a social and ecological development bonus, which they can use to assure potable water sources, basic medical care, the organization of the school system etc., and, during the last years, often only the Fairtrade system or method or way has made it possible to move on to ecological cultures.

Plantation workers have something to win because the Fairtrade initiative creates human working and living conditions, and a relation with the employers regulated by contracts assuring by law the minimum salary, work standards legally regulated, work protection and regulations meant to avoid the poisoning of the cultures and implicitly of the workers and of the environmental components by the dangerous chemicals used in agriculture, forbidding people's exploitation in the labor process and assuring minimum medical care, something that is not granted in the southern countries.

Consumers also win because they can enjoy in this way high-quality products coming from natural cultures. Fairtrade offers the guarantee of origin and controlled trajectory of products coming especially from limited territorial structures. These products are permanently taken care of, which is why their quality is so high. This thing can be felt, and people are content for having acted fairly. It is estimated that if just 10 people in the north were to consume Fairtrade coffee, a whole family in the south could survive.

Nature and the environment probably win the most because Fairtrade products are cultivated traditionally, respecting the environmental and nature regulations and acting sustainably, namely, by rotating cultures with other plants of domestic or industrial use, by using shading trees, by reducing the chemicals used in agriculture, by using natural fertilizers and fighting erosion. Moreover, by avoiding fires and an ecological removal of the residues, the tropical forest and the natural waters are protected. All these things have positive effects on the world in which we are all living, being consequently also useful to people everywhere.

Children in the southern countries also have something to win, because child labor exploitation is forbidden, and the family revenues can assure a decent living. The Fairtrade system bonuses are used for the construction of new schools.

There are already many raw matters carrying the Fairtrade mark: coffee, tea, chocolate, honey, bananas, sugar or rice. Next, we shall take the example of coffee to see how the principles delineated above are put into practice.

The following comment has also been made concerning the experiment presented on the webpage of the Austrian representative of the Fairtrade movement: "Coffee is the most important agricultural good on the north-south global market and, worldwide, it is the most important export matter, after oil".

Sustainable consumption is another important way in the examples of a sustainable way of acting. The sustainability principle designates the mechanism of the three action dimensions - ecological, economic and social. Combined with consumer behavior, the ecological dimension of sustainability becomes the most important. Economic development and social welfare are no longer possible, in the long run, except in a well-established framework, rising nature and its rules to the rank of vital element.

According to another line of reasoning, the economic and social aspects also have their role in the attempt of making ecology feasible: ecological production and consumption are elements that cannot be realized unless the consumer can afford them and unless both the consumption and the production are realized under acceptable social auspices.

Non-sustainable consumption and production models constitute a particularly important reason of environmental problems on all levels—from the local level to the global one—and, consequently, the preoccupations for defending nature and preserving the environment cannot ignore the subject: changing consumer habits.

Moreover, the theme sustainable consumption - as well as the topic sustainability, in general, is closely related to other subjects such as (worldwide) justice, distribution or globalization, aspects that a correct construction of the definition of sustainability as a new civilizing project cannot avoid.

Especially in the so-called rich industrialized countries usually dominate habits marked by exaggerate consumption, and ignorance of the resources available. Whereas in certain parts of the world people consume simply wastefully, there are poorer areas of the world population where people cannot meet even their basic needs. For this reason, a change in the consumption and production models supposes the elaboration of a strategy taking into account the misbalance noticed above.

There is no single principle valid for the consumption of the future. The individualization of the consumer decisions is a constitutive element of the modern, democratic and pluralistic society, which is not questioned by the scenarios foreseeing new sustainable lifestyles. Anyway, the consumers' decisions are and will always be strongly influenced by the framework-conditions. These include political decisions, prices, available technologies, revenues and their distribution, social norms and principles guiding the various groups of the society and, last but not least, the influence of advertising and marketing.

INTERDISCIPLINARY ACTIVITY FIELD

Sustainable consumption is an extremely stratified and interdisciplinary activity field. The change in consumer behavior is a process taking place with the participation of many social groups. Leaving aside the individual households, the largest consumer group, there are also the authorities, the economy, the educational institutions, the NGOs and many other groupings. For this reason, the authorities ought to create adequate framework-conditions, in exchange the process itself has to be developed first of all through the initiative and commitment of the various consumers (Popescu, C., 2008).

CHANGING CONSUMER HABITS

A change in consumer habits supposes first of all a fundamental transformation in values and lifestyle. Changing the consumers' way of thinking and acting, however, cannot be imposed by the hand of the authorities.

Living sustainably means living well, in partnership with the spring of resources, in a healthy manner, in collaboration and tolerance, admitting the value of things, savoring them and consuming them with joy. It also means valuing quality, not running after each tendency in fashion, without however neglecting them all—all of these things have to do with the quality of life. Consuming sustainably means remembering that the enemy of good is not necessarily 'worse'; remembering that community and individualism are parts of the same whole, just as partnership and autonomy. A sustainable lifestyle is the art of knowing to behave correctly in false structures. This is why we need both: politics at the top and our actions at the basis. Only by acting together can then appear sustainable economic structures, in point of production and consumption.

A STRATEGY OF EFFICIENCY AND SUFFICIENCY

To open the way to a sustainable (global) society, it is necessary to establish certain principles, such as those enumerated above, elaborated by the famous German institute Wuppertal Institute. To put these principles into practice, it takes a lot of courage and creativity. In this sense, we will discuss here two strategies coming to complete each other, as an increasing number of authors of the ecological economy sphere are explaining:

The strategy of efficiency aims to dramatically reduce consumption by redirecting technical progress. At its heart is the increase of resource productivity raised to the 4th power, and in the long term, even to the 10th power. A reduction of the natural resources consumption to a tenth is, naturally, a colossal challenge for creative and enterprising people, being considered "a new technological revolution, almost of the same proportions as the Industrial Revolution". This daring project is, however, compared to others, less controversial, and in many domains, it is even a subject of consensus.

The strategy of efficiency is nothing else, however, but a stage of the passage to a sustainable development. This level must be completed and supported by another dimension, which the authors from the Institute in Wuppertal call the strategy of sufficiency. It is only here that we meet necessities and lifestyles, a redefinition of life quality. This does not mean, however, the end of a good living. The key is the concept of "the new models of welfare".

"Half of what you had, in exchange twice as good": this resounding motto of the ecologist enterpriser of Munich, Karl Ludwig Schweisfurth, perfectly describes the situation (Schweisfurth, K., L., 2014). What he recommends concerning the consumption of food, can be applied as well in other daily life domains. The civilization guided by the sufficiency principle follows the "correct measure" and aims to attain a balance in the welfare assured by consumption goods, both temporal and spatial.

What do we actually need? This is the question that comes in handy here. Beauty is also something good that keeps us alive. We are advised to focus on the optimum, namely on better things, on quality, on sustainability, instead of following the maximal values. In this way, a culture of self-limitation and the elegance of simplicity is promoted – taking over the older ideas supported by the philosophy of the art of living.

Based on the idea of sustainability, a movement has been born and has increased, an ecological subculture on the world level, which developed definitions, perspectives and similar reforming propositions. It is a movement comprising small initiatives and enterprises, parties of the public administrations and scientific institutions, and which has built, based on numerous experiments, a capital of knowledge and skills constituting the fundament of the so necessary changes.

THE ENERGY ISSUE IN THE NEW CONCEPT

After consumption, if we refer to another fundamental issue, that of energy, we cannot help bringing back into discussion the solar energy.

Our civilization relies on raw matters, especially oil, coal and natural gas, fossil matters regenerated on very large spatio-temporal scales and which, inevitably, are going to be exhausted. Moreover, the burning of these fossil fuels decisively and doubtlessly contributes to climate change.

The vision of a solar epoch was brought into focus in the 1990s. The economic and political framework-conditions for the survival of the human race faced with a climate catastrophe were then in the focus of attention. The lifestyle, the cultural dimension - esthetic, ethical and spiritual - of the passage towards sustainability were, however, aspects that were largely overlooked. Only a few small circles, less known, pondered on these themes as well. Reference points in this context were, in the years 1985-1999, the Discussions of Toblach (Scherhorn, G., 1997).

This circle of discussions, applauded more in the German-speaking area and in Italy, turned their attention from the technical problems supposed by the return to ecological principles, focusing to a larger extent on the cultural dimension of sustainability. In 1992, the year of the world summit of Rio, the initiator of the Discussions of Toblach, the artist, sociologist and mountain man of South Tirol, Hans Glauber, proposed the coordinates of the new model of life: "Slower, less, better, more beautifully". Despite all the criticisms against the destructive development of civilization, this perspective takes seriously the power of attraction exerted by the slogan "faster, higher, further, more". It does no underestimate the power of this paradigm, which promises stability and safety. It does not deny the esthetic fascination and the promises of a better life of a consumers' world. Glauber believes that in an open competition between the two models, the new variant ought to become more attractive and "simply more beautiful".

"The vision is that of a solar epoch, the age of the new culture of sustainability." The fossil and nuclear age are but a short episode in the history of mankind. It starts with the beginning of industrialization and will end at the latest as soon as the fossil resources come to an end. Before that, mankind used only the power of the sun. And after that, the world will learn to live on it again. Anyway, the second solar age allows the development of a life to a much higher level of civilization. Due to the new technologies and especially thanks to the possibility of generating energy using the solar power, we will be able to use the sun's energy much more efficiently and much more flexibly.

The new civilization will be a decentralized, more democratic and more just one. Because unlike oil and the other fossil and nuclear fuels, controlled by the fewest, the sun shines for all of us. Nobody controls the sun and everybody has access to it. This source of energy, namely the sun, also has the advantage that it is extremely rich, even there where, today, poverty prevails. The utopia of a juster development consequently seems almost touchable.

The new civilizing project relies on the constitution of a new balance between material and non-material goods, on a comprehensive quality of life instead of a welfare unilaterally based on consumption goods. "The economy of a better life is constituted of a natural combination between moderate consumption and immaterial goods." (Gerhard Scherhorn, Toblach Discussions, 1997). The solar epoch will permit, in this way, the development of a civilization with easier access to resources. It will rely on a new method of production and consumption. It admits the fact that we will need to creatively accept its limits. Its concept relies on the confrontation with the quantitative limitations, looking for the potential for a continual and limitless growth in the sphere of immaterial goods and values. "The function of material goods finally resides in the fact of facilitating our access to immaterial assets and common goods." (Gerhard Scherhorn, Toblach Discussions, 1997). Yet, this very limitation finally becomes a resource, because we will have to make the best out of these limitations. Thus, an esthetics of the just measure shall be developed.

"Beauty, too, is a way of living." (Gerhard Scherhorn, Toblach Discussions, 1998). It is a basic need. Without beauty, one cannot have a fulfilled life. We have seen, out of experience, what happens when beauty is lost, you see landscapes destroyed and urban sadness, the other side of industrial mass production—this is where the commitment to a culture of sustainability comes from. It is characterized by a cautious resource handling. It focuses on the unique character and local traditions, and, at the same time, on natural and cultural diversity. Savoring ecological foods, understanding nature by the senses, the pleasure of recognizing a successful design and a good architecture mean joy of living (Popescu, C., 1999).

REFERENCES

Allan, D. (1994). *Stream Ecology*. Oxford.

Brown. (1997). State of the World and our Resources. New York: W.W. Norton & Company.

Georgescu-Roegen, N. (1979). Legea entropiei si procesul economic. Publishing House Politică.

Myers, N. (1993). *The World's Forests: Problems and Potentials*. Corvallis, OR: Pacific Rivers Council.

Odum, E. (1993). *Ecology and our endangered life-support system*. Sunderland.

Pimentel, D. (1997). L'écologie des fôrets. Ed. did. Paris.

Popescu, C. (1999). Protection and integration of the forest heritage of Romania-a problem of national and regional policy. The 24th Congress ARA, Liege.

Popescu, C. (2008a). Stări conflictuale generate de exploatarea abuziva a pădurilor lumii. Editura Bibliotheca.

Popescu, C. (2008b). The growth of the forest ecosystems role for the defence of the environmental components. The 32nd Congress ARA, Boston, MA.

Popescu, C. (2011). La durabilité en qualité de nouveau projet civilisateur. 57éme Congrès "Refondation financière, sorties de crise et nouvelles stratégies de croissance économique", Croatia.

Popescu, C. (2012). *The Evaluation of Climate Change Risks*. The XIII th Annual International Conference Risk In Contemporary Economy, Galaţi.

Popescu, C. (2014). *Reconsidering the Relationship Between Socio-Economic System and Natural Environment*. The 2nt International Conference ESPERA 2014 – Economic Scientific Research Theoretical, Empirical and Practical Approaches organizată de National Institute for Economic Research, Bucharest, România

Popescu, C. (2015). *Le développement durable en tant que concept multidimensionnel*. Le 59ème Congrés de l'AIELF Croissance, population, protection sociale. Faits et theories face aux enjeux", Paris, France.

Scherhorn, G. (1997). *Discuţiile de la Toblach* [The Discussions of Toblach]. Academic Press.

Schweisfurth, K. L. (2014). *Der Metzger, der kein Fleisch mehr isst Oekom Verlag*. München.

Chapter 3
Reducing Poverty and Sustaining Growth:
A Microfinance Approach

Nabila Nisha
North South University, Bangladesh

Afrin Rifat
North South University, Bangladesh

ABSTRACT

Microfinance institutions have been effective rural banking channels that extended financial services to low-income individuals, particularly women in developing country settings. Since its inception, microfinance has evolved as an economic development approach and has grown to enormous scale in Bangladesh, with a reported approximate 23 million borrowers in a country of roughly 150 million people. These numbers reveal the highest population saturation of microfinance in any country. However, with the maturity of the microfinance market in recent years, competition has subsequently increased among various financial and non-financial institutions. Against this backdrop of intense competition, this chapter aims to focus on the current institutions of Bangladesh that has made the microfinance service almost a sole option for the downtrodden segment of the low-income society. In particular, various approaches of microfinance and its operational structure by these institutions including the challenges and attributions of a dynamic micro credit concept will be highlighted.

DOI: 10.4018/978-1-5225-2081-8.ch003

INTRODUCTION

The concept of microfinance has evolved as an economic development approach targeted as a potential weapon in uprooting poverty and assisting the poor effectively to improve their living status and livelihoods significantly. The popularity of microfinance has made it the core activities of hundreds of microfinance institutions (MFIs) across the world, particularly in developing countries like Bangladesh. In fact, it was Bangladesh which pioneered and fostered the institutional development of microfinance and today it has reached an enormous scale with approximately 23 million borrowers in a country of roughly 150 million people.

Microfinance institutions have extended financial services mostly to rural areas where otherwise it would be more expensive and unprofitable to open branches of traditional banking institutions. Moreover, since the rural population living under the poverty line and the poor with lower income is still out of any formal credit services in Bangladesh, microfinance institutions have made it a point to provide credit to the poor through small savings under the dynamic microcredit concept. Microfinance has thus become the main form of rural finance in Bangladesh. The effectiveness of the microfinance concept is such in Bangladesh that its systematic, group-based and institutionalized operations have been replicated all over the world with local modifications and adaptations.

In the context of Bangladesh, microfinance institutions have gained credence as the providers of an effective poverty alleviation tool from both practitioners' donors and policy makers of the country. However, the case of microfinance in Bangladesh and its success as the largest and most efficient sector has only been achieved through the support of both government and non-governmental organizations, subsequently increasing competition among various institutions of the microfinance market. This chapter therefore aims to shed some light into the present status of the microfinance institutions currently operating in Bangladesh. To pursue this purpose, four prominent institutions involved in the provision of microfinance in the country have been highlighted. Findings of this chapter will provide further insights into understanding the microfinance models followed by these institutions, their operational structures and the generalized challenges they face. In addition, this study can assist various financial and non-financial institutions to understand the importance of microfinance and develop and implement microfinance concepts in a more profound way in Bangladesh.

BACKGROUND

Microfinance is generally known as a sustainable means of poverty alleviation leading to lasting, holistic development, particularly in the settings of developing countries. It has evolved from the time of its inception as an economic development approach that benefits the financially disadvantaged people, like those with low and unstable incomes, little or no land/assets and low social status in rural and urban areas (Maanen, 2004). The main idea behind microfinance is to provide these people with credit and other financial services of very small amounts so that they can raise their income levels and improve their living standards (Khalily, 2004). The concept of microfinance is a trial and tested one which believes that the involvement of lending-repayment process with different socio-cultural activities can result in the empowerment and social development of the overall community, especially the women (Yunus, 1998). Microfinance has also been viewed as a sustainable finance option and an effective rural banking channel for the unbanked population of developing countries.

Microfinance first evolved in the 1970s with the name "microcredit" and eventually became a tremendous movement of implementation by receiving the widest coverage compared to other poverty alleviation programs across the world (Ahmed, 2001). As such, around 160 million people in various developing countries are today served by microfinance. Historical context evidences that it was during the 1980s that non-governmental organizations (NGOs) came into existence and initiated the service offerings of small loans to women, so that they can invest in business, accumulate assets and increase their income to a substantial level (Zaman, 2013). Moreover, since banks could not afford to provide micro loans to poor people owing to the lack of collateral and financial assets, NGOs gained further momentum in this micro credit arena. Although there always have been other non-commercial and informal money-lenders like credit unions and lending co-operatives, lack of insecurity in the lending and borrowing process and mostly the absence of collateral made micro credit through NGOs a popular phenomenon.

The concept of micro credit was then transformed into a modernized version of microfinance and the credit of pioneering this goes to Dr. Mohammad Yunus. Yunus initially began experimenting with lending to poor women in the village of Jobra, Bangladesh and over time established an institutionalized version of the micro credit model, namely Grameen Bank (Rahman, Luo, Ahmed & Xiaolin, 2012). The Grameen model mainly involves small loans to women with fixed terms and amounts, group liability, weekly meetings, forced payments into a group savings account, etc. The basic idea is to provide the poor people of Bangladesh with credit without collateral (Shil, 2009). This simple yet classic method of delivering micro credit soon became a global movement and managed to capture publicity, billions of dollars of financing, large numbers of customers and even earned a Nobel Peace Prize for Dr. Yunus (Leikem, 2012).

According to Morduch (1998), Grameen Bank is the flagship of the international microfinance movement, whose model has been replicated on four continents and consequently, it became a formal tool for global poverty reduction across the world. With the progress of commercialization, microfinance facilities also got initiated in different institutions and other NGOs in Bangladesh in order to ensure smooth economic development. Thus, the golden era for the microfinance industry of Bangladesh begun in 1990s as various models of microfinance, with some local modifications and adaptations, converged towards the comparatively uniform "Grameen-model" of delivering microfinance to the impoverished without requiring any collateral (Alamgir, 2010).

Microfinance thereby became a popular economic development practice in Bangladesh, as a result of which, the microfinance sector of Bangladesh is currently considered as the most dominant and efficient one in the world (Zaman, 2013). This growth, however, took place during several distinct phases over more than three decades after the country got its independence. There was a time when commercial banks, agricultural banks and cooperative societies were the primary sources of small loans for various types of borrowers like farmers, traders and cottage industries, particularly before the arrival of micro credit concepts in Bangladesh. However, these institutions were more inclined to provide small loans to special borrowers rather than to the poor population. Moreover, these banks used to demand for collateral in order to sanction any loan and have rarely been interested in small loans with the exception of Islami Bank Bangladesh Limited which had large retail microcredit operations even at that point of time (Alamgir, 2010). On the other hand, there were agricultural development banks like Bangladesh Krishi Bank (BKB) and Rajshahi Krishi Unnayan Bank (RAKUB) that used to target and still targets only the small, medium and large farmers who could offer land as mortgage (Aziz, 2012). According to Hulme and Moore (2006), it is the microfinance industry, particularly the micro credit operations that has drastically changed this scenario and made it possible for more than 13 million poor households of Bangladesh to have access to credit. This easy accessibility of microfinance, in turn, has directly or indirectly affected the social conditions of the country to a large extent.

Today, there are four types of institutions involved in microfinance activities, namely Grameen Bank (GB): a member-owned specialized institution; NGOs like Bangladesh Rural Advancement Committee (BRAC), Proshika, Association for Social Advancement (ASA), BURO, etc; commercial and specialized banks like Bangladesh Krishi Bank (BKB), Rajshahi Krishi Unnayan Bank (RAKUB), Dhaka

Mercantile Cooperative Bank Ltd. (DMCBL), etc; and, government sponsored microfinance projects like BRDB, Swanirvar Bangladesh, etc. Even though there are hundreds of such organizations offering microcredit in Bangladesh, the bulk of the borrowers borrow from a handful of large organizations like Grameen Bank, BRAC, ASA, and Proshika. Hence, this study focuses on these four major institutions, which played revolutionary roles in alleviating poverty to a great extent from the rural areas of Bangladesh.

ISSUES, CONTROVERSIES, AND PROBLEMS

Bangladesh is often cited as the birth place of microcredit and one of those countries where the impact of the microfinance programs have been massive. Yet, the present coverage of the microfinance industry only stands about at one-third of rural households of the country through several hundreds of small to giant microfinance organizations (Mia & Ramage, 2011). This has resulted in yielding mixed impressions about the impacts of microfinance programs as rural banking channels in the context of Bangladesh.

In general, one of the major issues that surrounded the operations of MFIs has been the problem of overlapping. Since the concept of microfinance programs does not require documentary collateral against credit on the basis of the assumption that the targeted poor population owns no collateral, many borrowers tend to hide information about their current loans and try to obtain multiple loans from different sources in the same time periods. This causes a complex situation in this collateral-free lending system for people who are economically vulnerable and incapable of generating income from any other activities. Moreover, there are various other contextual controversies that are directly or indirectly related to this issue of overlapping in the microfinance programs. For instance, the profit-making objective of particularly the large MFIs resulted in high interest rates and an unhealthy competition among the operators in the microfinance sector. Additionally, the absence of regulatory authorities in this large and distributed financial market of the country further paced these competitions. Even the funds channeled by the Palli Karma Sahayak Foundation (PKSF), the world's largest apex microcredit funding institution, forced MFIs towards multiple lending to continue their operations. This is because the creation of high supply of micro credit through PKSF did not match the lack of demand for the MFIs in the borrower community of the rural areas. Consequently, the MFIs ended up taking probable borrowers into the grips of a higher degree of overlapping in Bangladesh (McIntosh & Wydick, 2005).

Besides high competition and pressures of disbursement, the information gap between the loan seeker and the loan provider also aggravated the issue of overlapping. As a result, the overlapped borrower became inclined to enter into a vicious cycle of loans, approaching local moneylenders, liquidating their remaining assets, and ultimately inviting a series of economic and social problems due to their over-indebting loans. It thus becomes imperative that the lack of control over this problem of overlapping is managed in the operational models of the microfinance programs. However, the MFIs have failed in managing this issue in countries like Bangladesh and this has been mostly evident in the operations of giant MFIs like Grameen Bank, BRAC, ASA and Proshika. In fact, concrete evidence of the effectiveness and efficiency of these four large MFIs is still inconclusive.

A number of studies have been previously conducted in order to examine the effectiveness and efficiency of the MFIs with regard to their operations, problems and challenges in Bangladesh. For instance, Khandker (2005) identified some major challenges that are faced by MFIs like overlapping membership growth, rising credit risk, etc. Barua (2009) further added some problematic issues encountered by the giant MFIs in Bangladesh like dependency on a single revenue generation model, multiple borrowing or overlapping, severe lack of training and education, lack of innovation and central database, misuse of credit by borrowers, sector-wise disbursement without technical expertise, etc. Alamgir (2010) supported these findings by highlighting other challenges faced by the MFIs like institutional capacity, quality and diversity of services, fallout from political and macroeconomic factors and so forth.

In line with the above studies, Mia & Ramage (2011) and Yuge (2011) also examined the nature, causes and consequences of overlapping in micro credit while Rahman et al. (2012) analyzed the operational mechanism and institutional innovation of large MFIs with regard to their outreach, outstanding loans, savings and efficient service deliveries. Alternatively, Zaman (2013) supported all findings of previous microfinance studies and provided evidence of problems like overlapping in multiple borrowing, lack of reliable database, lack of trained and skilled workforce, less concentration on ultra poor, etc as major issues that the MFIs face in Bangladesh.

Since the livelihood of a large number of people is affected by the microfinance programs of these MFIs, extensive and continuous research is necessary to keep track of their effectiveness. As such, this chapter focuses upon the present status of the microfinance institutions currently operating in Bangladesh, particularly the ones which have the largest micro credit operations across the country.

METHODOLOGY

In designing this research, a case study approach has been incorporated. According to Yin (2009), the case study approach is preferred to conduct exploratory investigations and one of the essential characteristics of using this approach is that it focuses on one instance of the thing that is to be investigated.

Case studies can actually employ various methods, including documentation, archival records, interviews, direct observations, participant observations and physical artifacts (Saunders, Saunders, Lewis & Thornhill, 2011). As such, a case study methodology is seen as an appropriate approach here since case studies can provide a rich understanding of the organization or organizations in question. Case study methodology also emphasize the ability of qualitative research to capture the real-life context within which events take place and to capture the essence of events, especially as they unfold (Gerring, 2007). In addition, Bryman & Bell (2015) argue that case studies can be valuable in situations where existing knowledge is limited, often providing in-depth contextual information, which may result in an in-depth level of understanding. Case studies can even be advantageous when the focus of the study is not typical but something unusual, unexpected, covert or illicit (Johnson, Onwuegbuzie & Turner, 2007). For instance, research on microfinance institutions and their operational activities are limited in number and most of them are simple comparative analysis of the success stories of such institutions. The focus on the activities and product portfolios of the selected microfinance institutions can provide further insights as to the operational structures of the microfinance programs in Bangladesh and the challenges surrounding such activities in the microfinance market. Based on the findings, recommendations have been proposed to promote the development and implementation of the microfinance programs at a larger scale in the country.

The research methods thus include in-depth interviews and secondary sources. Interviews were conducted with the officials and clerical staffs working for each of the microfinance institutions studied in this chapter. The representatives from the selected MFIs were particularly interviewed regarding the concept of microfinance, their offerings and how they operate, the problems and challenges they face in serving the rural market, and so on. Based on their responses, a general picture has been represented in this study which reflects the perceptions and perspectives of people involved in the microfinance programs and various aspects of the four large MFIs, currently operating in Bangladesh.

OVERVIEW OF MAJOR MICROFINANCE INSTITUTIONS

The following section provides an overview of the four major and giant institutions that took microfinance to a new height in the country, namely BRAC, Grameen Bank, ASA and Proshika.

BRAC

Bangladesh Rural Advancement Committee or more popularly known as BRAC is a finance-plus NGO that was established in 1972. BRAC was set up as a response to humanitarian need in order to help rural people in a war-torn Bangladesh during the post-independence period (Ahmed & Rafi, 1999). However, within a very short period of time after its inception, BRAC realized that relief work was a short-term measure given the multiple problems that the people faced. Thus, there was a shift in the objectives and BRAC evolved from a relief and rehabilitation organization to a development organization (Rahman et al., 2012).

Eventually, BRAC became a mainstreamed microfinance institution and started housing a very large range of non-financial social and supportive services such as functional, education, livelihoods training, logistical assistance and various social support services (Kabeer, Mahmud & Isaza Castro, 2010). It works particularly with the women from poor families whose lives are struck by acute poverty, illiteracy, diseases and malnutrition (Ahmed & Rafi, 1999). Besides, BRAC has contributed significantly to the educational sector of Bangladesh as well, by helping to achieve gender parity in enrolment and by targeting dropouts and non-enrolled children, particularly girls, in marginalized communities (Asadullah, Savoia & Mahmud, 2014).

Currently BRAC has its branches in all 64 districts of Bangladesh as well as in Afghanistan, Pakistan, Sri Lanka, Uganda, Tanzania, South Sudan, Sierra Leone, Liberia, Haiti and the Philippines. It works in over 68,000 villages and over 4,000 urban slums in every district of Bangladesh and employs over 100,000 people, roughly 70 per cent of who are women, reaching more than 126 million people (Kabeer et al., 2010). BRAC has thus gone through a series of evolutions and has now become one of the largest NGO-MFIs of the country in terms of the scale and diversity of its intervention.

Grameen Bank

The Grameen Bank is a finance-minimalist bank that offers a broad range of financial products and limited organizational support. It originated in 1976, in the work of Professor Muhammad Yunus, who launched a research project to study how to design a credit delivery system to provide banking services to the rural poor. In the beginning, the Bank was developed to experiment the hypothesis that if financial resources were made available to the poor at reasonable interest rates, they would be able to generate productive self-employment without external assistance (Wahid, 1994). The target groups for this experiment were the poorest of the poor, who are almost exclusively women (McDonnell, 1999). The reason behind targeting this group for loans, particularly for micro credit is that the poor have skills that are underutilized and with incentive they can earn more money. Besides, in order to develop a system of mutual accountability, Grameen Bank pioneered a peer group lending structure with joint liability, a mechanism that reduces problems of moral hazard and adverse selection where households are too poor to offer collateral (Morduch, 1999). Based on the positive results it achieved, Grameen Bank was authorized by national legislation as an independent bank in 1983.

Grameen Bank was always a provider of financial services to poor households, but it soon underwent a major change in its approach. In 2001-2, all Grameen Bank branches began to operate the new Grameen II (Grameen Generalised System) model more vigorously (Hulme & Moore, 2006). Under this new financial system, the bank started lending to both men and women, but their focus remained exclusively on women. This is because the bank believed women to be both more reliable in repaying their loans and more effective agents of change within the family (Kabeer et al., 2010).

Today, the success of the Grameen model has touched such a height that it has been replicated in various other parts of the world. Currently, it has approximately 6 million members in Bangladesh and around 96 per cent of them are women.

ASA

Association for Social Advancement or commonly known as ASA is the one of the largest and finest MFI of Bangladesh, whose transition from social movement to minimalist microfinance organization has been the most dramatic within the NGO sector (Kabeer et al., 2010). It established in 1978, with the objective to build consciousness and organize the poor and deprived people in realizing their rights. However, over time it realized that mere awareness-building motivation was not adequate enough for people who repeatedly asked for loans to invest in economic activities (Jain, 2007). This realization, later in 1989, paved way for the organization to transform into a microfinance provider through a cost-effective sustainable model.

ASA started its full fledged microfinance operations and reformed itself as a finance-only MFI in 1991. In the beginning, ASA introduced microfinance program as a pilot project where the sole focus was on using micro credit as its tool in fighting poverty. The distinctive feature of these microfinance programs has always been the easy credit access of the poor who get it at their doorstep in a flexible terms based on personal guarantee instead of group guarantee (Jain, 2007). Moreover, ASA also created employment opportunities by providing microfinance services for the socio-economic empowerment of the poor in Bangladesh.

Currently, ASA is the third largest MFI in the country, offering a range of savings, credit and insurance facilities. ASA has taken around 70000 villages under its wings by providing services to approximately 8.45 million people through its 3236 branch offices spread all over Bangladesh (Rahman et al., 2012). Also, there are 17 countries including India, Pakistan, Sri Lanka, Philippines, Ghana and Nigeria in which ASA has its own branches, where an appreciable number of workers are deployed to provide technical assistance and on-the-spot support to their microcredit programs (Jain, 2007). ASA's unique low-cost credit delivery mechanism has been replicated in several other countries and this particularly says a lot about its current success as a MFI (Hulme & Moore, 2006).

Proshika

Proshika was set up in 1974 by a group of student activists with a strong commitment to social mobilization, but it was registered as a formal organization in 1976 (Kabeer et al., 2010). Initially, it had a credit-program that was led and managed by its borrower groups and this borrower-driven feature of Proshika made it unique compared to other conventional microfinance organizations.

By the mid-1990s, it began to move in the direction of the financial sustainability model and started its microfinance programs, focusing mainly upon men and women from landless and marginal farming households. Like other large MFIs, Proshika also works closely with women, although around 30 percent of its membership remains male (Kabeer et al., 2010).

Currently, Proshika has its presence in 21,272 villages and 2,380 urban slums in 55 districts of Bangladesh. It works with nearly 1.36 million men and women members drawn from rural and urban poor households of the country. They have been organized into 104,295 primary groups and with an average 1.3 member from each household having 5.5 family members, this translates into over 5.77 million programme beneficiaries of Proshika (Daley-Harris, 2005). Moreover, it has created 12.33 million employment/self-employment opportunities for the poor and brought over one million households out of poverty while making over one million people literate and planting nearly one billion trees towards the greening of Bangladesh.

APPLICATIONS OF MICROFINANCE MODELS

There are various microfinance models used by MFIs throughout the world, but the four key models that have got immense popularity are: Grameen model, MC2 Model, Village Banking Model of FINCA and the SKS and Non Banking Finance Company (NBFC) Model. The following section discusses these four leading models of microfinance programs.

Grameen Model

One of the most successful models of microfinance that has been replicated around the world is the Grameen model. The Grameen model, introduced by the Grameen Bank of Bangladesh, is based on the voluntary formation of small groups of four to eight persons to provide mutual, morally binding group guarantees instead of the collateral required by conventional banks (Shil, 2009). As per the requirement of this model, the group has to self-select its members before obtaining a loan (Fotabong, 2011). After the formation of the group, the Bank grants loans to the selected members of the group first and then to the rest of the members. Moreover, the model requires the borrower to save 5 percentage of the loan beforehand, which basically acts as collateral. One of the best features of this group-based lending practice is the joint accountability that this model enforces. If one member of the group becomes a defaulter, the entire group will be ineligible and will not be entitled to receive further loans.

Besides, this model has placed strong focus on women on the basis of the belief that they are not only reliable borrowers but also perceptive and intelligent entrepreneurs as well. In this process, the bank has successfully developed a new banking system based on mutual trust, accountability, participation and creativity (Fotabong, 2011).

MC2 Model

The MC2 model originally stands for rural development micro-banking. The objectives of this model are one, economic and financial sustainability from the perspective of the micro bank, individuals and group members and two, social dimension (Atuya, 2014). In 1992, the first MC2 model was developed by drawing inspiration from Einstein's famous formula: Victory over Poverty (VP) is possible if the Means (M) and the Competences (C) of the Community (C) are combined (Atuya, 2014). Therefore, the formula VP= M x C x C = MC2 (Fotabong, 2011).

MC2 model has two versions: a rural version, MC2 and an urban version dubbed MUFFA (Rudrabhatla, Roy & Bose, 2015). The rural version of the model is exclusively for women who are most dominated by poverty while MUFFA is aimed at the disadvantageous women of urban areas. Both aim to provide easy access to financial services so that the two groups of women can become independent.

Developing MC2 microfinance model involves five stages. The first stage deals with sensitizing the poor and raising awareness among them regarding the importance of savings and self-reliance; the second stage deals with mobilizing resources through raising the startup capital, paying individual shares subscription and fees, registering the micro-bank, and opening of individual accounts; the third stage deals with financing individual income generating activities while stage four deals with financing common interest economic projects; and, the final stage deals with carrying out social development projects with the resources generated in stage three and four (Fotabong, 2011).

Village Banking Model of FINCA

The Village Banking model was first developed in the 1980s in Bolivia, wherein the village banking institution of Foundation for International Community Assistance (FINCA) first implemented the model in order to create financially-sustainable solidarity groups (Atuya, 2014). The policy of FINCA is to train small community groups in a 22-module program to establish Community Credit Enterprises (CCE), form groups of 30-60 members, mostly comprising of women and later permit these members to buy shares as shareholders and generate capital to offer sustainable credit and business models (Fotabong, 2011).

Under this model, the village bank usually receives its first loan from the implementing agency as soon as it gets inaugurated. Then, as per the requirement of the model, the first individual loan (usually US$ 50) needs to be repaid on a weekly basis in equal installments of principal and interest over a four-month period (Atuya, 2014). The village bank collects these payments at regular meetings. Besides, the village bank is required to repay the entire loan-principal plus interest-to the implementing agency at the end of the 16th week of the loan (Atuya, 2014). If the village bank repays the entire loan timely, it will be eligible for a second loan. However, if the bank cannot pay the amount due on time, the implementing agency stops further credit until reimbursement is made (Fotabong, 2011).

SKS and Non-Banking Finance Company (NBFC) Model

This model is one of the prominent microfinance models in the context of India. It is basically an investor-driven model with an objective of profit maximization (Fotabong, 2011). All MFIs that use SKS and NBFC microfinance model mobilize resource through capital market investments and borrowings from commercial banks. These NGO-MFIs believe that poor people are bankable and lending to them is a trustable and profitable venture without relying on low cost funds for lending (Rudrabhatla et al., 2015). Besides, they also collect capital from the capital market on the ground that their institutions need huge amount of money to finance micro projects where financial markets are the only way to mobilize resources. Hence, these NGO-MFIs use debts and mezzanine assets and mobilize debt at market interest rates (Fotabong, 2011). The funds they receive in turn are made available to the poor to finance their various business activities that very often end up pushing the poor further below the poverty line.

PRODUCT PORTFOLIOS

Generally, microfinance includes loans, savings, insurances, transfer services and other financial products for low-income clients. So, basically it represents all the financial (credit, savings, insurance, remittance, etc) and non-financial (non-formal schooling for disadvantaged children or community-delivered health care, training, legal aid and social awareness) services provided to different groups of poor and non-poor clients who are not fortunate enough to be served by the conventional financial institutions. This section therefore focuses upon the product diversity of the four major MFIs of Bangladesh. Even though all these four giant MFIs started out with the same goal of socio-economic development of Bangladesh, interestingly there is a hidden competition among them in innovating new products and services suiting to poor people livelihoods (Rahman et al., 2012).

Grameen Bank, BRAC, ASA and Proshika have experience in more or less all kind of microfinance services, currently providing micro-credit, savings, micro-insurance and educational services in the country. All of them have subdivided loan and saving products targeting different socio-economic strata. Beside some common services, they are also involved in providing some services which are only unique to them.

One of the most important features of the microfinance model that BRAC follows is its sustainability. Considering this, the main motto of BRAC's microfinance program is to make credit available to poor women at a reasonable price and to promote the economic development of the country by increasing the income level of the rural poor and operate self-sustaining credit activities (Rahman et al., 2012). The several financial and nonfinancial services offered by BRAC include credit, savings, insurance, education, health, training, social development, legal aid services program, research and development, human rights and advocacy, public affairs and communications, human resource development, etc.

On the other hand, apart from the regular savings, credit, micro-insurance and educational services, Grameen Bank has introduced many services that make them unique. For instance, special services for beggars that it has initiated as a part of its microfinance scheme were an outstanding innovation (Alamgir, 2010). Another excellent innovation by Grameen Bank has been the provision of guarantee to shop-owners to give goods of maximum of BDT 2000 on credit to a poor woman to sell door-to-door in villages. Furthermore, the Bank has education schemes for member's children and social businesses as well.

Alternatively, ASA functions as a pure MFI and is well-known for its innovative product portfolios, wherein it provides diversified loan products, deposit services, saving, insurance and educational products, health care services, etc (Kabeer et al., 2010). Moreover, with a pledge for making poverty-free society, ASA pursues a consciousness raising program to reduce health hazard and maintain sound health among its clients predominantly bracketed in low income and uneducated segment of the society (Aziz, 2012). Besides, to widen primary healthcare facilities, ASA launched Extended Health Program in the remotest and backward areas of the country where state owned and other public or private health services are inadequate (Aziz, 2012). ASA has initiated Water and Sanitation Program as well to develop sanitation facilities and improve access to pure drinking water to the people of lower segment of the society in Bangladesh.

Unlike BRAC, Grameen Bank and ASA, Proshika offers a loan portfolio that has a relatively large agricultural component - a sector which is usually shunned by most credit programs dedicated to the poor. Another distinctive but significant feature of Proshika's credit program has been the relatively large proportion of male group members in the total population unlike other MFIs where groups are almost 100 percent women. Even though Proshika's outreach is not broad enough, it still has its own share of innovation. This includes: Proshika Savings Scheme (PSS), which is based on principles such as security of savings, life insurance, risk coverage for damaged houses caused by natural disasters, accessibility, etc; and, Economic-Social Security Program (ESSP), which is a voluntary savings product that has been offered to group members of Proshika (Banking with the Poor Network, 2013).

OPERATIONAL STRUCTURES

Even though Grameen Bank, BRAC, ASA and Proshika were developed to provide financial and other nonfinancial services to the poor, their operational structure is quite different from each other.

The basic features of Grameen Banks' microfinance operation is poor people's access to credit with women as a priority by forming small solidarity groups of 5 members, exemption from collateral, small loans repaid in weekly installments, eligibility for higher loan amount for succeeding loans. Grameen Bank does not extend loans to all the members of the group at the same time. In the first stage, only two of them are eligible for a loan. If only the first two borrowers begin to repay the principals plus interest over six weeks, the other members of the group will be eligible for a loan.

On the other hand, BRAC forms group of 30-40 people which is known as Village Organization (VO). The purpose behind developing VO is basically to bring a group of poor, landless people together and improve their socio-economic positions. Besides, this VO works as a platform for launching and implementing BRAC's various activities (Rahman et al., 2012). Apart from the group approach, BRAC is also involved in providing individual credit facilities, wherein they consider the member's capacity to utilize the loan money, type of business and profitability of the Income Generating Activity (IGA)/business.

ASA's microfinance operation is slightly different from Grameen Bank and BRAC. It forms a similar group of 30-40 people for the financing purpose, but their operational mechanism is the most sustainable and cost-effective approach. The distinct feature of ASA is its decentralized nature. Each branch acts as its own cost and profit center. The branches have freedom to carry out all the activities as long as these conform to ASA's Operations Manual. For example, branch offices of ASA have no accountants; rather, it has simplified accounting and cash-handling for its branch offices by distributing the job between the branch manager and the three or four loan officers which is then monitored by senior staffs at four different levels leading up to the head office (Rahman et al., 2012). Moreover, each branch prepares its own annual work plan with fiscal targets and cash flow projection. As a result, funds are distributed evenly through the entire ASA structure.

Alternatively, Proshika's operation is based upon matching member savings with credit and to provide various forms of training, technical and skills development assistance. It also encourages members to expand their income-generating activities with credit provided by the organization (Kabeer et al., 2010). It typically works in those areas where many poor families live; a majority of people have a low level of education; sanitation systems are deficient or nonexistent and there is a low level of land ownership. Even though initially Proshika fulfilled its social intermediation objectives through group formation and consciousness rising rather than service provision, it has now moved into the provision of a wider range of social programmes. Proshika's credit microloan program now targets the agricultural workers, factory workers, small farmers, micro entrepreneurs and such others (Banking with the Poor Network, 2013).

CHALLENGES OF THE MICROFINANCE MARKET

An in-depth overview of the four MFIs, their product portfolios and their operational structures provide clear evidence for the success of the microfinance industry of Bangladesh. This growth of the microfinance market has given the poor access to credit and around 13 million poor households in the country today are provided with financial services like loan, savings, insurance, etc despite having low or moderate incomes (Armendáriz & Morduch, 2010). This saturation in the microfinance market of the country is truly remarkable, wherein approximately twelve hundred microfinance institutions function in several distinct phases, including the four large MFIs.

The MFIs currently host a variety of microfinance programs in the areas of agriculture, financial services, health, electricity, telecommunication, water, housing, tourism, handicrafts, consumer goods and services (Yuge, 2011). In the process, these NGOs have become the potent driver of financial inclusion for the poor; promoter of self-employment, poverty alleviation, savings and investment programs, empowerment of women; sources of human capital formation and employment of large numbers of graduates in the country, and so on (Ahmed, 2009). However, even after such achievements and success stories of the microfinance program, MFIs face a number of challenges and problems to operate in the rural areas.

Studies of microfinance programs through these four large MFIs show that the economic conditions of the poor people have greatly improved, yet there has not been any significant decline in the overall level of poverty of Bangladesh. Most of the poor population has been left out from the grasp of the microfinance programs due to the lack of sufficient creditworthiness and entrepreneurial ability necessary to handle money properly (Morduch, 1998). It can thus be stated that MFIs have not been able to reach effectively among the people of economically backward regions of the country (Sarder & Golzare, 2012). This implies that the MFIs have not very successful in including the entire population below the poverty line of the country.

Previous studies like Alamgir (2010) and Rahman et al. (2012) stated that the efforts of MFIs during the period of 1990-2006 reduced poverty at a rate of 1.8% annually, with an impressive economic growth of 7% in the country. A change in the scenario then occurred with an unprecedented price hike of food and other essential commodities in 2007-08, following which came recession (Chemin, 2008). Moreover, almost every year Bangladesh encountered natural calamities like floods and cyclones that resulted in the loss of lives, properties and livelihoods and created more poor people in the country. These external events, macro-economic instability and natural calamities have serious implications on the management and viability of microfinance institutions (Duvendack & Palmer-Jones, 2012). Several MFIs are forced to suspend microfinance operations like recovery and disbursement that leads to the loss of income and portfolio (Yuge, 2011). Some large MFIs even have to write off large amounts of loans and provide relief to the victims of the natural calamities (Ahmed, 2009). As such, MFIs often curb provision of loans and limit the withdrawal of savings, which create further problems for the poor people and results in the generation of an ultra poor level of population in Bangladesh.

Issues of weak governance and management often characterize the operations of microfinance programs in these large MFIs as well. For instance, Hulme & Moore (2006) mentioned about the Microcredit Regulatory Authority and claimed that it is the only supervisory body of the vast microfinance market of the country. However, lack of manpower, resource base and geographical concentration of this organization tends to aggravate governance and regulatory issues in large MFIs (Hassan, 2002). A crucial element that is therefore missing in the operations of these MFIs is the quality of leadership and management due to the interference of politicians and lobbyists. This is a major challenge for the MFIs particularly in a developing country like Bangladesh as the overpowering nature of lobbyists and governing bodies tend to alter decision-making in these institutions and change of rules with regard to credit and financial services targeted for the poor.

Additionally, a high dependence of these large MFIs on the availability of subsidies and donor funds tends to create further problems in the microfinance market. This is because if donor funding for microfinance diminishes, MFIs may have to charge higher interest rates to recover their operational costs and even look out for new avenues to fund their activities (Morduch, 1999). Lack of capital therefore poses quite a challenge for the MFIs. Owing to this, often these large institutions end up giving insufficient time for repayment to the borrowers. For example, most of the micro-loans from these four large MFIs are granted for a short period of time, following which the loan has to be rapidly repaid from the small amounts of cash flows generated from the business (Khandker, 2005). This step by the MFIs further creates hassles for the operations of these organizations, since shorter periods of repayments in majority of the cases results in the increase of the number of defaulters.

Moreover, instances of multiple borrowing or overlapping take place in large numbers due to this lack of time for repayment. Growing numbers of overlapping borrowers can destroy sustainable development among these large MFIs in the long-run (Zaman, 2013). This is because the MFIs highlighted in this study often compete to acquire new customers in order to expand their scale and maintain their operations. As a result, MFIs get engaged in excessive competition and end up lending multiple loans to a number of borrowers. This, in turn, encourages heavy debt which can later destroy many poor household economies. In fact, there are many reported cases wherein borrowers have misused these micro-loans in order to generate cash flows so that they can make repayments to the MFIs on time and avoid paying high interest rates (Godquin, 2004). On the other hand, multiple loans results in an increase in the amount of non-performing microfinance loans, irregular repayments among overlapping borrowers and a rise in the amounts of loan-loss reserves for these major MFIs (Karim, 2011). Overlapping borrowers thus often poses a systemic risk among major MFIs that undermines the basis of the entire microfinance industry in Bangladesh as a whole. Unfortunately, MFIs have failed to make any changes in their models which can provide corrective steps to cease these shorter periods of loan recovery (Ahmed, 2009). This need of innovation in the operations and microfinance models followed by these large MFIs is no less than a challenge in the current microfinance market.

Another burning issue for the large MFIs is the high cost of recruitment and training that they often have to undertake to run their organizations (Hulme & Moore, 2006). This is crucial since avoidance of training and education costs leads to the lack of skilled manpower within these MFIs and less research work on borrowers and the overall microfinance market of the country (Zaman, 2013). As such, this is yet another challenge for the MFIs in the context of Bangladesh.

Despite all these challenges, the activities and functionalities by these four large MFIs have evidenced that microfinance, on average and in general, did have a positive economic impact on the poor population in terms of income growth and reduced vulnerability and are continuing to do so even today. However, it is important that necessary steps be taken in order to reduce the impact of the identified challenges for the four players of the microfinance market.

SOLUTIONS AND RECOMMENDATIONS

Domination of the microfinance market by the four large MFIs is the root cause of many challenges that has been identified in the previous section. Encouraging new entrants can be a mainstream solution to the systematic risk of this sector in the context of Bangladesh (Hassan, 2002). Already there are many small NGOs and co-operative banks that are now part of the microfinance market of the country with an objective to work towards poverty alleviation, consumption smoothing and asset building of the poor (Hulme & Moore, 2006). While the new entrants can be a threat for the large MFIs, an overall outlook evidences otherwise. The joint effort of many microfinance institutions can not only bring in more development for the country, they can also establish an effective information sharing system in order to prevent overlapping borrowing among microfinance borrowers (Yuge, 2011). An example would be to initiate a credit bureau, wherein a screening effect can improve the risk assessment of all loan applicants. This will ultimately raise portfolio quality, which in turn, can reduce the rates of amounts overdue. In addition, the mere existence of such an information system can act as a deterrent which may prevent borrowers from taking a risk of borrowing excessive loans, particularly if they know the information available and the risks involved (Duvendack & Palmer-Jones, 2012). Moreover, if the large MFIs join hands with the new entrants and engage in informal information sharing activities like sharing the list of overlapping borrowers or households, this can safeguard the operations of the MFIs and reduce the number of non-performing microfinance loans and irregular repayments from the borrowers (Armendáriz & Morduch, 2010). It can also ensure accountability and transparency in the microfinance operations of these four MFIs.

Once the issues of overlapping borrowers are brought into control, these large MFIs can solve other minor issues as well. For instance, a major reason for the high interest rates of these MFIs is their high operational costs. The use of technology can reduce these operational costs and the institutions can plan to invest in staff training or educating their field staffs to further promote their microfinance programs in rural areas (Zaman, 2013). Trained staff can enable proper supervision and monitoring of loan disbursements and recollections in these MFIs and therefore prevent any kind of fraud and miss appropriations of funds. Additionally, if the credit officers are trained and educated, they can better guide borrowers about the various microfinance programs being offered in the microfinance market by these large MFIs. Adequate knowledge about microfinance programs and the overall market of these credit officers can even help the management of these MFIs to run a completely decentralized institution and target for expansion and cost-effective operations in the long-run (Karim, 2011). Besides, research platforms related to microfinance borrowers and micro-credit programs can be strengthened too, if operational costs are controlled by the MFIs.

It is also imperative that these four key players of the microfinance market consider providing flexibility in repayment schedules of their micro-loans and introduce flexible financial services for the microfinance borrowers (Meyer, 2002). The increasing number of overlapping borrowers indicates the lack of satisfaction from the financial services provided by the MFIs due to factors like weekly repayment schedules and loan sizes. Microfinance borrowers can actually make more productive investments if these MFIs meet their demands for loans by allowing more flexibility in loan disbursement and repayment schedules (Mallick, 2012). This will particularly be helpful for borrowers whose enterprises are entering an expansionary phase, since when the business is growing borrowers need more money to satisfy their financial demands of working capital. Due to high operational costs and even high interest rates, the four large MFIs often fail to satisfy such financial requirements and this inflexibility incurs the costs of multiple memberships among dynamic clients with good repayment capacity (Chemin, 2008).

Furthermore, the MFIs could offer new product lines for the most disadvantaged people by offering savings and insurance product portfolios under the microfinance programs. This can help the poor people to reduce vulnerability and deal with risks such as disease and accidents, thereby enabling them to avoid borrowing an additional loan (Khandker, 1998). In fact, the mobilization of funds through savings and insurance programs can strengthen the financial sustainability of the MFIs as well.

Currently, a growing number of poor people have access to financial market through microfinance. Hence, it is necessary to introduce financial education to these people, so that they know that excessive loans may cause serious damage to their household economies (Godquin, 2004). MFIs initially should ensure that loans are only given to those microfinance borrowers who are going to utilize it to earn a living rather than for any other purpose (Alamgir, 2010). Next, the MFIs should improve the financial literacy of their clients to maintain the quality of their portfolios by focusing upon financial options and strategies of poor individuals and households in the rural setting of Bangladesh. To enhance this outreach to the remote areas of the country, these four large MFIs can also use mobile financial services by establishing partnerships with mobile phone operators and banks to reach the unbanked low income people (Sardar & Golzare, 2012).

Since its inception, microfinance has made an important transition with various innovations in the market of Bangladesh. As such, it is highly likely that such continued endeavors and innovations can help the four large MFIs to deal with the problems and challenges of the microfinance market of the country. The introduction of a legal framework for information sharing may also be established within the umbrella of the Microcredit Regulatory Act (MRA) to help the MFIs in the combat process. This, in turn, can help these MFIs to survive the excessive competition posed by each other and other new entrants of the microfinance sector and work towards the continued development of Bangladesh.

FUTURE RESEARCH DIRECTIONS

The present study is solely based upon the four major microfinance institutions of Bangladesh, which includes mainly government and non-governmental organizations. Future research can examine other forms of organizations like co-operative banks or small-scale MFIs which have recently started taking interest in the microfinance concept. A similar research can also be conducted for a different developing country to do a more in-depth analysis of microfinance models and approaches. Moreover, this study has mainly emphasized on the assessment of the operational structures and challenges of the selected microfinance institutions. A longitudinal study can be adopted in future works to examine a research model in order to examine the perspectives and attitudes of officials of the microfinance institutions regarding the microfinance concept in Bangladesh. This will provide a better insight into the perceptions of people related to the implementation of microfinance and can help to enhance the understanding of individual users of microfinance institutions in the context of Bangladesh.

CONCLUSION

MFIs in Bangladesh have created innovative financial products and services to enable the poor, particularly in the remote or rural areas of the country, to become productive through various income-generating activities. Undoubtedly, this objective of the MFIs has created employment, leading to huge money circulation in the economy and thereby helping poverty alleviation across the entire country. This chapter therefore seeks to highlight the activities and present status of the four giant institutions – Grameen Bank, BRAC, ASA and Proshika – that are involved in the provision of microfinance in the context of Bangladesh. The study reveals the microfinance models followed by these institutions, their product portfolios, operational structures and the challenges they face in their operations. Findings of this chapter also state that these four MFIs commonly encounter problems like overlapping or multiple borrowing, lack of training and education, misuse of credit by borrowers, etc. However, they adopt a clear-cut strategy developed with experience gained over the years in order to deal with such problems and continue to contribute to the development of the economy. Bangladesh has thus become one of the most advanced countries in the field of microfinance today.

REFERENCES

Ahmed, S. (2001). *Poverty and microcredit: New realities and strategic issues.* Microcredit Operation Seminar. Bangladesh Bank.

Ahmed, S. (2009). Microfinance institutions in Bangladesh: Achievements and challenges. *Managerial Finance*, *35*(12), 999–1010. doi:10.1108/03074350911000052

Ahmed, S., & Rafi, B. M. (1999). NGOs and evaluation: the BRAC experience. *World Bank Conference on Evaluation and Poverty Reduction*, Washington, DC.

Alamgir, D. A. (2010). *State of Microfinance in Bangladesh.* Dhaka: Institute of Microfinance (InM). Retrieved from http://www.inm.org.bd/publication/state_of_micro/Bangladesh. pdf

Armendáriz, B., & Morduch, J. (2010). *The Economics of Microfinance.* MIT Press.

Asadullah, M. N., Savoia, A., & Mahmud, W. (2014). Paths to development: Is there a Bangladesh surprise? *World Development*, *62*, 138–154. doi:10.1016/j.worlddev.2014.05.013

Atuya, G. N. (2014). *Effect of microfinance credit on poverty alleviation at household level in Nakuru county* (Doctoral dissertation). University of Nairobi.

Aziz, M. A. (2012). ASA: Hope for the poor. *ASA University Review*, *6*(2), 248–258.

Banking with the Poor Network. (2013). *Proshika*. Retrieved from <http://www.bwtp.org/arcm/Bangladesh/II_Organisations/Microfinance_Providers/PROSHIKA.html>

Barua, P. (2009). *Targeting the poorest in microfinance: Poverty outreach of BDP ultra poor programme*. esocialsciences.com Working Papers.

Bryman, A., & Bell, E. (2015). *Business Research Methods*. Oxford University Press.

Chemin, M. (2008). The benefits and costs of microfinance: Evidence from Bangladesh. *The Journal of Development Studies*, *44*(4), 463–484. doi:10.1080/00220380701846735

Daley-Harris, S. (2005). *State of the Microcredit Summit Campaign Report 2005*. Retrieved from http://www. microcreditsummit.org/pubs/reports/socr/2005/SOCR05.pdf

Duvendack, M., & Palmer-Jones, R. (2012). High noon for microfinance impact evaluations: Re-investigating the evidence from Bangladesh. *The Journal of Development Studies*, *48*(12), 1864–1880. doi:10.1080/00220388.2011.646989

Fotabong, L.A. (2011). *Comparing microfinance models: MC2 model versus other microfinance model*. Available at SSRN 2007874

Gerring, J. (2007). *Case Study Research: Principles and Practices*. New York: Cambridge University Press.

Godquin, M. (2004). Microfinance repayment performance in Bangladesh: How to improve the allocation of loans by MFIs. *World Development*, *32*(11), 1909–1926. doi:10.1016/j.worlddev.2004.05.011

Hassan, M. K. (2002). The microfinance revolution and the Grameen Bank experience in Bangladesh. *Financial Markets. Institutions & Instruments*, *11*(3), 205–265. doi:10.1111/1468-0416.00051

Hulme, D., & Moore, K. (2006). *Why has Microfinance been a policy success in Bangladesh (and beyond)? Economic and Social Research Council (ESRC). Global Poverty Research Group*. GPRG.

Jain, P. S. (2007). *Maturing of microcredit movement: Some Pointers from ASA*. Dhaka: ASA.

Johnson, R. B., Onwuegbuzie, A. J., & Turner, L. A. (2007). Toward a definition of mixed methods research. *Journal of Mixed Methods Research, 1*(2), 112–133. doi:10.1177/1558689806298224

Kabeer, N., Mahmud, S., & Isaza Castro, J. G. (2010). NGOs' strategies and the challenge of development and democracy in Bangladesh. *IDS Working Papers, 343*, 1-71.

Karim, L. (2011). *Microfinance and Its Discontents: Women in Debt in Bangladesh*. U of Minnesota Press. doi:10.5749/minnesota/9780816670949.001.0001

Khalily, M. A. (2004). Quantitative approach to impact analysis of microfinance programmes in Bangladesh - what have we learned? *Journal of International Development, 16*(3), 331–353. doi:10.1002/jid.1081

Khandker, S. R. (1998). *Fighting Poverty with Microcredit: Experience in Bangladesh*. Oxford University Press.

Khandker, S. R. (2005). Microfinance and poverty: Evidence using panel data from Bangladesh. *The World Bank Economic Review, 19*(2), 263–286. doi:10.1093/wber/lhi008

Leikem, K. (2012). *Microfinance: A tool for poverty reduction?*. Senior Honors Projects. Paper 300.

Maanen, G. V. (2004). *Microfinance: Sound of Business or Development Instrument*. Voorburg.

Mallick, D. (2012). Microfinance and moneylender interest rate: Evidence from Bangladesh. *World Development, 40*(6), 1181–1189. doi:10.1016/j.worlddev.2011.12.011

McDonnell, S. (1999). *The Grameen Bank micro-credit model: Lessons for Australian indigenous economic policy. Discussion paper, Centre for Aboriginal Economic Policy Research no. 178*. Canberra: Australian National University.

McIntosh, C., & Wydick, B. (2005). Competition and microfinance. *Journal of Development Economics, 78*(2), 271–298. doi:10.1016/j.jdeveco.2004.11.008

Meyer, R. L. (2002). The demand for flexible microfinance products: Lessons from Bangladesh. *Journal of International Development, 14*(3), 351–368. doi:10.1002/jid.884

Mia, M. B., & Ramage, M. (2011). *Overlapping and information systems in microcredit: A Bangladesh perspective*. In *Second European Research Conference on Microfinance*, Groningen, The Netherlands.

Morduch, J. (1998). *Does Microfinance Really Help the Poor? New Evidence from Flagship Programs in Bangladesh. Research Program in Development Studies.* Woodrow School of Public and International Affairs.

Morduch, J. (1999). The role of subsidies in microfinance: Evidence from the Grameen Bank. *Journal of Development Economics*, *60*(1), 229–248. doi:10.1016/S0304-3878(99)00042-5

Rahman, M. W., Luo, J., Ahmed, S., & Xiaolin, W. (2012). The synthesis of Grameen Bank, BRAC and ASA microfinance approaches in Bangladesh. *World Applied Sciences Journal*, *20*(7), 1055–1062.

Rudrabhatla, R., Roy, S., & Bose, S. K. (2015). Role of microfinance and microfinance institutions model in improving quality of life: A critical review. *International Journal of Engineering, Business and Enterprise Applications*, *12*(1), 70–76.

Sarder, M.M.R., & Golzare, N. (2012). *Dynamics of Micro Finance Programs in Poverty Alleviation in Bangladesh: Present Status, Challenges and Policy Actions.* Research Report. Bangladesh Bank.

Saunders, M. N., Saunders, M., Lewis, P., & Thornhill, A. (2011). *Research Methods for Business Students*. Pearson Education India.

Shil, N. C. (2009). Micro finance for poverty alleviation: A commercialized view. *International Journal of Economics and Finance*, *1*(2), 191–205. doi:10.5539/ijef.v1n2p191

Wahid, A. N. M. (1994). The Grameen Bank and poverty alleviation in Bangladesh: Theory, evidence and limitations. *American Journal of Sociology*, *53*(1), 1–15.

Yin, R. K. (2009). *Case Study Research: Design and Methods*. London: Sage Publications.

Yuge, Y. (2011). *The Current Situation of Microfinance in Bangladesh: A Growing Concern about Overlapping Loan Problems–From a Field Visit to Rajshahi and Comilla. Student Research Series*. The Fletcher School, Tufts University.

Yunus, M. (1998). Poverty alleviation: Is economics any help? Lessons from the Grameen Bank experience. *Journal of International Affairs*, *52*(1), 47–65.

Zaman, M. (2013). Achievement and problems of microfinance of two leading MFIs in Bangladesh: A case study of GB and ASA. *ASA University Review*, *7*(2), 183–198.

ADDITIONAL READING

Battilana, J., & Dorado, S. (2010). Building sustainable hybrid organizations: The case of commercial microfinance organizations. *Academy of Management Journal, 53*(6), 1419–1440. doi:10.5465/AMJ.2010.57318391

Brau, J. C., & Woller, G. M. (2004). Microfinance: A comprehensive review of the existing literature. *Journal of Entrepreneurial Finance, 9*(1), 1–27.

Cull, R., Demirgüç-Kunt, A., & Morduch, J. (2009). Microfinance meets the market. *The Journal of Economic Perspectives, 23*(1), 167–192. doi:10.1257/jep.23.1.167

Hulme, D. (2000). Impact assessment methodologies for microfinance: Theory, experience and better practice. *World Development, 28*(1), 79–98. doi:10.1016/S0305-750X(99)00119-9

Hulme, D. (2000). Is micro debt good for poor people? A note on the dark side of microfinance. *Small Enterprise Development, 11*(1), 26–28. doi:10.3362/0957-1329.2000.006

Littlefield, E., Morduch, J., & Hashemi, S. (2003). Is microfinance an effective strategy to reach the Millennium Development Goals? *Focus Note, 24*, 1–11.

Milana, C., & Ashta, A. (2012). Developing microfinance: A survey of the literature. *Strategic Change, 21*(7-8), 299–330. doi:10.1002/jsc.1911

Robinson, M. S. (2001). *The microfinance revolution: Sustainable finance for the poor*. World Bank Publications. doi:10.1596/0-8213-4524-9

KEY TERMS AND DEFINITIONS

Microfinance: A general term that describes financial services to low-income individuals or to those people who do not have access to typical banking services. It includes services like loans, savings, insurance and other basic financial services to the poor. It mainly targets women entrepreneurs and aims to create employment, particularly in rural areas of developing countries.

Microfinance Institutions (MFIs): Institutions like small non-profit organizations, co-operative banks or in some cases, commercial banks that provides microfinance services to the unbanked or poor people of a country.

MRA: This Act is responsible for empowering, monitoring and supervising the microfinance activities of the MFIs. According to the Act, no MFI can operate microfinance program without obtaining license from this regulatory body.

Non-Governmental Organizations (NGOs): A non-profit organization that can operate on a national or international level without any government affiliations and is usually driven by people with common interest in areas like economic development, sustainability, human rights, environmental issues, etc.

Overlapping Borrowers: Includes the borrowers who take multiple loans within the same repayment period or secure loans from multiple MFIs. This is usually done by concealing the accurate information of their loans from the providers of microfinance.

PKSF: It is a public-private apex body that channels funds for microfinance to MFIs, and has been critical to the expansion and improved professionalism of the microcredit industry in Bangladesh.

Poverty Alleviation: Reduction of poverty in order to improve the livelihoods of poor people. A number of programs and strategic tools are used for this purpose so that any social and legal barriers to income growth among the poor can be removed. This primarily includes the use of microfinance to empower the poor and to increase their access to all factors of production, including credit.

Chapter 4
Green Performance Strategies in Romanian Economy in the View of EU 2020 Strategy

Violeta Sima
Petroleum-Gas University of Ploiesti, Romania

Ileana Georgiana Gheorghe
Petroleum-Gas University of Ploiesti, Romania

ABSTRACT

This chapter aimed to investigate green performance strategies in the Romanian economy. In the first part, authors exposed specific definitions and concepts related to the green economy, as they appear in the literature in the field. The European context and the main ways of implementation of the green economy are presented as they result from the objectives of The Agenda 2020 UE and The Agenda 2030 UNO. Green Performance in Romania during 2010-2014 is assessed by analyzing the environmental protection expenditures, environmental taxes, greenhouse gasses emissions, green jobs roles, and Environmental Performance Index. The sustainable economic growth effects are materializing in a major growth of the ecological productivity, an increased amount of energy derived from renewable sources, emissions reduction, improved air and water quality, widened access to the benefits of civilization - education, water sanitation. Thus, this green growth "can fight" against climate change. Also, green growth provides opportunities for creating new jobs requiring new skills.

DOI: 10.4018/978-1-5225-2081-8.ch004

INTRODUCTION

Ecological concern began to become apparent in the early 70s. It has gained consistency after summits in Rio (1992) and Johannesburg (2002) and especially after the signing of the Kyoto Protocol, becoming an important element in defining organizational culture. Thus, "Green Revolution, environmental protection, turning in "green", sustainable lifestyles, sustainable development, planet protection and many such manifestations have become a phenomenon increasingly evident in our current life" (Sima & Gheorghe, 2014). Businesses have started to be reshaped on the one hand to meet the legislative pressures on the environment, and on the other hand to take advantage of new trends.

The transition to the green economy involves implementing social investment policies and addressing concepts like economic development, green marketing, biodiversity, ecosystems preservation, climate change, health and welfare for the medium and long term. Green buildings, green products, eco-friendly companies - all these words have become increasingly used in recent years. People around the world are striving to keep the Earth healthy by driving hybrid cars or electric cars, using solar and wind energy, recycling.

The green economy is a model of economic development or an economy based on sustainable development and knowledge of the green economy. Karl Burkart (2012) defines green economy as being based on six main areas:

1. Renewable energy (solar, wind etc.);
2. Green Buildings (ex. Construction LEED - Leadership in Energy and Environmental Design);
3. Alternative fuels (hybrid electric vehicles etc.);
4. Water management (water treatment systems, rainwater collection, etc.);
5. Waste management (recycling, etc.);
6. Land management.

A 7th category can be identified. This is represented by "green markets", including green banking and financial investment services; carbon trading etc.

BACKGROUND

Specific Definitions and Concepts related to Green Economy

The concept of "green economy" began to become increasingly more present in the topics for debate of researchers across the world on sustainable development.

Reducing the level of non-renewable resources, climate change and, not least, the recent economic recession constitute challenges for academics, but especially for practitioners in economics. Thus, the tone was given by the UN Conference on the Human Environment (Stockholm, 1972), when The Environmental Programme of the United Nations (UNEP) was created. As a global player, the EU is in the forefront in international efforts to promote sustainable development, the EU applying some of the most advanced environmental standards in the world. Thus a UNEP Report in February 2011 released the following definition: "The green economy is defined as an economy that results in reducing environmental risks and ecological scarcities, and that aims for sustainable development without degrading the environment. It is closely related with ecological economics, but has a more politically applied focus."

The green economy can be a means to achieve sustainable development, representing an adaptation of the socio-economic system to the multiple challenges of the current period.

The transition to a green economy cannot be done instantly, but gradually through the elaboration and implementation of development policies and investments having as main goal to disconnect economic growth from increased consumption of raw materials and energy. Also, performances following the implementation of this model have proved that green economy was a good response to the global crisis of recent years, especially in managing social and environmental issues.

According to Andersen and Massa (2000) the economic growth and a sustainable use of resources do not exclude each other. Green economy implies the adoption of specific environmental policies. This should lead to structural changes of the production and consumption patterns for the long term.

Specific concepts have been defined in the literature. According to Loiseau et al. (2015), seven main concepts are associated with green economy. They are: Bioeconomy or Biobased economy, Cleaner Production, Waste hierarchy approach, Nature-based solutions, Industrial ecology, Circular economy, and Servicising, functional economy.

1. Bioeconomy or biobased economy was defined as the economy involving the development and use of biological products and processes. In Europe, this concept takes into account in especially the use of renewable resources, innovation, sustainable growth and creation of added value (OECD, 2009; Brunori, 2013; EC 2012).
2. Cleaner production is a concept introduced by The United Nations Environment Programme in 1990, as "the continuous application of an integrated preventative environmental strategy to processes, products and services to increase efficiency and reduce risks to humans and the environment."

3. Waste hierarchy approach. The Directive 2008/98/EC set out a priority order five stages in waste prevention and management legislation and policy, as follows: prevention, preparing for re-use, recycling, recovery and finally disposal.
4. Nature-based solutions (NBS) refer to the sustainable management of the natural environment to address current challenges in order to ensure public health and risk management in case of disaster (EC, 2015, p. 5).
5. Industrial ecology has been defined by Brad (2006) as a "systems-based, multidisciplinary discourse that seeks to understand emergent behaviour of complex integrated human/natural systems". This concept assumes that sustainable industrial systems design should be based on the analogy with natural systems (Frosch & Gallopoulos, 1989).
6. Circular economy represents a restorative or regenerative system by intention and design, aiming to design out waste. It replaces the end-of-life concept with restoration, shifts towards the use of renewable energy, eliminates the use of toxic chemicals, which impair reuse and return to the biosphere, and aims for the elimination of waste through the superior design of materials, products, systems and business models.
7. Servicising, functional economy was defined as one that optimizes the use of goods and services, aiming to create the highest possible use value for the longest possible time while consuming as few material resources and energy as possible (to create the highest possible use value for the longest possible time while consuming as few material resources and energy as possible (to create the highest possible use value for the longest possible time while consuming as few material Stahel, 1986).

In 2011 OECD has formulated a comprehensive definition for Green Growth, stating that: "Green growth is about fostering economic growth and development while ensuring that the natural assets continue to provide the resources and environmental services on which our well-being relies. To do this it must catalyse investment and innovation which will underpin sustained growth and give rise to new economic opportunities." According this definition, four main areas have been identified as representing landmarks in achieving green growth (Figure 1). These areas can be assessed by specific indicators.

European Context

All human activities may cause in some way environmental degradation. Ecosystems provide resources and services for human socio-economic system. Their use must be made within the limits of the supporting and self-regulating capacity of the ecosystems, their overcoming generating environmental degradation.

Figure 1. The main determinants of Green Growth
Source: Based on OECD approach

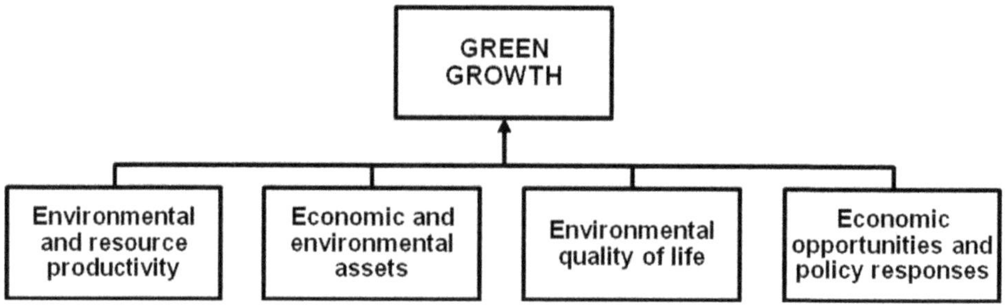

The Europe 2020 Strategy emphasizes increased competitiveness generated by a development model characterized by low emissions of greenhouse gases, effectively used resources and new technologies for environmentally friendly production and biodiversity.

The Europe 2020 emphasizes the opportunities and the role which SMEs can play in shaping a sustainable European economy.

Those companies that will be able to have an innovative and proactive management are those that will gain the winning positions at the 2020 horizon. The challenges are related to globalization, demographic change, natural resource depletion, climate change and acceleration of the use of new technologies. To maximize business contribution to the Europe 2020 targets and to strengthen its competitive advantages, the most important European network of social responsibility (CSR Europe) launched the Enterprise Strategy 2020 dedicated to business environment.

Green Economy is about using of natural resources, energy and new technologies together with new cleaner production methods, in order to promote economic growth and create new jobs. In this respect we need to communicate about sustainability of the enterprises, in order to respond to consumer demands for greener products and for more information about these products.

According classical economic approach, the entrepreneurship' role in society is to create new jobs and to pay more taxes, which leads to the emergence of new incomes, determining economic and social development and finally, increasing the welfare of the human society.

At the next level the entrepreneurs should have in sight social aspects by including of the social responsibility practices into their businesses.

The issue of Green Performance Strategies have become a topic of general concern for researchers worldwide. In implementing the performance management process the social and the environmental components hold important roles. Sustainable development and the fulfilment of the sustainable development indicators are dependent on how the refurbishment is designed, this substantiating the eco-performance. Thus, the eco-performance can be considered a multifaceted concept.

Ways of Implementation of Green Economy

Green economy, as it was cited above, is resulting in an increased level of "well-being and social equity, while significantly reducing environmental risks and ecological scarcity" (UNEP, Green Economy Reports: A Preview, 2010, p. 4-5). In order to achieve the specific objectives of the green economy specific policies and investments are required, able to decouple economic growth from increasing of current intensive consumption of raw materials and energy. In short, a green economy can be characterized by some main features as the Figure 2 shows.

The role of government occurs in both the public and in the private sector. Thus, in both cases, specific legislative regulations can constitute very effective tools, aiming to stimulate commercialization organic products with low environmental impact. Specifically, this can be achieved, as Gheorghe and Sima stated (2014), by "eliminating outdated subsidies, reforming policies and providing new incentives, strengthening market infrastructure and market-based mechanisms, redirecting public investment, and greening public procurement".

As shown in Table 1, the Agenda 2020 and The Agenda 2030 aim at common goals, so that certain correlations can be highlighted between specific objectives undertaken in the two documents (Figure 3). Raising the employment rate leads

Figure 2. The main features of Green Economy
Source: Based on UNEP approach

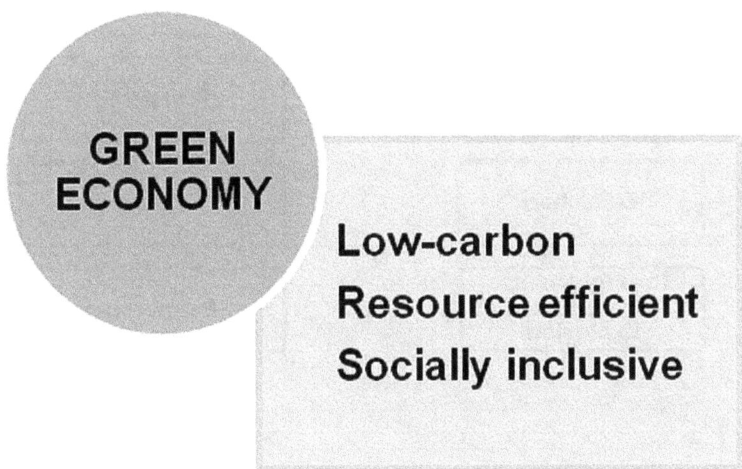

Table 1. Ways for the implementation of the green economy

Ways of Implementation	Objectives of The Agenda 2020 UE	Objectives of The Agenda 2030 UNO
Green jobs Green politics	1. Employment	1. People
Green jobs Green politics Green energy Green transport	2. Research and Development	2. Planet
Green jobs Green politics Green energy	3. Climate changes and sustainable energy use	3. Prosperity
Green jobs	4. Education	4. Peace
Green politics	5. The fight against poverty and social exclusion	5. Partnership

Source: Authors' own analysis based on literature survey

Figure 3. Correlations between objectives of the agenda 2020 UE and objectives of the 2030 UNO
Source: Proposed by the Authors

obviously to an increase of human welfare. All countries must cooperate to ensure labor mobility, which should contribute to a decrease of the disparities between countries in terms of employment. Investment in research and development is an important element. This area was affected in the period of economic crisis. Allocate a significant percentage of GDP is needed for this purpose. This is smart growth through the development of an economy based on knowledge and innovation which is able to ensure the protection of the planet, ensuring the prosperity of its people, which can be achieved only in peace. Achieving the objective of "20/20/20" in terms of energy and climate change is also important. This leads to sustainable growth by promoting globally, a green economy that is efficient and competitive. Education plays an important role in decreasing early school leaving among young people, helping to increase social welfare. Globally consistent policies are needed. These can lead to the implementation of social programs in this regard. Promoting an economy with high employment of labor is necessary in order to reduce social exclusion.

According to the latest documents adopted by the EU (Agenda 2020) and UN (Agenda 2030), the green economy aims to increase social welfare and the role of human capital by reducing environmental risks and ecological issues in order to achieve sustainable development. A highly ambitious UN goal is the eradication of poverty. The green economy, according to United Nations experts, providing an environment with fewer adverse environmental effects and substantial benefits on society and each person can contribute to achieving this objective. A new opportunity is represented by redesigning through greening of the national strategies, in terms of creating new green jobs, as a result of the expansion of green industries, which demand specific skills and competencies (Figure 4).

EU 2020 STRATEGY IMPLEMENTATION IN ROMANIA

Context

An extreme dynamics represents the essential feature of the current socio-economic environment. In this context, in 2010 the "Europe 2020" was launched, which represents the EU's growth strategy for the period 2010-2020. This strategy emerged in the context of a deep economic crisis and intensification of long-term challenges such as globalization, pressures on resources use and an aging population. The strategy "Europe 2020" has taken into account the peculiarities of each Member State, at the same time aiming a consistent reform program which had as a general goal to increase the competitiveness of Europe, based on the strengths of the EU - single market, common currency, and common policies. Through this strategy,

Figure 4. Effects on employment of the orientation towards sustainable economic
Source: Sima and Gheorghe, 2014, p.117

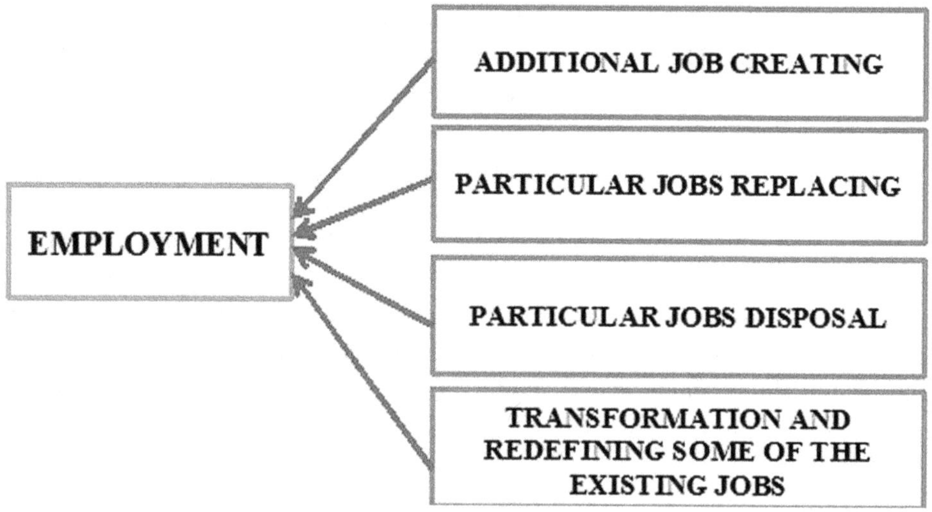

the EU aimed to become a smart, sustainable and inclusive economy. These three stated priorities are converging, supporting each other and being able to "help the EU and the Member States deliver high levels of employment, productivity and social cohesion" (José Manuel Durão Barroso, former Chairman European Commission). These priorities are:

- **Smart Growth:** Developing an economy based on knowledge and innovation.
- **Sustainable Growth:** Promoting a more resource efficient, greener and more competitive economy.
- **Inclusive Growth:** Fostering a high-employment economy delivering social and territorial cohesion (COMMUNICATION FROM THE COMMISSION EUROPE 2020, A strategy for smart, sustainable and inclusive growth, p.5).

The Headline Targets of "Europe 2020"

This strategy has targeted five areas considered as the biggest challenges for the contemporary world:

1. **Employment:** Ensuring an employment rate of 75% for people aged 20 to 64 years;
2. **The Role of Research and Development:** An increase of the investment in R&D to 3% of the EU GDP;

3. **Climate Change:**
    a. Limiting the emissions of greenhouse gas by at least 20% compared to 1990;
    b. Providing of 20% of the demanded energy by using renewable resources;
    c. Improving the energy efficiency by 20%;
4. **Education:**
    a. Reducing early school leaving to below 10%;
    b. An increased share of population with higher education, for people with ages between 30 and 34 years;
5. **Fight Against Poverty and Social Exclusion:** Reducing the number of Europeans suffering or being at risk to suffer from poverty and social exclusion with 25% (reducing the number of people at risk of poverty by 20 million).

In developing the Europe 2020 objectives, the EU Commission took into account the heterogeneity of its members so that objectives were relevant to all 27 states, as were in 2010 and 28 today. For this purpose a flexible approach has been chosen, the European objectives being translated into national targets, reflecting the peculiarities of each country.

In March 2010, Romania established the National 2020 targets, under the coordination of the Department for European Affairs of the Romanian Government, based on the conclusions of the European Council. The main fields of action targeted by Romania are:

1. **An Increase in the Employment:** In order to achieve this, a reform of the legal framework is required to encourage employment and continuous training of the labor force considered being relevant instruments in this field. Romania has assumed only an increase of up to 70%, given that, in 2008, the employment rate was 64.4%.
2. **The Allocation of 2% of GDP for Research and Development:** This is a target difficult to attain in Romania because the current structures of research and development in our country show a very low intensity of the field. The share of expenditures for research and development in Romania's GDP in 2008 was 0.45%, but the economic crisis has reduced it to 0.30% in 2009 and 2010, which has caused significant damage to ongoing research projects.
3. **A Reducing of the Greenhouse Gasses (GHG) Emissions:** In this field, Romania has assumed, realistically, only a decrease of 19% compared to 2005, due to the current possibilities compared with the value stipulated by the European standards (30%).

4. **An Increase by 24% in the Share of Renewable Energy in Final Consumption**: For Romania, the target means 6.2% more than in 2005 (when the share of this category in final energy consumption was 17.8%).
5. **An Increase of the Energy Efficiency by 10%:** Romania's objective in this area aimed at reducing the primary energy consumption, this sector having a great potential for saving.
6. **A Reducing of the Early School Leaving**: In this field, Romania has assumed a decrease of 11.3%. Some progress has been made, in part due to the implementation of social programs (reducing the school leaving rate from 22.9% in 2000 to 15.9% in 2008, but the indicator rose again in 2009 to 16.6%, due to the economic crisis).
7. **An Increase in the Share of Population under 30 Years Old Having Completed Tertiary Education to 26.7%:** For this purpose, reforms are needed, not only in education but also in the economy designed to support education expenditure.
8. **Increasing the Social Inclusion**: This objective envisages primarily the ensuring of the social and territorial cohesion. Romania has assumed to reduce the number of people at risk of poverty by 580 000 persons. For this purpose, Romania is expected to increase funds for social assistance and to continue the healthcare reform.

Stage of Implementation of the Europe 2020 Strategy in Romania

Regarding the employment rate, as it has been shown above, for people aged 20-64 years, the proposed EU target is 70%. In 2015 Romania reached 70.8%, higher than in 2014 when the employment rate was 70.4% (Figure 5). This trend confirms that Romania has made progress in this area, the assumed goal being practically achieved. This was due to the fact that the National Plan on Stimulating Youth Employment was implemented. An ongoing project is important to mention, namely, related to the Development of Local Economies and New Jobs Creation.

This project has the following objectives:

- To decrease undeclared work (undeclared);
- To decrease youth unemployment and increasing employment.

To achieve these objectives, three directions are envisaged:

Figure 5. Employment rate, 2010-2015
Source: Data provided by EUROSTAT (t2020_10)

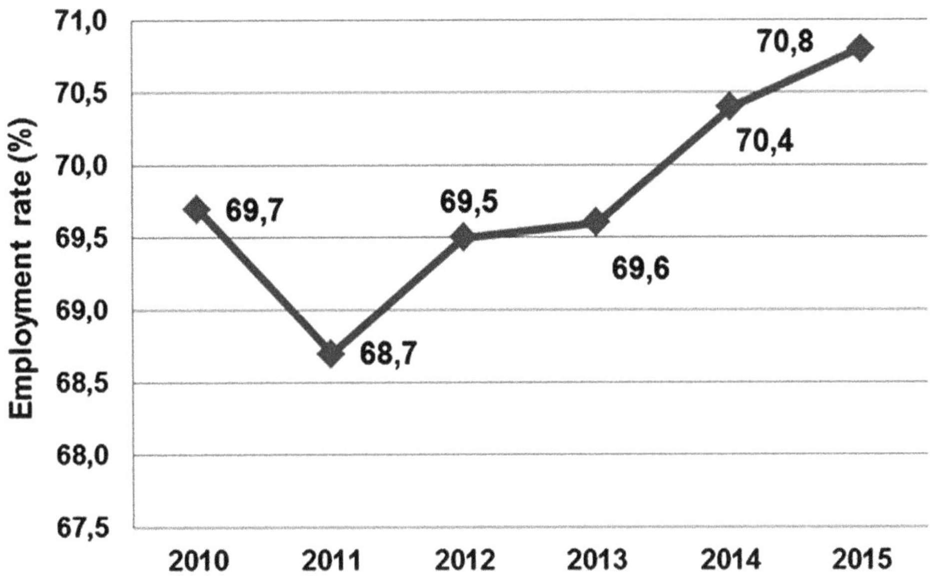

- A continuous training of young people, especially those in rural areas;
- The development of micro-enterprises, both in the non-agricultural sector, but especially in agriculture;
- The integration of people who left school early by recognizing their skills.

Regarding Total intramural R & D Expenditure - the target assumed by Romania was to reach 2% of GDP. In this area, Romania registered a growth of 0.39% in 2013 and 0.38% in 2014. There is a downward trend in values (Figure 6), even if over 750 projects were with Romanian and international participation were supported in this domain. The public sector was the one where cuts in expenditure were higher Thus, to achieve the objective, Romania will have to increase R & D Expenditure on average by 31.7% per year between 2015 and 2020.

To increase on average by 31.7% per year between 2015 and 2020 in the future two main issues are taken into account:

- To develop the relationship between theory (research) and practice (businesses) by promoting R & D activities in economic sectors with growth potential and public importance;
- To upgrade the national R & D investments to increase efficiency in administration.

Figure 6. Total intramural R&D expenditure, 2010-2014
Source: Data provided by EUROSTAT (rd_e_gerdtot)

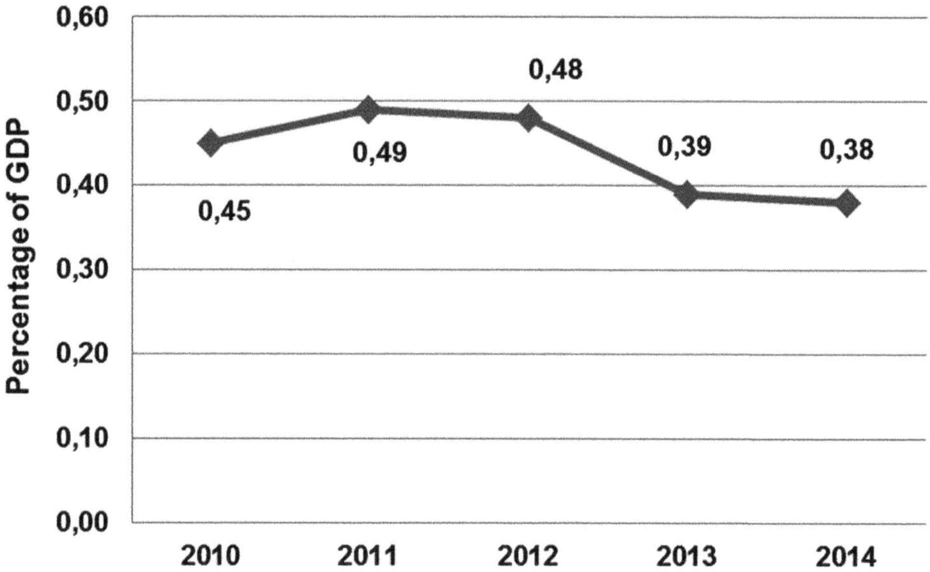

Regarding Greenhouse gas emissions reduction the target assumed by Romania is 19%. Figure 7 shows the evolution of Greenhouse Gas Emissions. Thus, after 2005, the highest value of Greenhouse Gas Emissions was recorded in 2011 (48.33%), followed by a continuous decrease. The lowest value was being recorded in 2014 (43.68%). The contraction of the national economy has essentially contributed to this decline, due to the economic crisis. On fields, the causes of this trend are:

- **In the Energy Sector:** The following issues are to be mentioned: increasing the share of energy from alternative sources, upgrading of major combustion plants and stimulate energy production from clean sources - Program for increasing energy production from renewable sources, Program "Green House."
- **In the Transport Sector:** A determinant factor was the stimulation of the national car park renewal and monitoring of the road transport vehicles clean and efficient energy - Program Rabla.
- **The Increase of the Afforested Areas:** Program for improvement of the environment quality through afforestation of degraded lands, ecological restoration and sustainable management of forests.
- **Expansion of Green Areas in Towns:** National Programme for improvement of the environment quality by creating green spaces in cities.

Figure 7. Greenhouse gas emissions, base year 1990, 2010-2014
Source: Data provided by EUROSTAT (t2020_30)

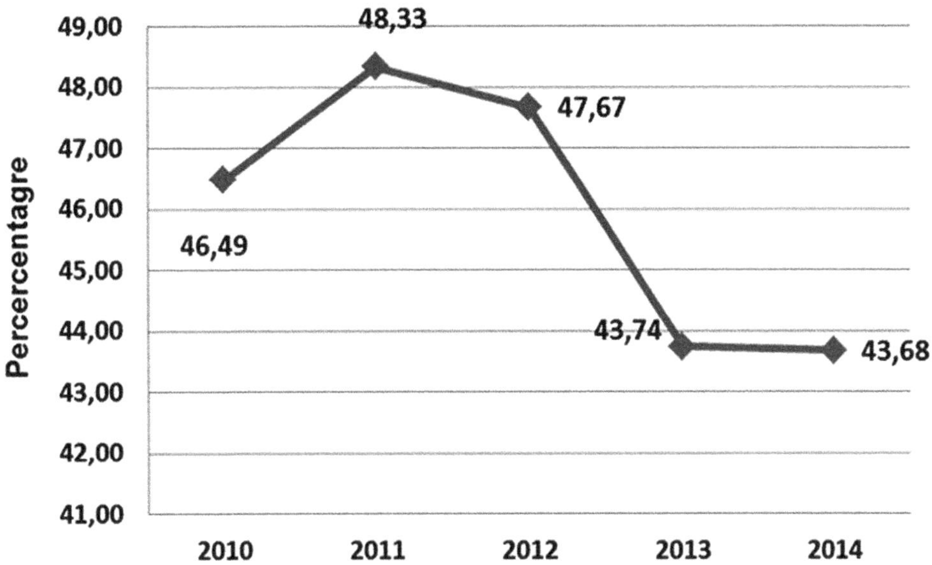

Some national programs are to be mentioned here, namely: Green House, Rabla, accreditation of The International Airport Henri Coanda Bucharest according to the standard of certification of the CO2 emissions management.

Regarding Share of renewable energy in gross final energy consumption (Figure 8), the target assumed by Romania is to cover 24% from the necessary of energy using renewable resources. A share of 23.9% was reached in 2013 and in 2014 one of 24.9%. Thus, we can affirm that Romania has already exceeded the target for 2020, although, from a legislative point of view, there still may be emphasized certain vulnerabilities. The economic crisis had a major contribution also in this domain but the implementation of some energy efficiency measures is also to be mentioned. The most important are:

- SRE promotion by means of green certificates;
- Modernization and achievement of new capacities of producing electric and thermic energy;
- SRE promotion by means of Medium Fund, the program regarding the installing of the heating systems which use renewable energy, inclusively the replacement and the completion of standard heating systems (Green House);
- Elaboration of some equivalent certification systems or qualification systems for the electricians working in the SRE domain, introducing 4 new qualifications in the Romanian Professions' Classification (fitter for heating pumps,

Figure 8. Share of renewable energy in gross final energy consumption, 2010-2014
Source: Data provided by EUROSTAT (t2020_31)

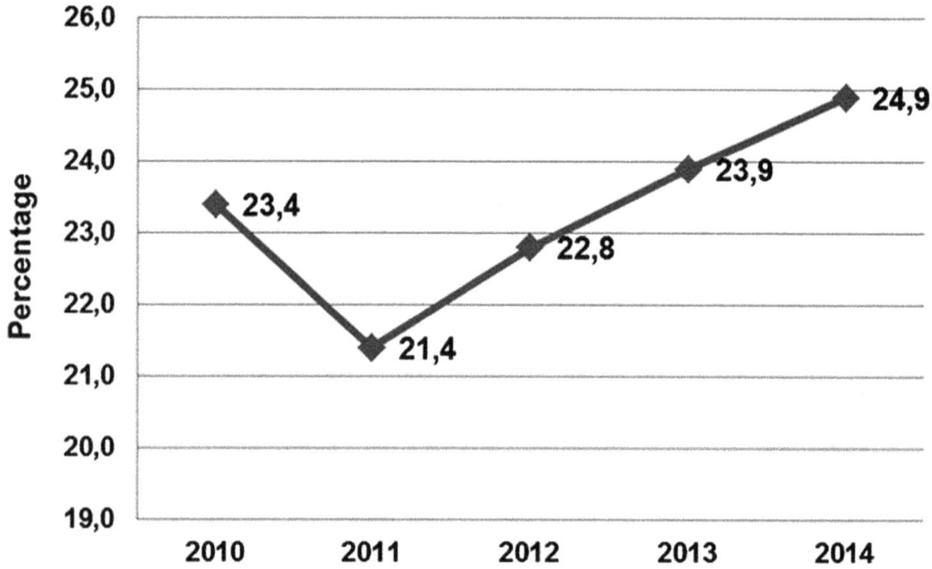

geothermal systems, PV solar systems and for thermic solar systems) and the elaboration of 2 new occupational standards (fitter for systems of thermic use of SRE and fitter for PV systems);

- Modification of the support scheme regarding the promotion of the energy resulting from renewable energy in order to avoid overcompensation;
- Supporting the measures aiming at the modernization and rehabilitation of the transport and distribution network in order to obtain a better take over in the network of the energy produced from renewable energy sources.

Regarding Primary energy consumption, Romania target for energy effectiveness in 2020 is of 43 Mtep, expressed in primary energy consumption (30.3 Mtep expressed in the final energy consumption). In Romania, after 2008, there may be noticed a constant lowering of the primary energy consumption (Figure 9a). This lowering was the result of some measures:

- The implementation of the state support scheme for the promotion of the high efficiency cogeneration;
- Popularizing campaign to inform the population and business medium regarding the importance of the increasing of the energy efficiency; there were organized eight seminaries in six towns, with a total of above 370 participants;

Figure 9. (a) Primary energy consumption, base year 2005, 2010-2014; (b) Final energy consumption, base year 2005, 2010-2014
Source: Data provided by EUROSTAT (t2020_33)

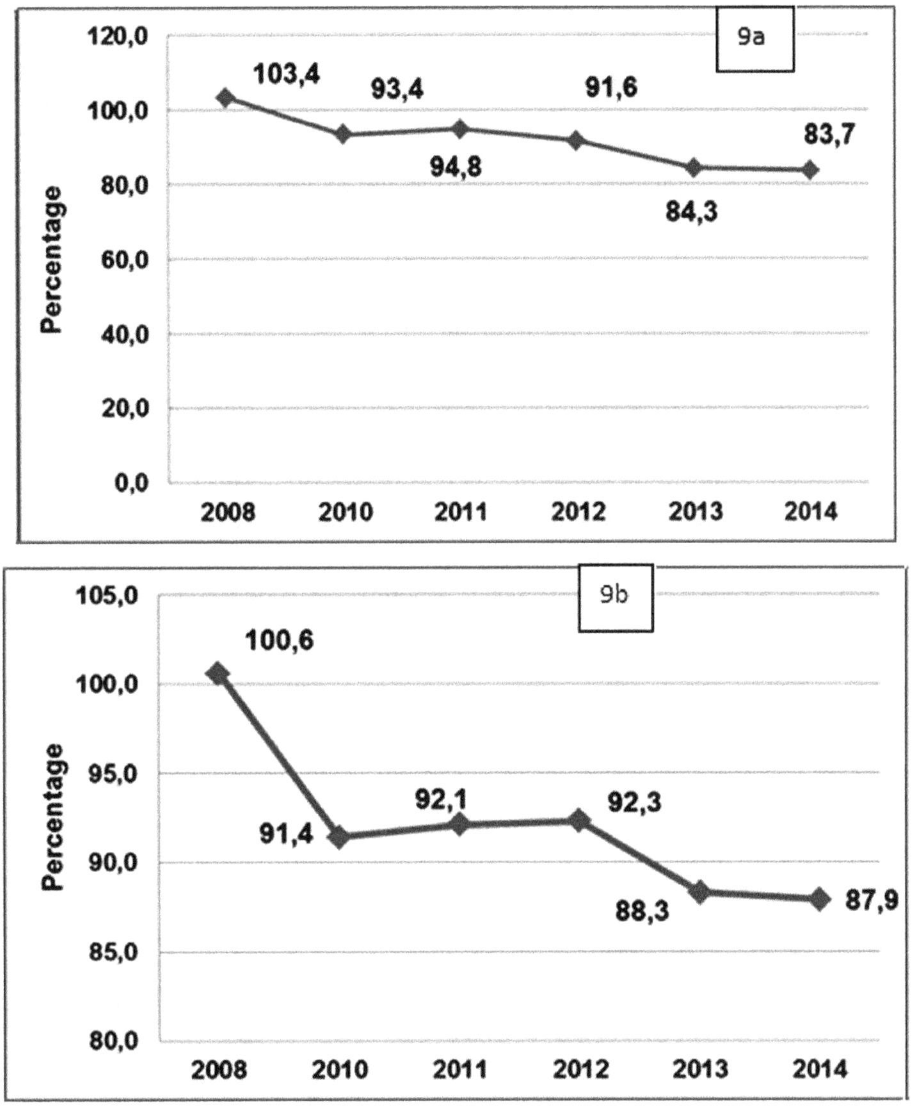

- The Program "Heating, Heat and Comfort";
- The modernization and realizing of some units and new equipment in the industry plants;
- Thermic of the buildings;

- The improvement of the energy efficiency in the communities with low income from Romania;
- Promotion of some projects regarding the intelligent counting at the level of the electric energy distribution systems.

As concerns Final energy consumption there is to be noticed approximately the same evolution (Figure 9b). The highest level was registered in 2008 (100.6%), and the lowest in 2014 (87.9%).

As concerns Early leavers from education and training status, after a relatively linear decrease during the period 2010-2013, starting with 2014, an increase tendency may be ascertained (Figure 10). Therefore early leaving school rate, increased at a level of 18.1% in 2014 and, respectively, at 19.1% in 2015, in spite of the measures approved by the government (the implementing of the social programmes in order to support the pupils from the disadvantaged regions – School Supplies, Money for High School, Euro 200, and Roll and Milk, Honey and fruits, Refunding of the Transport Money and School Buses, implementing of some programmes, stipulated in the National Education Law for the support of the coming back to school and the increasing of the liquidation of illiteracy level for population.

The second chance, School after school, the liquidation of illiteracy programmes, assurance of the educational process quality within the secondary school education,

Figure 10. Early leavers from education and training status, 2010-2015
Source: Data provided by EUROSTAT [edat_lfse_14]

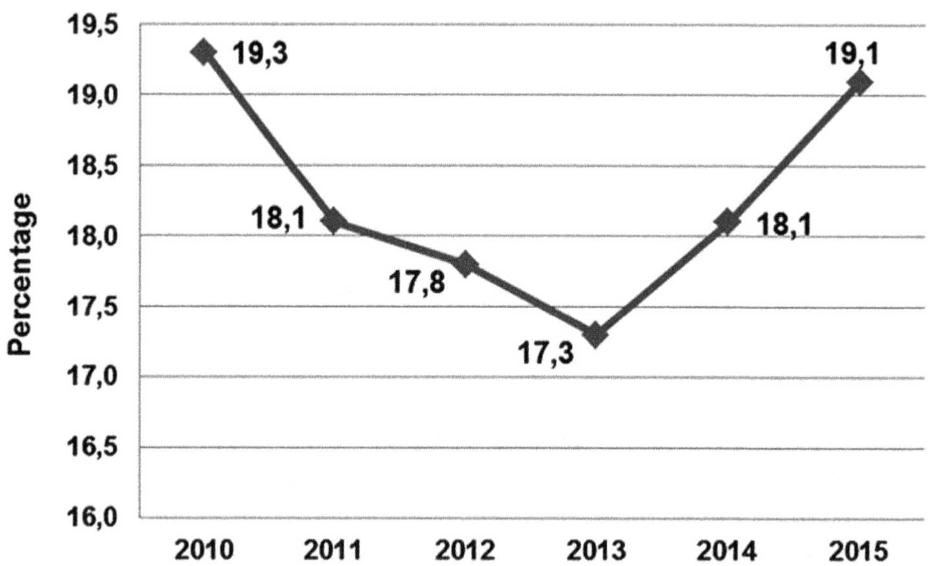

the development of the vocational education, high school education (technological type) and college education. This evolution situates Romania among the countries with the highest rates of early school leaving in EU, Romania being moved away from its target. It also has to be mentioned the fact that there are gender and residence discrepancies (a higher rate among boys and in the rural area compared to girls and urban area).

Regarding Population by tertiary education (levels 5-8) attainment, Romania registered progress and an increasing tendency of this index may be noticed (Figure 11), the value of this index substantially improved, reaching the quota of 25.6% in 2015. Therefore, Romania is on its way to reach the assumed target.

The measures which contributed to this evolution:

- Adapting the academic education to the labour market demands by means of elaborating an analysis of the indexes reported by the universities and the implementing of specific projects;
- The Management of the correlation of the educational system with the labour market and public policies inserted in the academic education: a necessary premise for Romania development;
- Implementing of the social programmes for the students;

Figure 11. Population by tertiary education (levels 5-8) attainment, 2010-2015
Source: Data provided by EUROSTAT [edat_lfse_03]

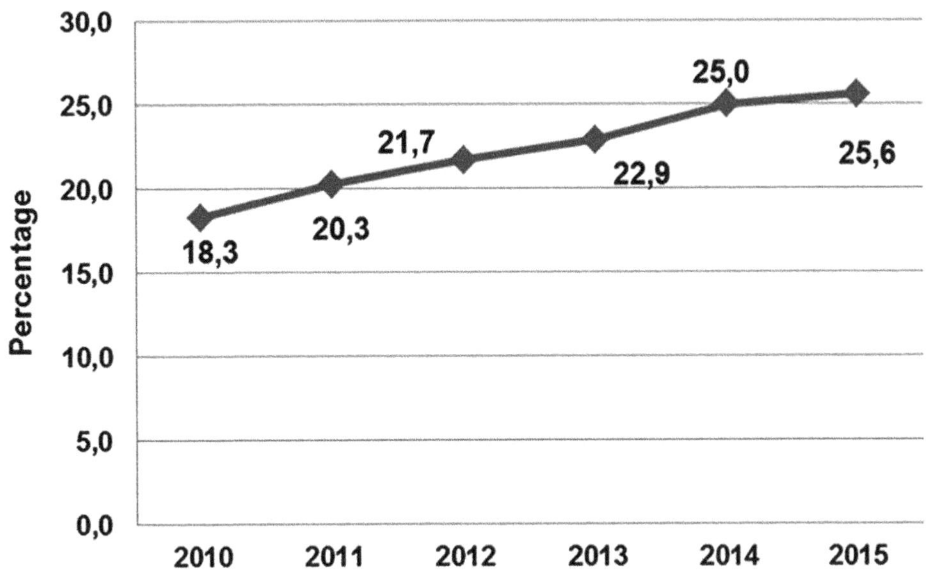

- The development of the national systems of qualifications for the academic education in Romania by means of the operationalization of the National Academic Education Qualifications Register (RNCIS) and adopting The National Qualifications Framework.

Concerning Reduction of the number of people at risk of poverty or social exclusion, in Figure 12, it may be noticed that the target has already been surpassed. This important progress was possible due to:

- The support of the poorest families with children;
- **The Assurance of the Social Protection and of the Most Vulnerable Population Categories:** Granting of an allowance for the support of the family, insurance of a minimum guaranteed income;
- **Social Protection Measures for the Vulnerable Consumers and for the Diminishing of the Energy Poverty Risks**: Support for the heating with natural gases and for the heating with electric energy;
- **Increasing of the Children Social Services Quality**: Improvement of the care services, closing of the old institutions and founding recovery centers and houses of family type;

Figure 12. Reduction of the number of people at risk of poverty or social exclusion, 2010-2015
Source: Data provided by EUROSTAT [ilc_peps01]

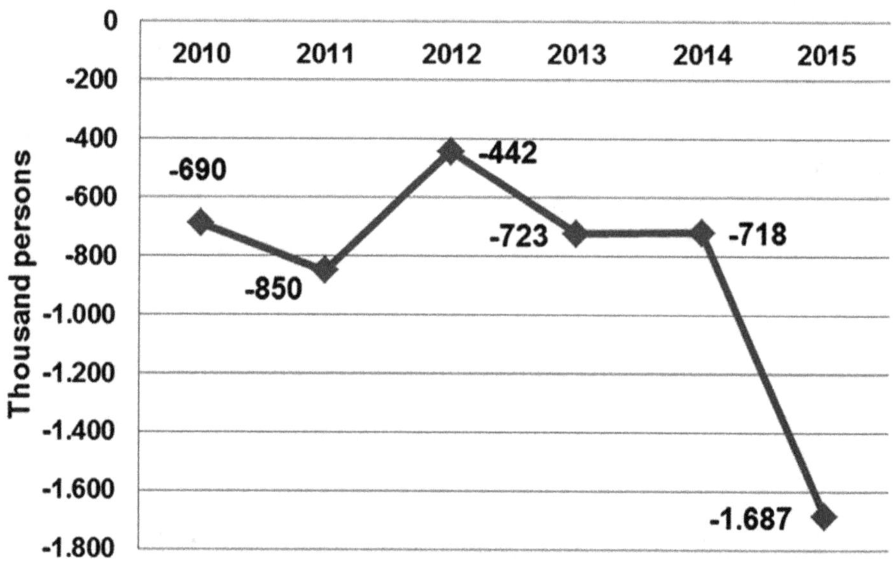

- **Facilitating the Access and Participation of the Individuals Taking Part in Vulnerable Groups on the Labour Market**: Implementing some qualification/re-qualification;
- The development of the social substructure and education substructure;
- **The Improvement of the Access for the Vulnerable Persons to Health Services**: Implementing health national programmes (Screening Programme for the early active identification of the col cancer), the assurance of the access to the medicaments ambulatory provided to the pensioners with low income;
- **Economic Efficiency of the Health System**: Computerization of the health system by implementing the National Health Framework and of the programme the Electronic Card of the patient.

GREEN PERFORMANCE IN ROMANIA

Environmental Protection Expenditures Evolution during 2010-2014

As concerns the expenses for the medium protection in Romania, it may be noticed that, taking into account the activity sectors, the specialized producers own the highest quota which records, generally, over 50% of the total environmental expenditures (Figure 13).

This category is followed by the category of the specialized producers in public administration. It has to be mentioned that, starting from 2012, the percentage represented by the public sector was drastically reduced.

From the total of these expenses, the amounts assigned to the investments have a different evolution (Figure 14). In this respect, the nonspecialized producers are the one who assign the highest percentage for investments in medium protection, excepting 2011. Starting with 2012 the figures have become increasingly higher, showing an increased concern for the environment. As for manufacturing, in the 2010-2013, it represented about a half of environment protection expenditure of unspecialized producers.

After 2013 their share decreased, to 25.3% in 2014. Specialized producers assigned for the investments the highest quota in 2011 (25.9%). Starting with 2012 their assignments for the investments continually decreased reaching 8.8%, in 2014. The public sector manifested similar trends.

Figure 13. Environmental protection expenditures, by activities, 2010-2014
Source: Data provided by National Institute of Statistics (TEMPO_PMI105A_16_9_2016)

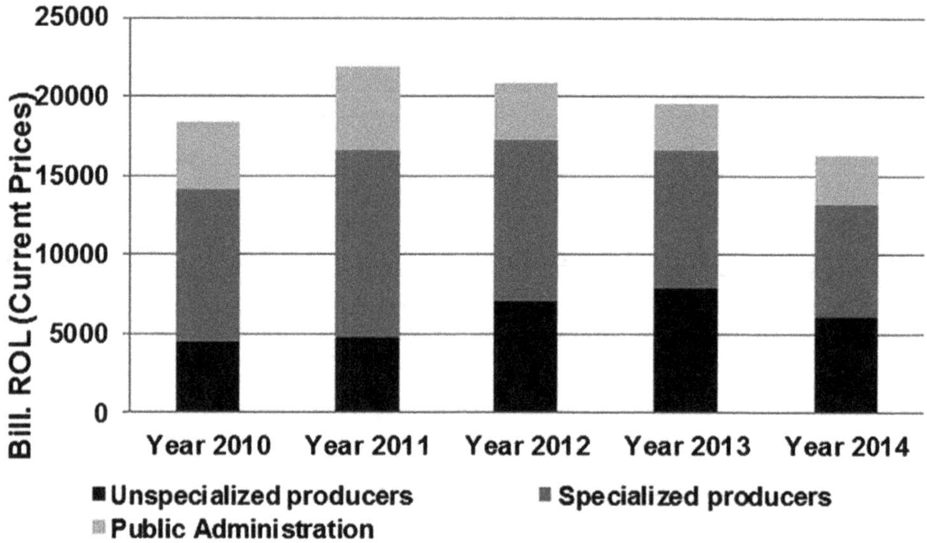

Figure 14. Environmental protection expenditures for investment, by activity sector, 2010-2014
Source: Data provided by National Institute of Statistics

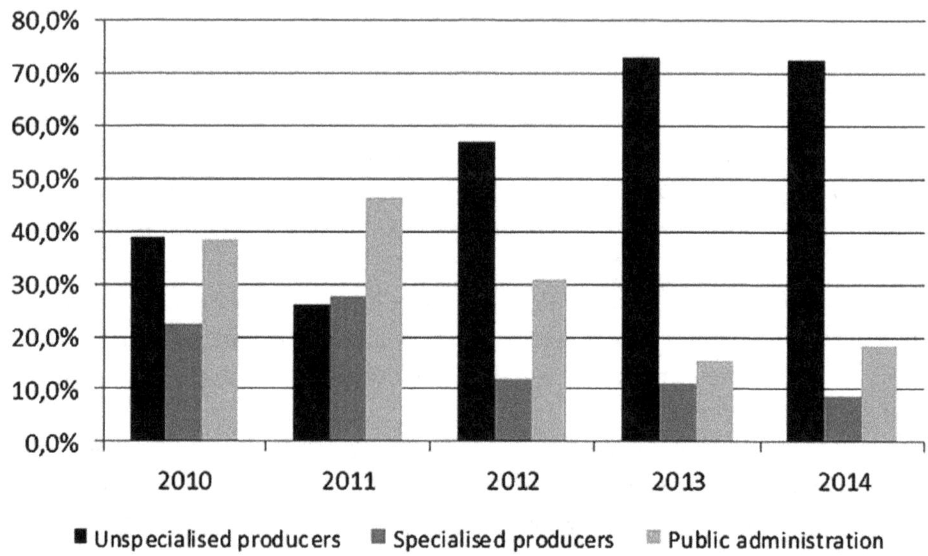

By environment field, the highest share of expenditure was recorded for waste management, more than 50%. It was followed by water protection expenditure (Figure 15).

Environmental Taxes Evolution in Romania and Efficiency of Revenue Generated by Them During 2010-2014

Romania has an inefficient economy from the energy point of view. Energy has among the lowest cashing obtained from environmental taxes as PIB percentage both at general and activity sectors levels (energy taxes, transport taxes and environmental and pollution taxes). The Table 2 shows the evolution of the energy taxes in Romania compared to EU. A first observation is that the level is under 2.5% from PIB, being under the European media. In 2011 (the year when in Romania manifested the strongest economic crisis in all activity domains) registered the lowest value for the analyzed period, namely 1.69% from PIB, and in 2014, the highest

Figure 15. Environmental protection expenditures, by environmental domains, 2010-2014
Source: Data provided by National Institute of Statistics (TEMPO_PMI105B_16_9_2016)

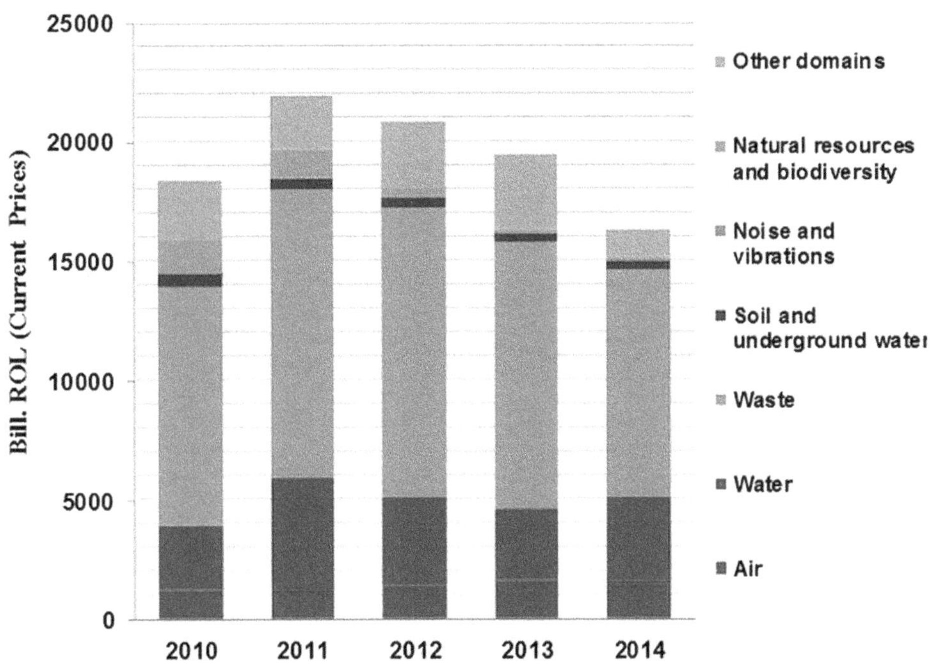

**For a more accurate representation of this figure, please see the electronic version.*

Table 2. Environmental taxes by economic activities, 2010-2014 (% of GDP)

Year	2010		2011		2012		2013		2014	
	Mil. €	(% of GDP)	Mil. €	(% of GDP)	Mil. €	(% of GDP)	Mil. €	(% of GDP)	Mil. €	(% of GDP)
Energy taxes	2235.53	1.76	2247.69	1.69	2272.76	1.7	2545.73	1.76	3237.75	2.16
Transport taxes	400.03	0.01	314.19	0.00	351.58	0.01	397.67	0.00	393.52	0.00
Pollution taxes	7.72	0.32	6.37	0.24	8.77	0.26	6.11	0.28	5.24	0.26
Resource taxes	7.53	0.01	5.28	0.00	4.33	0.00	5.00	0.00	4.23	0.00

Source: Processed by authors using data provided by EUROSTAT [env_ac_tax]

value, namely 2.16% from PIB. In the case of the transport taxes and environmental and pollution taxes the value is under 1% from PIB.

This situation may be explained by the intention of the state to maintain the taxes and excise duties at minimum duties. Moreover, in the case of the pollution and use of the resources taxes, the collecting capacity for the majority of taxes is diminished in comparison to the charging potential basis. This thing is even more serious as the pollution and use of the resources taxes are, in fact collected in order

Figure 16. Total environmental taxes, 2010-2014
Source: Data provided by EUROSTAT [env_ac_tax]

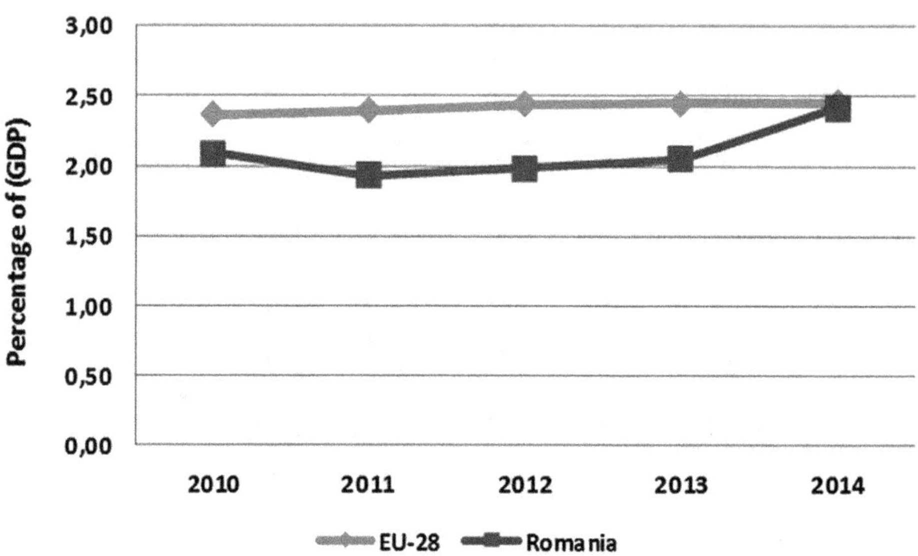

Figure 17. Environmental taxes revenues (% of Total Revenues), 2010-2014
Source: Data provided by EUROSTAT [env_ac_tax]

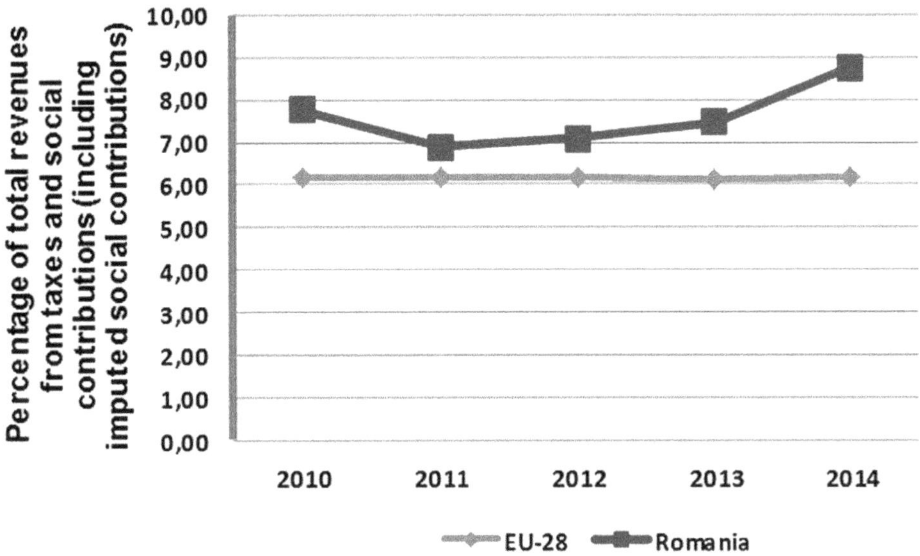

to finance projects meant to diminish the negative effects of the human activities against the environment.

The competitive advantage offered by a low level of the charging is not exploited in Romania at all. As a matter of fact European Union recommends a change of the accent from the work charging (where Romania emphasizes a high fiscality level) to the charging of the consumption and pollution.

Within this context it may be noticed that the evolution of the taxes and contributions in Romania has an increasing tendencies and the registered values are over the European mean of 6%. It may be also emphasized the year 2011 with minimum values. As concerns the Energy taxes, it registered an increasing tendency during the studied period, reaching in 2014, at the level of 7.79%, which surpasses the European mean (Table 3).

Evolutions of Greenhouse Gas Emissions

According to The European Environment Agency (EEA), the five main emission source sectors of greenhouse gasses include:

- Energy (fuel combustion and fugitive emissions from fuels), which also includes transport;
- Industrial processes and product use;

Table 3. Percentage of total revenues from taxes and social contributions (including imputed social contributions), 2010-2014

Year	2010	2011	2012	2013	2014
Energy taxes	6,56	6,01	6,1	6,44	7,79
Transport taxes	1,17	0,84	0,94	1,01	0,95
Pollution taxes	0,02	0,02	0,02	0,02	0,01
Resource taxes	0,02	0,01	0,01	0,01	0,01

Source: Processed by authors using data provided by EUROSTAT [env_ac_tax]

- Agriculture;
- Land use, land use change and forestry (LULUCF);
- Waste management.

According to European Environment Agency (EEA), emissions of greenhouse gas in Europe declined by 19% from 1990 to the present, despite a 45% increase in economic output. European Environment Agency (EEA) published a report in 2014

Figure 18. Greenhouse gas emissions per capita, 2010-2014
Source: Data provided by EUROSTAT (t2020_rd300)

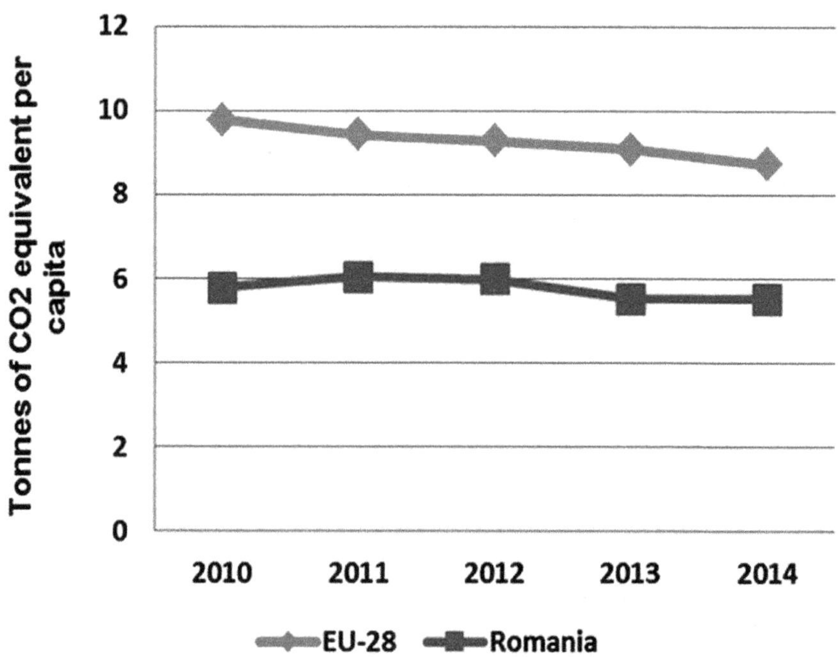

that evaluated the greenhouse gas emissions in the European Union from 1990 to 2012. It showed that the commitments of the EU countries to reduce the amount of greenhouse gas emissions in 2020 was close to being met (Figure 18). It is expected that, by the deadline, they can be overcome. Romania has reduced its emissions of greenhouse gasses, especially after 2012.

The main reasons that led to these changes are:

- Decrease of CO2 emissions in road transport;
- The economic crisis and the economy contraction. Emissions have decreased primarily in countries most affected by the economic recession: Italy, Spain, and Greece;
- The drop in CO2 in manufacturing and cement production. The drop was 11 million tons, representing 3% compared to 1990. The countries with the biggest reductions were Italy, Germany, Britain, Spain, and Portugal;
- The reduction in the production of solid fuel.

But there were sectors where the amount of GHG emission increased. The most important are related to electricity consumption in public space and heating plants, which led to an increase of 3%. The highest increases were in Germany, Great Britain, and Spain. Another significant increase was recorded in consumption in households and services, bringing a plus 4%. Experts claim that winters are becoming colder so that the increasing demand for heating could represent an explanation of these changes.

"In Europe, supply and use of energy is the most important source of GHGs emissions (80%). Agriculture has a sectorial share around 9%. So, impact of agriculture on climate change is modest" (Matei, Stancu & Vuković, 2009).

In Romania, more than 13% of the greenhouse gas emissions come from the transport sector, and 96% of them are caused by road transport. According to Greenpeace (2014), 18% of greenhouse gas emissions in Romania come effect of coal power plants.

As a result of the economic downturn after 1989, in Romania, a significant reduction in GHG emissions was recorded. Total emissions of CO2 equivalent (without LULUCF) for Romania accounted for 2.61% of total EU emissions. Table 4 shows the sectoral contributions to GHG emissions in 2014. Table 3 shows the sectoral contributions to GHG emissions in 2014. Thus, in 2014, the energy sector contributed about 83% of GHG emissions representing a priority for reduction. The transport sector has grown rapidly - by over 35% compared to 1990. This trend is likely to continue, indicating that this sector, especially road transport, deserves attention in terms of limiting the increase in GHG emissions.

Table 4. Greenhouse gas emissions by source sector, 2010-2014

	Year	2010	2011	2012	2013	2014
Energy	EU-28	3794960.92	3646230.22	3599940.98	3515317.95	3323934.71
	Romania	82881.97	87745.92	86548.74	76996.24	76302.13
Industrial processes and product use	EU-28	386605.76	382432.12	369807.85	368676.97	373403.9
	Romania	12260.33	12504.39	11551.79	10376.58	10856.15
Agriculture	EU-28	426939.07	426945.64	424392.67	428068.7	434937.7
	Romania	16271.06	16425.64	16446.56	16860.21	16844.63
Land use, land use change, and forestry (LULUCF)	EU-28	-317274.89	-316224.63	-311686	-316262.36	-302559.77
	Romania	-18496.75	-18805.03	-17937.19	-18232.47	-18258.18
Waste management	EU-28	169196.44	163352.68	158454.28	150743.02	145701.36
	Romania	5584.37	5015.4	5519.73	5798.94	5756.73
Other sectors	EU-28	15.69	15.23	12.92	13.19	14.02
	Romania	:	:	:	:	:

Source: Processed by authors using data provided by EUROSTAT (source: EEA) [env_air_gge]

In urban areas, 56% of the population lives and most of the economic activities are conducted. This is a diverse and complex sector, with a wide range of opportunities to reduce the GHG emissions by improving energy efficiency in buildings, a more efficient urban transport, and implementation of waste management. Agriculture is responsible for over 18% of total GHG emissions. It is worth mentioning that net absorption of CO2 from the atmosphere by forestry offsets about 20% of emissions in other sectors at the national level. It offers a wide range of mitigation measures - conservation and enhancement of existing C deposits, improvement of the absorption rate of atmospheric CO2 and land use change.

Green Jobs in Romania

Millions of green jobs could occur if the green economy were more emphasized.

In Europe, there are over 20 million jobs linked to the green sector.

In our country, the number of "green" jobs is becoming increasingly higher in the following areas:

- Renewable Energies;
- Ecological Agriculture;

- Food Industry;
- Transport.

In this context, a revolution takes place in the labor market, "green" jobs representing a lifebelt. People trained in fields concerned with the environment are beneficiaries of some extra employment opportunities. Romania has a potential for growth, particularly in the non-renewable energy sources - the wind and solar energy: environmental consultant, environment manager, energy buyer, technical operator, responsible for maintaining and wind turbines and solar panels. Also, in 2014, in Romania, there were over 2,000 companies in the recycling and waste management field, and their number is growing.

EU 2020 strategy includes the increasing employment rate among its objectives. Green sector has a clear upward trend, which requires new training programs and an adaptation of sustainable business practices. Green products are increasingly requested. These changes contribute to an increase in the number of green jobs. In specialty literature, the concept of "green collar" has appeared. In this context, green jobs can be a way to support the economy. They can contribute to economic growth.

Environmental Performance Index (EPI) in Romania

Environmental Performance Index (EPI) measures the performance of countries in terms of human health protection from harm and protection of the environmental ecosystems, using 25 indicators grouped into ten categories as follows:

- Health Impacts;
- Air Quality;
- Water and Sanitation;
- Water Resources;
- Agriculture;
- Forests;
- Fisheries;
- Biodiversity and Habitat;
- Climate and Energy.

In 2014 Romania was ranked 86. Figure 19 shows that the best result for Romania had been registered in the field of Health Impacts, with a score of approx. 85 and the weakest one, in the field of Water Resources, with a score of approx. 13, despite the government's efforts, demonstrated by the increasing expenditures in this area.

Figure 19. Environmental Performance Index in Romania, 2014
Source: http://www.epi.yale.edu/epi/country-profile

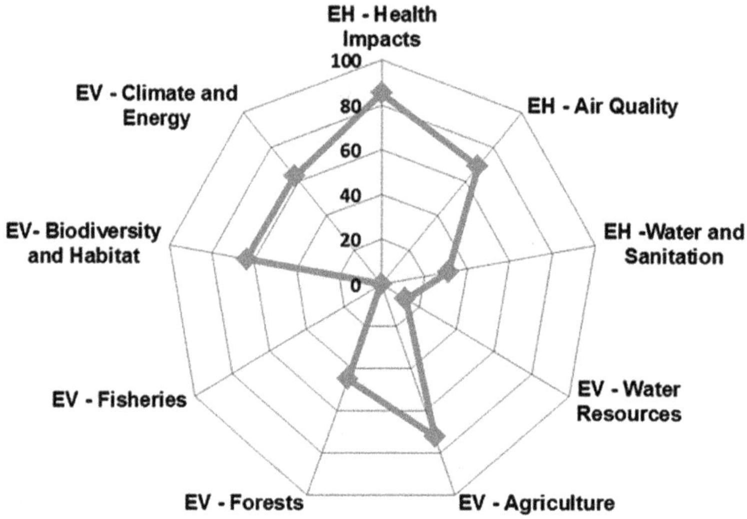

According to Sima and Gheorghe (2014), the value of the correlation coefficient (0.74) confirms a moderate direct link between the environmental performance index and the GDP /capita, a better air quality, etc.

CONCLUSION

Specific indicators are designed to measure sustainable economic growth. Its effects are materializing in a major growth of the ecological productivity, an increased amount of energy derived from renewable sources, emissions reduction, improved air and water quality, widened access to the benefits of civilization - education, water sanitation. Thus, this green growth "can fight" against climate change. Also, green growth provides opportunities for creating new jobs requiring new skills. Romania has the chance to be among the EU countries that will practice this social model based on these new skills that could lead to an improved quality of life.

In the latest statistics, there are some fields in which Romania holds honorable positions, as follows:

- According to the European Wind Energy Association, in 2014 Romania ranked 9 in the EU depending on the capacity of wind farms with an installed capacity of 2,952.9 MW. Germany ranked first with 39,127.9 MW.

- According Eurostat data, in 2014 Romania ranked 10 in the EU depending on the amount of carbon dioxide emissions in the energy sector. Germany, the leader, emitted 12 times more pollutants than Romania.

There are also fields in which Romania is at the end of the list, as follows:

- After the amount of municipal waste generated by population, Romania ranks 22 in the EU, with 389 kg per capita, in a ranking led by Denmark with 668 kg per person.
- In terms of recycling, Romania ranks last in the EU. Romania recycles only 1% of its waste, while Germany recycles 65%.

There is a close relationship between environmental taxes and efforts to protect the environment. Romania has low energy taxes. However, paradoxically, Romania is a country with low CO2 emissions. Despite the fact that the environmental taxes have lower levels than the EU average, and the capacity to collect these fees is quite limited, Romania is in a very good situation in terms of the overall level of CO2 emissions. Deindustrialization, the economy contraction, a decrease of the synthetic fertilizer use, the drop in growing areas could explain this.

REFERENCES

Alexander, M. (2013). Management Planning for Nature Conservation, A Theoretical Basis & Practical Guide (2nd ed.). Springer eBooks.

Allenby, B. (2006). The ontologies of industrial ecology? *Progress in Industrial Ecology-An International Journal*, *3*(1/2), 28–40. doi:10.1504/PIE.2006.010039

Andersen, M. S., & Massa, I. (2000). Ecological modernization — origins, dilemmas and future directions. Journal of Environmental Policy & Planning. *Journal of Environmental Policy and Planning*, *2*(4), 337–345. doi:10.1080/714852820

Bell, S., McGillivray, D., & Pedersen, O. W. (2013). *Environmental law* (8th ed.). Oxford, UK: Oxford University Press. doi:10.1093/he/9780199583805.001.0001

Brunori, G. (2013). Biomass, Biovalue and Sustainability: Some Thoughts on the Definition of the Bioeconomy. *EuroChoices*, *12*(1), 48–52. doi:10.1111/1746-692X.12020

Burkart, K. (2012). *How to define the green economy*. Available at: http://www.mnn.com/green-tech/researchinnovations/blogs/how-do-you-define-the-green-economy

Carter, N. (2007). *The politics of the environment: Ideas, activism, policy* (2nd ed.). Cambridge, UK: Cambridge University Press. doi:10.1017/CBO9780511819179

Cato, M. S. (2009). *Green Economics: An Introduction to Theory, Policy and Practice*. London: Earthscan.

Deanna, J. R. (Ed.), *(n.d.). The Industrial Green Game: Implications for Environmental Design and Management*. Washington, DC: The National Academies Press; doi:10.17226/4982

Dobson, A. (2007). Environmental citizenship: Towards sustainable development. *Journal of Sustainable Development, 15*(5), 282–283.

Frosch, R. A., & Gallopoulos, N. E. (1989). Strategies for Manufacturing. *Strategies for Manufacturing Scientific American., 261*(3), 144–152. doi:10.1038/scientificamerican0989-144

Gheorghe, I. G., & Sima, V. (2014). Transition to Green Economy in Romania. *Annals of the Constantin Brâncuşi, 3*, 32-39. Retrieved from http://eur-lex.europa.eu/legal-content/EN/TXT/PDF/?uri=CELEX:32008L0098&from=ROhttp://www.unep.fr/scp/cp/

Loiseau, E., Saikku, L., Antikainen, R., Leskinen, P., & Pitkänen, K. (2015). Conceptual framework and methodological tools used by green economy. In *Implementing the green economy in a European context – lessons learned from theories, concepts and case studies*. PEER Report. Helsinki: Partnership for European Environmental Research, Juvenes Print. Available at http://www.peer.eu/fileadmin/user_upload/publications/PEERreport_ImplementingTheGreenEconomy.pdf

Matei, M., Stancu, A., & Vukovic, P. (2009). *The interdependence between agriculture and climate change-a European perspective.* Paper presentato al 113th EAAE Seminar, Belgrado.

Sima, V., & Gheorghe, I. (2009). *Eco-Efficiency – A Romanian Perspective*. The 12th IBIMA Conference, "Creating Global Economies through Innovation and Knowledge Management", Kuala Lumpur, Malaysia.

Sima, V., & Gheorghe, I. G. (2014). Analyze of environmental performance in Romania based on environmental performance index. *Annals of the Constantin Brâncuşi, 3*, 101-104.

Sima, V., & Gheorghe, I. G. (2014). Labour market trends in România in the context of green economy. *Annals of the Constantin Brâncuşi*, 116-123. Retrieved from http://www.utgjiu.ro/revista/ec/pdf/2014-04.Special/22_Sima,%20Gheorghe.pdf

Stahel, W. R. (1997). The Functional Economy: Cultural and Organizational Change. In Cultura civică şi dreptul antreprenorial. Editura Lumina Lex.

Wind in Power. (2015). *European Statistics: The European Wind Energy Association*. Retrieved May 24 2016 from https://windeurope.org/wp-content/uploads/files/about-wind/statistics/EWEA-Annual-Statistics-2015.pdf

ADDITIONAL READING

European Commission. (2015). *Towards an EU Research and innovation agenda for nature-based solutions and re-naturing cities*. Brussels: CEC.

OECD. (2009). The Bioeconomy to 2030: designing a policy agenda. OECD Publishing, Paris.EC (European Commission), 2012. Communication from the Commission of the European Parliament, the Council, the European economic and social Committee and the Committee of the Regions: "Innovating for Sustainable Growth: A Bioeconomy for Europe." Brussels.

OECD. (2011). *Towards Green Growth: Monitoring Progress. OECD Indicators, OECD Green Growth Studies* (p. 9). Paris: OECD Publishing.

Towards the Circular Economy 1: Economic and Business Rationale for an Accelerated Transition; January 2012, Cowes, Isle of Wight: Ellen MacArthur Foundation. Towards the Circular Economy 2: Opportunities for the consumer goods sector; January 2013, Cowes, Isle of Wight: Ellen MacArthur Foundation. 'Hidden innovation' in: Science & Public Policy, London, vol. 13 no. 4, August 1986.

UNDP (United Nations Development Program). (2010). Green Economy Report: A Preview

KEY TERMS AND DEFINITIONS

Environmental Performance Index: It measures the performance of countries in terms of human health protection from harm and protection of environmental ecosystems, using 25 performance indicators grouped into ten categories including: Health Impacts, Air Quality, Water and Sanitation, Water Resources, Agriculture, Forests, Fisheries, Biodiversity and Habitat, and Climate and Energy.

Environmental Protection Expenditures: "Statistics on environmental protection expenditure present data on the economic resources devoted by resident units to environmental protection" (Eurostat).

Environmental Quality: A state of environmental conditions, expressed in terms of indicators or indices, which measures environmental health, referring to air and water purity or pollution, noise, resources, flora and fauna.

Environmental Tax: A tax whose base is a physical unit (or a proxy of a physical unit) of something that has a proven, specific negative impact on the environment. Environmental tax statistics present data on taxes in the following areas: Energy, Transport, Pollution, and Resource (Eurostat).

Green Economy: A means to achieve sustainable development, representing an adaptation of the socio-economic system to the multiple challenges of the current period.

Green Growth: "Green growth is about fostering economic growth and development while ensuring that the natural assets continue to provide the resources and environmental services on which our well-being relies. To do this it must catalyse investment and innovation which will underpin sustained growth and give rise to new economic opportunities." (OECD, 2011).

Greenhouse Gasses Emissions: A group of compounds which are able of absorbing infrared radiation to trap heat, keeping the Earth's surface warmer than it would be if they were not present.

Green Jobs: A "work in agricultural, manufacturing, research and development (R&D), administrative, and service activities that contribute(s) substantially to preserving or restoring environmental quality. Specifically, but not exclusively, this includes jobs that help to protect ecosystems and biodiversity; reduce energy, materials, and water consumption through high efficiency strategies; de-carbonize the economy; and minimize or altogether avoid generation of all forms of waste and pollution" (2008).

Chapter 5
Aggressions of the Socio-Economic System on the Natural Capital

Constanţa Popescu
Valahia University of Târgovişte, Romania

Constantin Popescu
Valahia University of Târgovişte, Romania

Maria Luiza Hrestic
Valahia University of Târgovişte. Romania

ABSTRACT

Nearly 250 million years ago, the Earth was shaken by the amplest extinction known so far, which led to the extinction of up to 96% of all the marine species, 70% of the vertebrate species, and almost all the insects. This extinction affected the whole range of biodiversity so much. Nature took almost 10 million years to recover after this event. Life was really in danger on our planet at that moment, due to the dismal conditions that were created, and the current research shows that these dire conditions continued to occur, in the natural environment, after that, triggering numerous outbreaks that occurred for five to six million years following the initial crisis, triggered by the carbon rise and the repeated shortages of oxygen, the increased warming and other such adverse effects, which, once initiated, were uncontrollable and had disastrous effects. When life returned to normal and, gradually, after several million years, a new beginning was possible, the significant elements that caused the disaster - global warming, acid rain - sound strangely familiar to us today.

DOI: 10.4018/978-1-5225-2081-8.ch005

MAN'S BELONGING TO NATURE

In time, for a very long period, nature in general, but especially forests, have been considered empty areas, some even hostile, which could become valuable only when the trees were turned into timber and/or the land freed (evidently, deforested) acquired a deforested land, acquired an agricultural use, or settlements or infrastructure elements were built on it.

Human perception and attitude to nature and its components is a key element for understanding the relations between nature, mankind and culture. This perception, aware or not, guides the attitude, the actions and the ecological footprint of different individuals, groups or cultures, on the environment in general and especially on nature. Yet, at the same time, this perception has consequences on man himself, directly influencing his mental and physical health.

Unfortunately, often science and, on these grounds, also education, tend to intellectualize, in the sense of complicating, the feeling of nature and implicitly man's relation to nature.

The genetic information related to man's ancestral belonging to nature comes back intuitively or culturally and produces feelings, often contradictory ones, in the relations between man and nature and even in relation to human naturalness.

In is almost unanimously acknowledged that the increase of the human population, accompanied by the growth of the needs for goods and services of the members of the different communities are the main drives of the human society's development, which determined the diversification, the improvement and the increased capacity of the means and technologies of access and use of the resources and services provided by the natural systems.

The concept of structural unity between biocenosis and the physical and chemical components of the area it occupies anticipated and actually substantiated the concept of "organization" in a given space, which is much more comprehensive and constitutes the backbone of the ecology theory. In this way, it has been possible to integrate the study of the populations in the study of the ecosystems - basic productive units.

The research carried out on the energetics of the ecosystems and, implicitly, on the energetics of the natural populations, highlighted the need to research the circulation of the mineral elements and, first of all, of carbon, nitrogen and phosphorus, to be able to explain the primary output dynamics.

From this new perspective, the bioindividuals, the populations or the species, interconnected in biocenoses, and also the structural entities resulting from their interaction with the abiotic environment, become integrated units, functioning based on cybernetic principles and self-regulable (Popescu C., 2008).

PRODUCTIVE CAPACITY AND CARRYING CAPACITY

This conceptual progress permitted to investigate and know the productive and carrying capacity of ecosystems or ecosystems complexes. Errors have also been committed, like those of the period 1960-1985, when, without a sufficiently consolidated basis, a series of sub disciplines were differentiated, such as: ecophysiology, ecotoxicology, biochemical ecology, biophysical ecology, agroecology, urban ecology, human ecology etc., which, operating each with many, often conflicting concepts, created confusions, undermining the coherence and credibility of ecology as a science.

During the same period, the theoretical basis of ecology was consolidated and completed with dynamic systems mathematics, attaining during the last two decennia of the 20th century the systemic conception that gave ecology the force and means necessary to perceive and interpret the physical and biological environment as a hierarchy of complex ecosystems, dynamically influencing one another. At the same time, the passage from the analythical method to systemic analysis allows identifying ecological systems as real entities and identifying, at the same time, ways of investigating them and of describing their behavior.

Systemic analysis supposes an integrated holistic approach both in the research and especially in the management of natural ecological systems and of those dominated by the human species.

During the present stage, after the conceptual clarification of ecology as science of the ecological systems, an ample process of identification of the ecosystems organized in hierarchies, from simple to complex, also comprising anthropized systems, has been started, to be able to project and then develop support information systems and especially organize their integrated management.

This is how for us, forest administration people, understanding climate change as a direct effect of deforestation was unfortunately the first practical evidence of the accuracy of the systemic approach (Popescu C., 2008).

The many conflictual states created in the world in relation to the forests are caused by the fact that, unfortunately, people have understood too late that when forests vanish they do not lose only wood but first of all the effects of their first functions.

The very ample studies of the American researchers coordinated by professor Robert Constantza (University Professor of Sustainability in the Institute for Sustainable Solutions at Portland State University, 1997) demonstrate that the environmental services of the world's natural ecosystems go even over the world GDP and, under these conditions, during the last 200 years, about 3 billion hectares of forests have disappeared, namely almost half of the forests covering back then the Earth's land.

The increasing conflicts related to forests and forest lands and highlighting their implications on the political and managerial decision is part of the new arena delineated by the complex interaction between public processes and phenomena and between them and local ones, which are getting more numerous and call for solutions.

The topicality of the subject is also accentuated by the fact that, increasingly more, the relations citizen-administration will be defined by new directions and implications related to natural resource management, and only the integrated approach will be the one able to solve them competitively (Constantza, R., 1997).

The great ecological accidents, as well as the ecological crisis we are going through, are first of all due to the anthropocentric economic conception according to which plants, animals, forests, waters and ecological systems in general are important only to the extent to which they are the object of the interests of human communities.

The deeply negative effect of such an approach is that very few restrictions have been imposed on the way people deal with the environment in general and especially with forests. Practically, since times out of mind, and apparently even today here and there, in their relation with nature, the only limit of those people mastered by the desire of overexploitation of the natural resources has been only the result of their interplay with the interests of other individuals.

This is why the next step in the direction of a deeper approach was considered as "huge"; it is a step by which ethics has been extended to the analysis of all the areas and not just of those dominated by man. This is how the concept of "Earth ethics" was launched by the American forester and ecologist Aldo Leopold even since the middle of the 20th century.

Leopold's principles are today acknowledged by an increasing number of specialists in the theory of ecology and not just by them, as these principles have introduced new values:

- Nature and the environment have an intrinsic value, just as any value put in the service of man, or even in opposition to this
- Not just people and the projects put in their service carry value
- Something is correct when it tends to preserve the integrity, stability and beauty of the biotic community, and incorrect if, on the contrary, it has a different orientation
- Earth ethics simply extends the boundaries of the community, also including the soils, the water, the plants and the animals from all over the Earth
- The ethical community is therefore extended so that it overlaps the ecological community.

Starting from these concepts, the Norwegian Arnei Naess issued in 1978 the postulate according to which mankind is inseparable from nature. In other words, nature as a whole has moral value—not the human individuals or other living organisms, taken separately.

The conclusion of such an approach is that the environmental issues will be solvable only by those able to emit judgements of value, beyond the narrow limits of human interests.

GOODS AND SERVICE PRODUCTION

Continuing this logic, today, is unanimously accepted the thesis according to which "the goods and services production increase, in order to answer, on the one hand, the basic needs of the population, and, on the other hand, the increasing "desires" manifested in the developed countries have always been assured based on the absorption of matter and energy resources or services, assured by primary producers. In other words, it is admitted that the socio-economic system is strictly dependent on the energy performances of the natural and seminatural ecological systems.

Primary producers – the populations or species of plants and photosynthesizing and chemosynthesizing bacteria, concentrating solar energy and chemical energy, produce biomass that, after the decrease of their own consumption of energy, constitute an energy source for the heterotrophic species that are part of the structure of a biocenosis or human population.

Here, in Table 1, we see the gross primary production of the main ecological systems on our planet (Popescu C., 2008; Vădineanu, A. 1998).

Table 1. Gross primary production of the main ecological systems

Categories of Ecological Systems	Area ($10^6 km^2$)	PPB $kcal/m^2/year$	% of ecosphere PPB
Planetary ocean (depths > 200 m)	326	800	30
Desert and tundra	40		
Coastlines (altitude < 200 m)	34	4000	32
Grazing fields	42		
Coniferous forests	10		
Temperate forests	10		
Waters and wet temperate forests	5		
Traditionally managed agrosystems	10		
Estuaries, deltas, reefs	2	18000	38

Therefore, natural and seminatural ecological systems produce biological resouces (concentrated energy) and recycle the raw matter needed by the biological production, using solar energy. The processes by which goods (renewable resources) and also services (water quality, soil formation and protection, carbon absorption and climate control etc.) are produced are relatively costly in point of energy, yet, solar energy, which is free, is the source covering these expenses. Consequently, it results that natural and seminatural ecological systems are the most efficient dissipative structures.

Dissipative structures accumulate, concentrate, transform and dissipate energy, the result being an increasingly complex organization, namely they behave anti-enthropically, and their main outcomes are the production of renewable resources and services.

It is precisely the increase of the organization degree and the productive capacity that are assured by the specific of biological systems, which are part and parcel of the ecological systems. It results, therefore, that natural and seminatural ecological systems are the only productive units and carrying units for life on the planet.

Unlike in them, in the systems transformed and controlled by man (agrosystems, farms, intensive aquaculture etc.), energy expenses are realized from considerable subsidies obtained by burning energy stocks concentrated in fossil fuels, constituted in time, via long geological processes.

The systems created by human populations (urban systems, industrial complexes), as energy are parasite systems, depending on the concentrated energy and raw matter stocked in natural systems.

Recycling raw matter needed by primary producers to absorb and concentrate solar energy in organic matter by photosynthesis, or chemosynthesis, is the most important ecological process on earth.

The recycling compartment, represented by the trophic structure of the biological systems, taken as parts of the ecological systems (beginning with biocenoses and ending with the biosphere) is closely interconnected with the elements of the hydrogeomorphological units (soil, lithosphere, water) forming the toposphere. In their turn, these components are interconnected by physical-chemical mechanisms and phenomena and constitute the support of the local, regional and global biogeochemical circuits.

The productivity of any ecological system depends on both the stock of macro and microelements available in the mass of water and sediments of acquatic systems, or in the soil and water of terrestrial systems, and on recycling speed of the respective stock by the ecological systems' biological elements.

Under these circumstances, the ecological systems availing themselves of relatively small stocks of macro and microelements, especially nitrogen and phosphorus, but having a very dynamic recycling system, realize great productivities of goods and services.

Such are the forests, the most productive biocenoses of our planet, which beside profitably using the lands that are poorest in micro and macroelements, often totally impossible to be used for other uses, provide fundamentally important services for the key components of the ecosphere, such as: lithosphere, hydrosphere or troposphere, namely they become carrying units of life.

It has been demonstrated in this way that the deterioration of the vegetal layer by deforestations and overgrazing, along with draining, damming, channaling, soil compaction through intensive agriculture have modified the amplest essential phenomenon on the planet: the water circuit in nature.

The development of the socio-economic system has been and will be dependent on the hydrological circuit, but it is regrettable that it is precisely many human activities that have significantly affected the key mechanisms of this circuit.

EVALUATION OF THE RISK DETERMINED BY CLIMATE CHANGES

On Risk and Uncertainty

The consequences of most human activities are almost unforeseeable, because we often do not know the nature of these consequences. Here we have in view the extreme case of uncertainty regarding future events. As our knowledge improves we can express our uncertainty by the probability of occurrence of such consequences, namely we can transform our uncertainty into risk. Consequently, risk can be defined as measurable uncertainty.

Many ecological processes are, however, insufficiently understood so far, so that one cannot precisely foresee the impact of the economic activities on them and implicitly on the environmental components. One can understand and foresee the type of potential impact, but not its amplitude or the moment when it is going to occur. Particularly difficult is the anticipation of the possible impact of an event triggering a chain reaction. Irreversible effects, such as the disappearance of a species, damages on the ozone layer or landscape changes have become main concerns for the ecologists.

In order to face uncertainty, one can act in several ways:

- Stimulating investments in information
- Presenting eventual consequences and their probabilities of occurrence (evaluating risk)
- Carrying out analyses on the perceptions and preferences of the decision-maker and/or the public concerning the risk (the perception of risk and subjective preferences)
- Determining the rules regarding decision-making and investment strategies

Risk evaluation is the process by which uncertainty is turned into risk and answers questions such as:

- "How risky is the situation?"
- "What are the risks associated to the different ecological problems?"

Complementarily, risk management answers questions such as:

- "What should be done in this situation?"
- "What solutions can be found to reduce the risks associated to the various ecological problems?"

The aim of risk evaluation consists in analyzing and hierarchizing the risk levels associated to some ecological problems, based on the best information and scientific judgements available.

Ecological problems can represent a risk both for people, and for the ecosystems; they can also lead to the degradation of the quality of life. Each risk category is important and must be analyzed separately. For example, the heating of the atmosphere induces the heating of the waters, which has a negative impact not just on the biocenoses of the ecosystems, but also determines a loss of some recreational opportunities of the communities (diminishing the quality of life). For this reason, it is important to look at the ecological problems from all the perspectives: of the risks for human health, for the ecosystems, and for the quality of life.

Comparative Risk Evaluation (CRE) is also a useful tool for hierarchizing the priority actions in environmental protection. For this reason, the solving of the global environmental problems, such as climate changes or irreversible biodiversity loss, has to be approached, if not simultaneously, at least according to the order of their priority.

CLIMATE CHANGE

Indices of the Impact of Climate Changes

The average air temperature worldwide has risen by 0.3-0.6o C since the end of the 19th century. In the year 1997 (the hottest year), the average temperature was 0.43 degrees higher than the average recorded during the period 1961-1990. Europe has been confirmed as matching the global trend, the 1990s being the hottest years. According to the estimates, the average temperatures of the year 2010 will be two degrees Celsius higher than those of the 1990s. At the same time, in Europe, it is estimated that the warming is going to be more significant in the northern than in the southern areas (Allan, D., 1994).

Global warming has been dilating the seas and oceans and accelerating the melting of the icecap. All these have led to an increase of the seas and oceans' level of 10-25 cm during the last 100 years. The estimates indicate the fact that in the year 2020, the sea level will be 50 cm higher than the level of the 1990s (with a variation ranging between 15 and 95 cm), the uncertainty degree being increased by the lack of knowledge regarding the contribution of the polar ice.

The increasing sea level can have consequences such as:

- Flooding and dislocating the marshy or low lands
- Increasing salinity in estuaries
- Deteriorating the potable water sources

From this perspective, the riskiest areas are deltas, beaches, islands and estuaries. In Europe, they include the coastlines of the Netherlands, Germany, the Balkan States, Ukraine, Russia and some Mediterranean deltas.

Coastal areas can also be affected in other ways than just by the rising of the sea level. For example, in the Netherlands, a 10% storm intensity rise, accompanied by changes in the wind direction, could bring more damage than a 60 cm sea level rise.

The cost of the adaptation and protection against a one-meter sea level rise has been estimated to US$12,300 million for the Netherlands, US$1,400 million for Poland and US$23,500 million for Germany.

Precipitations

In the Europe of the 20th century, the precipitations regime has been changing continually. Thus, precipitation quantities have grown, in general, in the Northern half of Europe and have decreased in its Southern half.

While in Northern Scandinavia, precipitations have increased by 5%, the southern parts of Italy and Greece have recorded, since the year 1900 till now, a decrease of about 5%.

All the attempts of modelling the climate modifications forecast an increase in the average annual precipitations; at the same time, global warming influences soil humidity, by accentuating water evaporation. The modelling of these processes suggests the fact that, in Europe, soil humidity is going to decrease.

Hydrology and Water Resources

Even since the middle of the 19th century, the glaciers of the Alps have begun to "withdraw" (it is estimated that during the next hundred years, global warming will melt up to 95% of the glaciers of the Alps), which will influence the seasonal pattern of the river courses (Constantza, R., 1996). During the last decennia, their volume increased in Northern Europe, which agrees with the precipitations growth observed.

The climate change will probably accentuate the "hydrological stress" of some already sensitive European areas: the Mediterranean region, the Alps, Northern Scandinavia, the coastlines and central and Eastern Europe. The consequences of the hydrological cycle changes are hard to estimate; they include a possible increase in the frequency and intensity of flooding and a possible water quality decrease, by the infiltration of salty water in the underground water of the coastal areas.

Agriculture and Forest Ecosystems

The ecosystems' reaction to the changes of temperature, precipitations and soil humidity and of other factors that change along with the climate is hard to forecast.

The main impact on the species will be concretized in the modification of their geographic distribution. A one-degree Celsius rise of the annual average temperature is equivalent to a shift northwards of 200-300 km or in altitude of 150-200 m. A two-degree Celsius temperature rise in 50 years in Europe would lead to a shift of the climate zones northwards at a faster pace than the migration ability of most plant species. Moreover, in the alpine areas, the plants' location will be forced upwards, yet there may be no room available for their migration. Besides, the possibilities of migration in many parts of Europe are limited due to the intensity of the land use.

Climate change can have various effects on agriculture and forestry, namely on the plants' periods of growth and productivity. The growing variability of the climate can endanger certain crops due to the occurrence of late frosts. Some studies and especially simulation and modelling have shown that climate changes can trigger richer crops in large areas of Europe (Leopold, A., 1949).

CLIMATE CHANGE REASONS. MAIN GREENHOUSE GASES: EMISSION SOURCES, CONCENTRATIONS

Carbon Dioxide

The greatest anthropic source of CO2 is the burning of fossil fuels for the production of electricity, heat, in transports and industry. The natural ecosystems emit and absorb, by photosynthesis and respiration, large quantities of CO2.

In time, these processes have been balanced and have not given rise to extra emissions on either side. Human activities and the socio-economic system in general have disturbed, however, these balances, when they generated and as they continue to generate important supplementary net emissions. For example, by the destruction of the forests, carbon is freed, and this evil could be remedied, generating a significantly higher net absorptions, for example if deforested areas were reforested or if forests were allowed to reach greater ages and sizes.

On a global level, the main CO2 sources are fossil fuel burning (77%), industrial processes such as cement production (2%) and modification of the land use (21%). In Europe, the contribution of these sources is slightly different: fossil fuel burning (98%), industrial processes (2%), while the land use can actually be a sponge absorbing 13% of the carbon dioxide emitted in Europe. At present, Europe generates 29% of the global carbon dioxide emissions.

CO2 emissions depend on the economic development degree of the different countries. Thus, the CO2 emissions level per GDP unit in the year 1994 shows that, excepting some parts of the former Yugoslavia and Albania, this indicator is considerably higher in Central and Eastern Europe (3.3 tons/US$) and in the new independent states (2.4 tons/US$), than in Western Europe. The numbers reflect the inefficient use of energy and the predominance of the heavy industry, consuming significant quantities of energy, in Eastern Europe.

Methane

The global anthropic emissions of methane total 375,000 tons/year, out of which 27% result from the use of fossil fuels. European emissions represent about 11% of this total. The main sources are: leaks from gas transport and distribution networks, coal extraction and agriculture - especially ruminants breeding and rice fields. Natural sources (e.g., marshes) contribute by about 20% to the global methane emissions.

Nitrogen Protoxide

The global anthropic emissions of N_2O range between 3 and 8,000 tons/year. The existing uncertainties regarding the evaluation of these emissions results from the insufficient understanding of the processes involved and of their distribution around the globe. Worldwide, the greatest emissions are generated by the fertilization of the agricultural lands. In Central and Eastern Europe, N_2O emissions in agriculture have decreased due to the reduction of the use of fertilizers; to a lesser extent, due to the restructuring process, the emissions coming from the industry have also recorded a decrease (the production of nitric acid and nylon).

Halogenated Gases

The emissions of halogenated gases, such as CFC, are rapidly decreasing due to their suppression according to the protocol of Montreal. Consequently, the emissions of replacing gases, especially HCFC and HFC, both greenhouse gases, have been growing. The data on these emissions are too limited to establish their evolution in time, yet their long-term remanence in the atmosphere and their high global warming potential, can increase their importance.

The contribution of greenhouse gases to global warming, and therefore their influence on the sea level, precipitations and ecosystems, depends on their concentration and period of remanence in the atmosphere and their efficiency in retaining radiations. For example, although CFCs are present in the atmosphere in very small concentrations, they are important because their period of remanence is around 100 years, and each molecule determines a greenhouse effect many times higher than one of CO_2. To be able to compare the impact of various gases, the indicator called global warming potential relative to CO_2 has been used, carbon dioxide being attributed the value one. The dimensions of this indicator depend on the time horizon considered. Examples of such values calculated for a period of 100 years are: 21 for CH_4, 310 for N_2O and several hundred for halogenated compounds. The measurement units of these emissions, which take into account the values of the global warming potential are called equivalent (carbon).

Moreover, the tropospheric ozone can contribute to global warming, the estimates showing that they add 16% to the total effect caused by the anthropic greenhouse effect gases mentioned.

The aerosols, which can be emitted directly (primary aerosols), or formed in the atmosphere out of SO_2, NO and NH (secondary aerosols), have a cooling effect, both directly, through the dispersion of the sunlight, and indirectly, by modifying the features of the clouds. The size of the cooling effect is not known for sure; it has been estimated that aerosols annihilate almost half of the warming triggered by greenhouse gases. However, unlike the main greenhouse gases, aerosols have a short period of remanence in the atmosphere. Their effect is therefore regional and short-term and appears especially over Europe, USA and China. As in Europe the level of SO2 and NO emissions is decreasing, the quantities of secondary aerosols generated are also decreasing, simultaneously to their cooling effect.

The great variations of the duration of remanence in the atmosphere of the various greenhouse gases shows a contribution in time to global warming that can vary from 20 to several thousand years. Consequently, there is a considerable temporal gap between the period when the emissions reduction takes place and the stabilization of their concentration in the atmosphere. Therefore, the actions undertaken today will need a long time to have some effect.

Global warming is not, however, the only effect that greenhouse gases can trigger. Thus, the actions meant to control the climate changes can have beneficial or negative side-effects on the environment:

- The reduction of CFC emissions meant to protect the stratospheric ozone also diminishes their greenhouse effect
- The decrease of the methane emissions meant to slow down the global warming phenomenon is concomitantly lowering the level of the tropospheric ozone
- The diminution of the SO2, NOX and NH3 emissions will reduce acidification

On the other hand, a side-effect will be the decreasing production of sulphate and nitrate aerosols, which have a regional cooling effect (Lester, R. Brown, et al., 1997).

OBJECTIVES AND POLICIES OF GREENHOUSE GASES REDUCTION

The Decision no. 406/2009/EC of the European Parliament and of the Council of 23 April 2009 regarding the effort of the Member States of reducing the greenhouse gas emissions so that they may respect the Community's commitments to reduce greenhouse gas emissions until 2020 is the central document regulating the position and the commitments of the EU States in relation to greenhouse gas emissions reduction.

The supreme objective of the UN Framework-Convention on Climate Change (UNFCCC), approved on behalf of the European Community by the Decision 94/69/EC of the Council JO L 33, 7.2.1994, p. 11, consists in the stabilization of greenhouse gas concentrations in the atmosphere at a level preventing any anthropogenic disturbance of the climate system (Popescu, C., 2011).

According to the opinion of the Community, expressed most recently especially by the European Council of March 2007, in order to be able to attain this objective, the global increase of the average annual temperature on the ground should not go over the preindustrial levels by more than 2°C, which means that the world greenhouse gases emissions ought to be reduced, until 2050, by at least 50% compared to the levels recorded in 1990.

The Community's greenhouse gas emissions, regulated by the present decision, ought to continue to be reduced annually after 2020, as part of the Community's efforts of contributing to this global emissions reduction goal.

The developed countries, including the EU Member States, ought to continue to constitute an example, committing to reduce, until 2020, their greenhouse gas emissions by up to 30% compared to the levels recorded in 1990. They ought to realize the same thing in order to attain the collective goal of emissions reduction of 60% to 80% until the year 2050, compared to the levels recorded in 1990.

All the economic sectors ought to contribute to the realization of this emissions reduction goal, including the international transport by sea and the aviation sector. The aviation sector contributes to these reductions by its inclusion in the EU' emission quota trading system (henceforth called "Community system"). If, until 31 December 2011, no international agreement including the emissions coming from the international transportation by sea among its reduction goals is approved by the Member States in the framework of the International Maritime Organization or by the Community in UNFCCC, the Commission ought to submit a proposition coming into force until 2013 and including these emissions in the frame of the Community's commitment of emissions reduction. Such a proposition ought to reduce any negative impact on the Community's competitiveness, while considering the eventual benefits for the environment.

At the same time, in order to attain this objective, the European Council of March 2007 reiterated the community objective of reduction by 30% compared to the levels of 1990 of the greenhouse gas emissions until 2020, as a contribution to the conclusion of a global and comprehensive agreement for the period following the year 2012, on condition that other developed countries should also commit to realizing comparable emissions reductions, while the developing countries with a more advanced economy ought to contribute adequately, according to the responsibilities and capacities of each of them.

The European Council of March 2007 highlighted, at the same time, the Community's pledge of transforming Europe in a highly energy-efficient economy, with low greenhouse gases emissions, and decided that, until the conclusion of a global and comprehensive agreement for the period following the year 2012 and without affecting its position in the international negotiations, the Community takes on this firm and independent commitment of realizing a reduction of at least 20% compared to 1990 of the greenhouse gas emissions until the year 2020.

An improved energy-efficiency is an essential element for the accomplishment by the Member States of the present decision's demands. In this context, the Commission ought to closely monitor the progresses recorded in order to attain the objective of energy consumption reduction by 20% until 2020 and propose further actions in case of insufficient progress.

Directive 2003/87/CE

The Directive 2003/87/CE of the European Parliament and of the Council of 13 October 2003, instituting a greenhouse gas emissions trading system in the Community (JO L 275, 25.10.2003, p. 32) has created a greenhouse gas emissions trading system in the Community, which regulates certain sectors of the economy (Allan, D., 1994).

Paris 2015

The main objective of the conference is to sign a treaty by which all the participant countries will take on to reduce their polluting gas emissions. So far, the only document of this type was the Kyoto protocol, of 1997. Only a few industrialized countries have committed, however, to respect the provisions of this protocol. Meanwhile, these countries produce only 15% of the greenhouse gas emissions worldwide. Moreover, the Kyoto protocol expires in 2020.

Here are the main results of the final agreement of the Paris Climate Change Conference of December 2015:

- Limiting global warming to maximum 2 degrees Celsius compared to the average temperatures of the preindustrial epoch
- Checking all the commitments assumed by the signatory States every 5 years
- Financial help for developing countries, especially for those in the south, from the developed ones

The text of the agreement explicitly mentions a limitation of the global average temperature growth to up to maximum 2 degrees Celsius and a continuation of the efforts of lowering this increase limit down to maximum 1.5 degrees Celsius. The objective of 2 degrees Celsius, related to the preindustrial epoch, was established in 2009, in Copenhagen, and imposes a drastic reduction of the greenhouse gas emissions (GGE) and also energy saving measures and investments in renewable energies, as well as afforestation plans for large areas.

Numerous countries, especially Island States, which are the first threatened by the perspective of the rise of the planetary ocean, are in danger if average global temperatures rise by more than 1.5 degrees Celsius.

Out of the 195 States represented at the Conference of Paris, 186 announced measures meant to limit or reduce their greenhouse gas emissions until the horizon 2030. But even if these measures are respected perfectly, they would lead to an increase of the global average temperature of about 3 degrees Celsius.

To attain the objective of 2 degrees Celsius, the text proposes a peak of the greenhouse gas emissions as low as possible and the adoption, as fast as possible, of rapid pollution diminutions to attain a balance between the emissions resulted from anthropic activities and those that can be absorbed, a possible reference to the forests, but also to the new technologies meant to capture and store carbon dioxide.

One of the key provisions of the agreement refers to the constitution of a voluntary mechanism checking the respect of national commitments. Such a check-up will take place every 5 years and will "represent a continuation of the previous report". A first obligatory revision is to take place in 2025, after a collective action assessment foreseen for the year 2023. Meanwhile, a first discussion on the actions undertaken and the measures taken is foreseen for the year 2018.

The UN Climate Convention of 1992 introduced a strict distinction between the developed and the developing countries regarding the sharing of the obligations in this domain. Industrialized countries, such as the USA, want to fragment this clear separation line, and developing countries, such as India, refuse to accept the renunciation to this delineation in the name of their right to development and of the historical responsibility of the northern hemisphere for excessive pollution and climate changes.

Regarding the greenhouse gas emissions reduction, this "differentiation" remains active: the developed countries "need to be about to adopt objectives of polluting emissions reduction in absolute value", while developing countries "must continue to improve their efforts" in the fight against global warming, according to their national situation.

Another important provision is that of granting financial aid to the countries of the austral hemisphere. In 2009, the developed countries promised they would discharge 100 billion dollars a year, starting with 2020, for funding climate policies in developing countries. The latter asked for a progressive increase of this sum and a greater clarity concerning the means of implementation of this provision.

On the other hand, the developed countries do not wish to bear these costs on their own and ask for contributions from countries in full economic expansion, such as China, South Chorea and Singapore or from the countries with rich oir reserves. The formula proposed is: "developed countries ought to assure financial resources to help developing countries" adapt to the effects of climate change and take measures to reduce their greenhouse gas emissions (Constantza, R., 1997).

THE PREMISES OF A NEW ENDEAVOR

In Paris, the participants have tried to conclude a new global climate treaty, entering into force in 2020. The 2009 Climate Summit of Copenhagen failed in a similar attempt. Experts like Christophe Balls are, however, more optimistic regarding the summit of Paris.

"Political will is much greater than in Copenhagen", as the political leader of the NGO German watch declared for DW. "Second, negotiations are more advanced than in Copenhagen. Third: the real world evolutions are much better than before Copenhagen. Last year, for example, the polluting emissions caused by energy production no longer increased, even though there was a little economic progress worldwide."

All the economy sectors ought to contribute to attaining a 20% reduction of the greenhouse gas emissions, compared to 1990, until the year 2020, in a cost-efficient way. Consequently, the Member States ought to implement further policies and measures in their effort of limiting even more the greenhouse gas emissions from other sources than those regulated by the Directive 2003/87/EC.

Each Member State's effort ought to be established in relation to the level of the greenhouse gas emissions recorded in the year 2005 nationally, which are under the influence of the present decision; this level ought to be adjusted to exclude the emissions in the atmosphere of the installations that existed in 2005 and which were included in the community system for the period 2006-2012. The annual level of emissions allocated for the period 2013-2020 expressed in tons of carbon dioxide equivalent ought to be established based on analyzed and verified data.

The Member Sates' emissions reduction efforts ought to rely on the principle of solidarity between the Member States and on the need of a sustainable economic growth throughout the territory of the Community, considering the Member States' GDP per capita. The Member States recording, at present, a relatively low level of the GDP per capita and, consequently, important expectations regarding the increase of their GDP, ought to be authorized to increase their greenhouse gas emissions level in relation to 2005, but also to limit this growth so as to contribute to respecting the independent commitment of Community emissions reduction. The Member States recording, at present, a relatively high level of their GDP per capita ought to reduce their greenhouse gas emissions levels in relation to 2005.

To be able to continue to assure an equitable distribution of the Member States' efforts of contributing to the implementation of the Community's independent emissions reduction commitment, no Member State should be obliged to reduce its greenhouse gas emissions until 2020 by more than 20% compared to the levels recorded in 2005, nor should it be authorized to increase its greenhouse gas emissions until 2020 by more than 20% over the levels of 2005. The greenhouse gas emissions reduction ought to be attained in the period 2013-2020. Each Member State ought to be authorized to transfer from the following year a volume of up to 5% of its annual level of emissions allocated. When a Member State's emissions are lower than its annual level of emissions allocated, the respective Member State ought to be authorized to transfer to the following year the emissions reduction supplement.

To balance the Member States' emissions reduction costs differences, which would offer a greater geographic flexibility and at the same time improve the general efficiency of the costs incurred by the total community commitment, any Member State ought to have the possibility to transfer to other Member States a part of its annual level of emissions allocated. The transparency of these transfers ought to be assured by the notification of the Commission and by the recording of each transfer in the registers of both Member States involved. The respective transfers can be realized by a procedure convenient for both parties, including by tender, by market intermediaries acting as agents, or by means of a bilateral agreement.

The European Union ought to record a significant reduction of its greenhouse gas emissions. The use of credits coming from project activities ought to be limited, in order to complete the internal actions. The Union renews its pledge to continually improve its Clean Development Mechanism (CDM) and will try to improve it via adequate international procedures. It is important for the credits coming from the project activities used by the Member States to represent real, supplementary and permanent, verifiable emissions reductions, to present net advantages for sustainable development and no significant negative impact on the social or environmental level. The Member States, at the same time, ought to report on the qualitative criteria they apply for the use of such credits.

To grant the Member States a certain flexibility in the accomplishment of their pledges, to promote the sustainable development of third countries, especially of developing countries, and to offer security to investors, the Community ought to continue to recognize a certain number of credits from greenhouse gas emissions reduction projects undertaken in third countries before the adoption of a future international agreement on climate change (henceforth called "the international climate change agreement"). The Member States ought to make sure that the national policies of acquisition of these credits facilitate an equitable geographic distribution of the projects, especially by the increase of the Certificate Reduction Emissions (CER) ratio bought from the Least Developed Countries (LDC) and from Small Island Developing States (SIDS) and the conclusion of an international climate change agreement.

Consequently, the Member States ought to use the greenhouse gas emissions reduction credits granted for reduction realized during the period 2008-2012 and resulting from types of projects eligible for use in the community system during the respective period. At the same time, the Member States should be able to use greenhouse gas emissions reduction credits for the reductions realized after the period 2008-2012, resulting from projects recorded in the period 2008-2012 and from types of projects eligible for use in the community system during the respective period.

In the least developed countries, a very small number of CDM projects have been implemented. Considering the support given by the Community to the equitable distribution of CDM projects, including by means of the Global Climate Change Alliance, established by the Communication of the Commission of 18 September 2007 entitled "Building a global climate change alliance between the European Union and poor developing countries most vulnerable to climate change", it would be good to guarantee the acceptance of the credits coming from projects launched after the period 2008-2012 in the least developed countries, for types of projects eligible to be used in the community system during the period 2008-2012. Such an acceptance ought to continue until 2020 or until the date of the conclusion of an agreement with the Community, if this date comes earlier than 2020.

To assure a greater flexibility to the Member States and to promote the developing countries' sustainable development, the Member States ought to be able to use supplementary credits coming from projects based on agreements concluded by the Community with third countries. In the absence of an international climate change agreement, establishing the quantity attributed to the developed countries, Joint Implementation (JI) projects cannot continue after 2012. The greenhouse gas emissions reduction credits resulting from these projects could continue to be recognized, however, in the framework of agreements with third countries.

The Member States' continual capacity of using credits in the framework of CDM is important, contributing to the assurance of a market for the respective credits after 2012. In order to assure such a market and new greenhouse gas emissions reductions in the Community, encouraging, in this way, the realization of the community goals in the domain of energy from renewable sources, energy efficiency, safe energy provision, innovation and competitiveness, it is proposed to authorize an annual use, by the Member States, of the credits coming from greenhouse gas emissions reduction projects carried out in third countries, within the limit of a volume representing 3% of the greenhouse gas emissions of each Member State non-regulated by the Directive 2003/87/CE in the year 2005, or undertaken in other Member States, until the adoption of an international climate change agreement.

The Member States ought to be authorized to transfer the unused part of this volume to other Member States. Certain Member States recording a negative limit or a positive limit of maximum 5%, according to the present decision, should be authorized to use, beside the above-mentioned credits, supplementary credits of 1% of their emissions checked in 2005 coming from projects undertaken in LDC and in SIDS, under the reserve of their respect of any of the four conditions foreseen in the present decision.

The present decision should not affect more stringent national objectives. If, to accomplish a more stringent objective, the Member States limit the greenhouse gas emissions level regulated by the present decision more than the obligations assumed based on the present decision, the limits imposed by the present decision regarding the use of greenhouse gas emissions reduction credits should not apply to the supplementary emissions reductions realized in order to attain the national objective.

The United Nations' Green Climate Fund has raised for the moment only US$ 2.3 billion, out of which one billion promised on Tuesday by France", as the Secretary-General of the United Nations declared in the conclusion of the reunion. This sum is far from the objective proposed, of 10 billion dollars until the end of this year, to reach 100 billion per year beginning with 2020.

The United Nations' high official also announced that private banks have pledged to issue green bonds worth 20 billion dollars and the insurers intend to "double their green investments" by 2015, reaching 82 billion dollars.

The American president called, from the summit's pulpit, to the conclusion of an "ambitious" agreement at the Conference of Paris of the end of 2015, promising that the United States will take on their part of contribution in "the urgent and increasing climate change threat".

In his turn, the French president affirmed that France will contribute with a billion dollars to the Green Fund, created in 2009 to aid developing countries in their efforts of facing climate change. Germany had announced, even since July 2015 a contribution of a billion dollars.

The Chinese Vice Premier declared that his country – one of the greatest polluters, along with India and the United States – "will collaborate with other states for the edification of a better future". He reaffirmed, however, that the industrialized countries need to "respect their obligation to support, by their finance and technology, the developing countries".

China and India sent to the New York summit lower rank representatives, casting a shadow over this reunion, exceptional by the number and diversity of its participants: 120 heads of state or government, over 200 companies and numerous NGOs.

The reactions to the announcements of financial support from some countries were prudent. Oxfam-France appreciates that the billion announced by the president Hollande "is a first timid step that risks being insufficient"' and "there are many details still in suspense". Greenpeace considers that the announcement is "an important signal of support to the most vulnerable countries", yet regrets the fact that "the details remain unclear". The organization also regrets that "the Obama administration continues to allow the industry to prospect and exploit coal, oil and gas on public land".

According to a survey made by Chicago Council for Global Affairs and published on Tuesday, half of the Americans interviewed appreciate that the government does not make enough efforts in relation to climate change.

The Secretary-General of the United Nations, Ban Ki-Moon, who asked the participants to the opening of the summit to "demonstrate leadership", received support from the actor Leonardo DiCaprio, who took the floor and said that "clean air and a liveable climate are inalienable human rights" and that investing in renewable energies is "a good economic policy". DiCaprio, called by the UN "messenger of peace" for the climate, recommended the heads of state or government "to answer the greatest challenge of our existence with courage and honesty".

THE OBJECTIVE OF GLOBAL TEMPERATURE INCREASE OF JUST 2 DEGREES CELSIUS

Even if a new treaty is signed, including new climate protection measures, it is very likely to miss the objective of limiting global warming until the end of the century to just 2 degrees Celsius over the level previous to industrialization, although the international community had adopted this objective at the Cancun Climate Summit of 2010.

The consequences of a global warming of maximum 2 degrees Celsius are considered still moderate and controllable. The physicist Anders Levermann from the Postdam Institute for Climate Impact Research warns: "With increasing warming, some physical systems or ecosystems may be at risk. If we continue as we have begun, until the end of the century, our global temperature will be 5 degrees Celsius higher. This means the loss of most alpine glaciers. The Arctic Sea Ice will also disappear. Corals, determining for the existence of 600 million people worldwide, will also die."

According to the UN calculations, even if all the pollution reduction measures discussed were applied, the planet will grow warmer by 2.7 degrees Celsius until the end of the present century.

NEED FOR IMPROVEMENTS

Some States are asking that the summit of Paris ought to give birth to a process of revision and improvement of the climate goals every five years. The German chief-negotiator Karsten Sach is expecting tough discussions on this topic. According to him, the EU would like the environment goals to begin to be reviewed already starting with 2020, while other countries, however, would like this process to begin later.

Controversial are also the regulations that ought to be adopted in this dynamic revision and improvement process. The head of German watch Bals draws the attention on the different calculation standards: "Some countries take into account the forests in their estimates; others do not." "The countries also have different factors regarding the polluting emissions for different fossil sources of energy."

EU negotiators are asking for more transparency on a global level, which bothers some, especially among the great emerging economies. "China and India are not the greatest friends of transparency and taking on responsibilities", says the speaker of the evangelical association "Brot für die Welt", Sabine Minninger.

NATURAL CAPITAL FROM THE PERSPECTIVE OF ECOLOGICAL ECONOMY

It has been demonstrated that what supports the sustainable development of the socio-economic system is the natural capital and biodiversity.

Practically, the natural capital of a country, region or of the planet, in general, is the network of ecological systems operating in a natural and semi natural regime and the anthropized systems, constructed through the transformation and simplification of the first two categories.

For this reason, renewable natural resources, including water and the soil, and non-renewable ones on the time scale at which the development assured by the natural capital elements is projected, are key factors of the economic system's production function and support of sustainable development.

Continuing this logic, the natural capital becomes part and parcel of the diversity of the ecological and biological systems and includes, beside the components operating in a natural regime, the human species, as part of the biosphere, together with their environment.

Therefore, natural capital has a certain productive capacity that has to be known by the economic activities' managers, in order to avoid overexploitation, namely a certain carrying capacity – an essential parameter, necessary in the process of dimensioning the anthropic pressure, namely of the human society, avoiding the degradation of the environment.

It logically results that, to guarantee a sustainable socio-economic development, it is absolutely necessary to assure the conservation of a diverse and balanced natural capital structure and a use of the resources and services produced by it within limits bearable for the natural capital components.

Beginning with the years 1970, when the Club of Rome began discussions on the limits of growth, for the first time, the issue of the need of modifying and transforming the economic growth model was brought up, in the sense that this growth cannot be unlimited.

A series of theories followed, concerning the concept of economic growth and the way of quantifying the degradation of the environment, differentiated by the theories that generated them:

The general economic theory interprets the natural capital either as a circulating monetary fund, or as a stock of technical means existing at a certain moment, which can be reproduced and diversified to support a goods and services flow necessary to development. The so large interpretation of the monetary capital in monetary and physical terms led to the conclusion according to which the natural capital might be a metaphor harder to quantify and use in designing an economic development model.

The neo-classic economic theory characterizes the economic systems as being designed and developed based on the principle of their independence to the environment, in the sense that the environment is not a factor limiting the development of the socio-economic system, because resources are renewable and can be assured endlessly, while the resulting wastes can be absorbed without restrictions. The theory was soon fought against and amended by its very supporters, as soon as they noticed that the deterioration of the environment is a reality, directly connected to the economic development. The supporters of a growth at all costs tried to argue that the resources provided by the natural ecosystems can be gradually replaced by those produced by the components of the environment created by man, based on the technological progress, namely the world can exist as well without natural resources.

In other words, a series of theories that had the gift of encouraging the economic development based on the maximization of the profit and on the relation demand-offer, tried to find arguments to support a development at all costs, going even up to modalities of substituting the natural capital. They supported either the direct substitution, when a component of the capital created can assure a service equivalent to that provided by the natural capital or an indirect one, generically defined as "efficient growth through technological progress".

The two modalities were impossible to defend except by a new approach – the systemic approach of the environment – which will be able to demonstrate that the environment is a hierarchy of simple systems or grouped systems that develop based on a stability hierarchy.

NATURAL CAPITAL FROM THE PERSPECTIVE OF SYSTEMIC ECOLOGY

The definition of the natural capital through the prism of the way the physical, chemical and biological environment is perceived, as representing the totality of the natural and semi natural ecological systems, permits a new approach of the ecological systems' management.

Natural ecological systems are, in this case, interpreted as self-regulatory systems with no or very limited direct anthropic influence (generally activities meant to meet the 1st order needs of the local population, research needs, and, more recently, ecotourism).

Semi natural ecological systems are represented by systems that, although bearing a direct anthropic influence (especially by the industrial exploitation of renewable resources), preserve their structural and functional features, by which they maintain themselves and develop themselves.

The basic feature of the natural and semi natural ecological features is that their productivity and stability does not require any supplementary input of energy produced in other systems.

The direct activities of exploitation of the resources from semi natural systems or of control of certain command factors, call for a current management process.

These ecological systems operating in a semi natural regime are represented by:

- Agro systems responsible for producing cereals, vegetables, fruits, technical and fodder plants
- Secondary forests or forest plantations for wood production
- Farms for the production of animal-based foods and raw matter for the leather industry, farms for aquaculture, in general, and for intensive fisheries, in particular
- Storage lakes created for the exploitation of the hydro energetic potential, renewable water source and exploitation of fishing potential etc.

The anthropic intervention is direct both during the stages of creation of these types of ecological systems by removing or totally eliminating the components of the natural ecosystems and affecting some physical and chemical environments and especially the bio-geo-chemical mechanisms starting with the sawing or plantation stages, species improvement, fertilization, pests fight etc.

We shall underline the fact that the semi natural ecological systems produce resources and services, by concentrating the solar radiant energy and maximizing the density of the energy flow. For example, wet areas are ecological systems with intermediary position, between the terrestrial systems and the aquatic ones and characterized by their capacity to purify surface waters, due to mechanisms such as: periodically or permanently the soil is covered by hygrophyte species in which a specific fauna develops, able to recycle nutrients.

Practically, the natural capital is therefore made up of natural and semi natural ecological systems and anthropized ecological systems.

All systems making up the natural capital preserve the productive function of resources and services based on fundamental ecological processes. For this reason, the energy flow from the radiant solar energy which is free, and the recycling of nutrients—the fundamental mechanism for maintaining the bio-geo-chemical circuits – are defining elements of the natural capital structure.

At the same time, we consider that maintaining the spatio-temporal organization, the productive function, and controlling the dynamics of these ecological systems can be realized only if the human populations' direct and significant intervention is assured permanently and non-destructively.

Practically, anthropized systems are characterized by a strict dependence on the human populations' direct and complex intervention, associated to a flow of auxiliary energy, produced in other systems, such as those for energy conversion.

Consequently, one can state that these ecological systems have specific structural and functional features and, as a result, we can consider them an essential part of the socio-economic systems.

In essence, a third of all agrosystems, for instance, are intensive and super intensive production structures, calling for a very large auxiliary energy input, of up to 10 kcal/m^2/year. For this reason, such ecological systems are assimilated to anthropic capital components (built by human populations).

Finally, we consider this last category of ecological systems as representing natural capital (NC) components dominated and controlled by human populations and, consequently, one can state that these ecological systems are subordinated structurally and functionally to the socio-economic system's development strategies, actually proving that they are practically integrated in the socio-economic system (SES).

Moreover, we consider that the weight of this category of ecological systems increased exponentially during the last century, as the population and the 1st order needs of the members of the human societies increased, and the numerical growth of these systems is the result of a process of substitution of the natural and semi natural systems.

Therefore, we do not exclude the possibility of substituting, between certain limits, some components of the natural capital, by others, in order to increase productivity, yet the massive substitution of the ecosystems functioning in a natural and semi natural regime, producing for free renewable resources and services, by anthropized ones (super intensive cultures, urban centers, transportation infrastructure elements etc.), which cannot function except based on the significant increase of the energy flow produced in other systems is not allowed.

The comments on the so controversial issue concerning, on the one hand, the possibility and opportunity of substituting the natural capital components by components created by the human populations, and on the other hand, the obligatory need to guarantee complementariness, must lead to the conclusion that, always, the normal progress is towards the harmonization of the spatial relations and the matter and energy flows circulating between the natural capital and the socio-economic system.

We reiterate the fact that all the components in a natural and semi natural regime and the anthropized ones are dissipative systems, maintaining and maximizing the energy flows and recycling raw matter, producing resources and services.

Thus, all the ecological systems are dynamic on large geological time scales and develop by going through different growth stages, depending on which they produce resources and services. It logically results that on ecological and geological time scales (over 100 000 years), all resources are renewable.

Practically, however, the socio-economic systems' management is based on strategies emitted for much smaller time scales (5-15 years); in this case, their management cannot be operated based on a comparison to the scales at which resources are renewable.

For this reason, in the category of renewable resources we cannot include anything else but the vegetal and animal biomass, most soil and water reserves and partially the mineral resources usable as building materials, for example.

Ores and fossil fuels (coal, oil, gas) have a replacement time of the order of hundreds of thousands or millions of years, which determines their inclusion in the category of non-renewable resources.

Managerially, the distinction between renewable and non-renewable resources is extremely important, as it leads to the conclusion that renewable resources need strategies meant to preserve their functional integrity and the productivity of the natural capital components, maintaining the exploitation rate under or very close to the rate at which these resources are produced or regenerated (Lester, R. Brown, et al., 1997).

For non-renewable resources, however, flexible strategies are needed, involving measures limiting the exploitation rates, identifying alternative sources and especially, technical measures of bio-geo-chemical recycling of the products obtained and of the residues.

One of the essential features of the natural capital, almost always neglected, is its structural and functional diversity.

The presentation of the problems up to this stage is giving us the possibility to highlight the structural and functional aspects of the ecological systems, which are actually arguments in the substantiation of the new model of socio-economic development: sustainable development.

Thus, Sustainable Development does not suppose only the need to maintain the natural capital as ratio over a critical level, but supposes especially the need for it to preserve a maximum level of structural and functional heterogeneity, on which long-term development opportunities will actually depend.

Thus, the issue of preserving biological and ecological diversity is not a collateral problem representing just a small defect for the political decision factor, but is the very issue of preserving the natural capital as development support and sustainability guarantee.

The last 3-4 decennia of the past century were marked, incomparably more than any other period in the history of mankind, by the evident process of deterioration of the perceptible environment, via the toxic, often lethal effects, of the by-products and final products resulted from the processes of the socio-economic system. These products have come together and have become concentrated in the major compartments of the environment (troposphere, lithosphere, hydrosphere) and have affected the taxonomic hierarchy of the biosphere, degrading at the same time the abiotic environment.

The reactions to the tendencies of degrading the environment by damaging anthropic activities have diversified as the effects were seized, assessed and linked to a series of concrete human activities.

Consequently, actions delimiting the pollution effects, and, very recently, actions meant to diminish and prevent pollution, have been designed and have increased in diversity.

Compared to the alarmingly growing tendency of the process of elimination of various plant and animal species, a phenomenon generating the worrying narrowing of biodiversity, the answer was mainly actions of identification of the vulnerable and endangered species and the elaboration of special protection programmes.

At the same time, for endangered habitats, the answer was ecological reconstruction actions, consequently also avoiding the elimination process.

The real process of erosion of biological diversity following the aggressions of the socio-economic systems could not be stopped by sectorial protection actions regarding certain species or the reconstruction of some endangered habits. For this reason, organisms such as E.U. or U.N. have found themselves obliged to adopt regional or global conventions on biodiversity protection, climate change, reducing greenhouse emissions etc.

Two mentions are needed, helping us to make a distinction between biodiversity in a broad sense and in a restrained sense, the latter being promoted by those supporting a "development at all costs":

- For a long time, this concept designated only the richness of species without taking into account the diversity of the structural and functional units of the abiotic environment.
- The socio-economic systems, which include a great diversity of the social, cultural and patrimonial capital, were not taken into account when biodiversity was discussed.

BIODIVERSITY AND ECOSYSTEM SERVICES AS FUNDAMENTS OF SUSTAINABLE DEVELOPMENT

While in its broad sense the concept of biodiversity includes the totality of the organized units constituting the natural capital, including the human species and the totality of the capital created by them, it results that the syntagm "diversity of the ecological and biological systems" would be more adequate for the concept of biodiversity in a broad sense.

Diversity needs to be analyzed and quantified at least on four distinct levels

- Of the species and species hierarchy
- Of every development level along the hierarchic line
- Of each system with supraindividual organization
- Of each genetic structure (Popescu C., 2003)

Consequently, biodiversity conservation ought to be designed and realized based on strategies, programmes and methods, pursuing on the one hand a sustainable use, namely within the limits of the carrying capacity of the natural capital components, and, on the other hand, a management of the development of the socio-economic system, namely of the capital created by the human populations.

Therefore, the diversity of the biological and ecological systems ought to be analyzed at least on these levels:

- Diversity as support of life
- Diversity of the biological systems in the species' hierarchy
- Diversity of the genetic structure of the population and of the species, including of Homo sapiens
- Ethno-cultural diversity of the socio-economic systems

The extension and operationalization of the biodiversity concept was necessary given the numerous attempts of reducing the diverse biodiversity forms, by supporting new ecosystem degradation techniques.

Governmental experts, as well as those of important financial organisms, still have the tendency, even to this day, of interpreting biodiversity restrictively, stating that affecting the environment is a natural process of technological development, and the solution is possible by new developments.

We need to mention that the 2002 Johannesburg meeting is a proof that the political decision factors have understood that they need to give up on speculative arguments and have seen themselves obliged to adopt, at least formally, clear measures meant to prevent environmental degradation.

Political decision factors and managers have had to admit that important for long-term development is the creation of the conditions needed for a sustainable development and implicitly for preserving biodiversity.

The large recognition of this need has been supported at least by the following arguments:

- The effort for preserving biodiversity cannot focus only on the ecological systems, arguing that they would integrate almost all the species, of which the great majority are unknown.
- It is equally necessary to preserve the habitats assuring the complex ecological-fundamental processes, and, naturally, to avoid the elimination of certain species.

Out of the total of about 50,000,000 species existing on Terra, over 90% are invertebrate species (fungi, bacteria), not yet studied, whose salvation would not be needed, since their contributions to the functioning of the ecological systems have not been quantified yet.

Conserving or maintaining the structural-functional integrity within the stability domain of a given natural or semi natural ecological system involves, to the same extent, maintaining the trajectory of the abiotic compartments' dynamics and the dynamics of the biotic compartments' trajectory, but also the interactions between them.

Thus, the term interconnectivity is introduced, representing the necessity of permanent intercommunication of the components, in the sense of support of life, one for the other.

When analyzing the development of each ecological system as a complex long-term process, the general tendency is to assure the mechanisms by which the number of species or populations can increase, without considering the necessity that, within them, specializations and interactions need to intervene, able to intensify the environmental services, such as maximizing the energy flow, recycling nutrients, and regulation, balance and stability mechanisms etc.

The result of such a process appears, therefore, in the extension of the stability domain on a spatial level, while the analysis on a time scale specific to large systems would be obligatory.

Therefore, one cannot at all speak about the existence of useless species within a complex model, but in different growth stages, the functioning of the ecosystem relies successively on some or the other of the species comprised in the taxonomic hierarchy.

Consequently, even though, at the same time, not all the elements composing the ecosystem on the spatio-temporal scale of analysis are equally important, each species has its distinct role.

It logically results that to preserve the ecological structures on the level of the national and macro regional complexes, one has to take into account the maintaining of a mosaic of natural and semi natural systems, to include all the types of ecosystems and preserve at least half of their surface. The conservation of the ecological systems therefore involves their interconnectivity, assured via natural corridors or, where they do not exist, the technological and ecological reconstruction of such corridors is needed (Popescu C., 2003).

The connectivity of the natural and semi natural systems is an essential condition for the dispersion of the species within their area, for their movement, for the directions of the new gradients modified given the climate change, the consideration of the elements highlighted having to be done in fact by operative policies and strategies, on each State or State Union level.

The European Council established, on the occasion of the environmental ministers' summit of Sofia, in 1996, that on the level of Europe it is necessary to create a European network of ecological systems interconnected through management programmes, comprising the conservation of the natural and semi natural systems specific of their different European regions, the reconstruction of some endangered habitats, the rehabilitation of certain ecosystems and their reconnection, and special programmes of sustainable management for the anthropized systems.

All these are necessary since the biological systems' diversity actually holds a huge genetic fund (an immense genetic information bank), a fund assuring, on the one hand, the natural process of species dynamics and, on the other hand, information for the technological research concerning the correct dynamics of the anthropized systems and the correction of their trajectories, imitating nature.

Very recently, the syntagm bioindustrial development has emerged, in the sense of avoiding the negative tendencies generated by the idea that man masters nature. It is acknowledged in this way that the anthropic factor, though being the command subsystem, is part and parcel of the ecosystem.

Moreover, during the last decennium, there emerged the idea of creating a complementariness between the high-performance industries of the developed countries and the diversity of the genetic resources of the underdeveloped countries, in the sense that by the "Convention on Biodiversity" the developed states are obliged to return at least 20-25% of the profits obtained by exploiting the genetic patrimony to the underdeveloped countries.

These financial resources would have the role of funding the increase of the territories called "protected areas", namely precisely of preserving this invaluable genetic patrimony, the main support of life on our planet.

REFERENCES

Allan, D. (1994). *Stream Ecology*. Oxford.

Brown. (1997). State of the World and our Resources. New York: W.W. Norton & Company.

Constantza, R. (1996, October). Gross world product from International Monetary Fund (IMF). *World Economic Outlook*.

Constantza, R. (1997). The Development of Ecological Economics. London: Academic Press.

Georgescu-Roegen, N. (1979). Legea entropiei si procesul economic. Publishing House Politică.

Kumari, K. (1996, November). Sustinable Forest Management: Myth or Reality? Exploring the Prospects for Malaysia. *Ambio*.

Leopold, A. (1949). A Sound Country Almanac. Oxford.

Pimentel, D. (1997). L'écologie des fôrets. Ed. did. Paris.

Popescu, C. (2003). *Economia protectiei mediului*. Târgovişte: Editura Bibliotheca.

Popescu, C. (2008). Stări conflictuale generate de exploatarea abuziva a pădurilor lumii. Editura Bibliotheca.

Popescu, C. (2011). La durabilité en qualité de nouveau projet civilisateur. 57éme Congrès "Refondation financière, sorties de crise et nouvelles stratégies de croissance économique, Croatia.

Popescu, C. (2014). *Reconsidering the Relationship Between Socio-Economic System and Natural Environment.* The 2nt International Conference ESPERA 2014 – Economic Scientific Research Theoretical, Empirical and Practical Approaches organizată de National Institute for Economic Research, Bucharest, România

Vădineanu, A. (1998). *Sustainable development.* Press University of Bucharest.

Vădineanu, A., Negrei, C., & Lisievici, P. (1999). *Sustainable development.* Press University of Bucharest.

Chapter 6
The Role of Forest Ecosystems in the Economy of the Rural Area

Silvia Elena Iacob
Bucharest University of Economic Studies, Romania

ABSTRACT

We have presented the forest as an ecosystem, the socio-economic development of the forest ecosystems in the rural area and the sustainable management of the forest as an ecosystem. The debate on the public assets of the forests and on climate change will nourish the discussions related to the future form of the Common Agricultural Policy at a moment when the European Union is preparing its new forest strategy. A new sustainable rural development policy will need to rely on a strong will, based on the support of the States for the most disinherited rural areas in point of location, accessibility, economic development and services for the population. "The rural world" represents an opportunity for our country (until 2020); we only need to want to take advantage of these resources for a more sustainable development.

DOI: 10.4018/978-1-5225-2081-8.ch006

THE FOREST AS ECOSYSTEM

For a long time, in people's perception, forests have been just empty or even hostile areas, which were appreciated only to the extent to which their felled trees provided timber, and the deforested land was cultivated for agriculture, or new settlements were built.

Extremely few were the examples of sustainable management of the forests, based on understanding them as vital ecosystems, the most common relation that people have had with the forests being expressed by destructive practices, persisting almost everywhere.

In the ancient times, the Mediterranean region was more humid and more fertile, being forested; the 13th-16th centuries meant an irreversible disaster of deforestation for the sake of wood used for ships and as fuel, grazing lands, agriculture, etc.

The loss of 90% of the forests in the Philippines in just 20 years of impetus of the processing industry is the most eloquent example of "shortsightedness" in the management of some renewable resources as well as the most brutal ongoing attitude.

As soon as the forests have been "opened", a new phenomenon began in the wet forests. Fires, the inestimable damages caused in Indonesia, Brazil, North America and more recently in SE Asia, where the fires of the years 1997-1998 gave shivers, if we consider only the fact that smoke darkened Indonesia, Malaysia, Singapore, Brunei, the south of Thailand and the Philippines for several months, interrupting the activity of schools, firms, transport, etc. Tens of millions of people grew ill and several hundreds died, and the habitats of some endangered species, such as the orangutan, were devastated.

Certainly, now changes in the forest landscape occur much faster, due to the modern exploitation technologies, and fires have begun to occur naturally, often following the deforestations occurred so far, triggering terrible storms and whirlwinds, accompanied by unimagined natural outbursts.

Very late, people have realized that, when forests disappear, they lose not just wood, but first the effects of the first functions of the forest—vital regeneration functions.

The first 150 products obtained from the forests, other than wood, traded internationally, are worth more than $11 billion /year, without considering the local value of these products which is even higher, if we think just about the fact that they offer, simultaneously, more than 8 million jobs.

At the same time, forests house countless species and offer habitat to millions of valuable organisms that decompose organic substances, create soils, pollinate cultures and control disease-carrying pests. Then, very late, people have realized the effect of the forest as a defender of the soil against erosion and as a protector of the hydrographic networks, regulating the water courses and offering stability to storage lakes. The lack of forests leads to soil erosion in the areas with high relief energy, while runoffs trigger high floods, and the water circuit in nature is damaged, generating true catastrophes.

Frequently, it has been considered that the greatest value of a forest is given by the wood crop that can be obtained, for timber or paper paste, along with the transformation of the respective area into land for agriculture or for other uses.

It has been admitted, at the same time, rather formally, that there are also other important functions of the forest such as: protection, regeneration, social, but which can be considered free or are simply ignored, although, supported in the long term, could be beneficial for the whole community.

For instance, when alternative management strategies for the mangrove forests of the Bintumi Gulf (Indonesia) were weighed, the value of the fish and of the other local marine crops obtained by avoiding erosion was analyzed, and the conclusion reached was that the most adequate solution would be to preserve the forest, which yields a constant revenue of $ 4800 /ha, compared to the wood exploitation, which brings only $ 3600 /ha. At the same time, keeping the forest would have permitted to continue the local, agricultural and fish exploitations, yielding about $ 10 mil. / year, i.e. over 70% of the local revenue, and protecting the local fishing, which used to assure a yearly revenue of more than $ 25 million. Unfortunately, all these arguments have been ignored (Iacob, 2015).

Beside the many products they provide, forests offer habitats to bees and other pollinators, and birds that keep agricultural pests and disease-carriers under control.

They are, then, home to most animals, and support for water life in the rivers crossing and flooding them. In purely financial terms, one can appreciate that only the protection of the hydrographic basins is more valuable than the value of the wood of the whole forest area.

Then, reminding of their functions of water pump protecting the earth, nutrient recyclers, climate stabilizers and oxygen plant, it is very hard to understand how, in the world, more than 12 mil. hectares of forests disappear every year.

All the scientific forums admit that the planetary water in its circuit falls under the form of precipitations at the surface of the soil, then moves down gently, forming springs, rivulets and rivers and, at the same time, feeding the underground water-bearing structures, while most of it, along this trajectory, is absorbed by plants and restored to the atmosphere.

Anthropic activities have modified even the most fundamental force of nature by removing the plant cover, by draining and baffling, and getting to "pave the landscape", as stated by a FAO report, presented at Oxford in the year 1997.

The slow drainage of the water at the surface of the soil is vital to the constant refilling of the natural underground or aquiferous reserves, vital sources of drinkable water.

The most common conflicts related to the hydrological function come from the formal recognition by the political factor of a forested hydrographic network's value: its capacity to absorb and purify water, recirculate nutrients in excess, settle soil and avoid flooding.

David Pimentel, a French ecologist in the domain of agriculture, affirms that "the speed at which unprotected soils are eroded can get several thousand times higher than that of forested ones". Under natural conditions, each hectare of land loses, by erosion, between 0.004 and 0.05 tonnes/year, meaning, more often than not, more than the quantity that the pedogenesis processes are able to generate. On forested lands, loss by erosion is virtually inexistent, and the fitting option forest-and-exposed land diminishes the erosion to less than half.

On recently deforested slopes, erosion washes away yearly about 17 tonnes/ha in the USA and in Europe, and 30-40 tonnes/ha in Asia and South America. On lands with marked degradation processes, erosion washes away up to 100 tonnes/year, the eroded soil transporting fodders and sediments that would have been useful for the ecosystem they are leaving, but often damaging for the ecosystem they reach.

The same ecologist appreciates that "erosion, landslides, sediments and higher water temperatures, caused by deforestations, affect the aquatic ecosystems for decennia after deforestation" (Popescu C, 2013).

The cost of lost forest services shows how valuable these "free" services really are.

The deforestations of the Gange Valley (India) caused, for more than 10 years, floods whose damages were estimated to $ 1.2 billion/year.

According to governmental estimates of the year 1998, soil erosion triggered by deforestations caused in the Canadian province British Columbia damages of $ 80 mil./year. In the Pacific Northwest (USA), 94% of the annual landslides are caused by deforestations, and the damages on the level of the year 1996, for instance, were estimated at $3.2 billion.

The forests' control of the global climate is one of the most important services that drew the attention of the public during the last few years of the past millennium. It is generally acknowledged that the most important ecosystemic service of our planet is its production of its oxygen, vital for the organisms to evolve, along with carbon lock-in.

Starting with the industrial revolution, people began to disturb the control system of the global climate, by burning fossil fuels, reducing the forested area and implicitly the recyclable carbon quantity, which has gradually diminished compared to the emitted one.

The felling and burning of forests and also peat deposits added even more carbon in the atmosphere, and, the effects being accumulated, triggered climate changes, which generated serious ecological troubles (winds, early or late frosts, tornados, storms accompanied by high floods and landslides) in forest ecosystems, which highlighted their capacity of supporting and controlling the climate.

To have an idea about how much carbon the forests can store, it has been estimated that an old oak can lock in about 3 tonnes, a hectare of plantation aged between 5 and 10 locks in around 200 tonnes of carbon, a hectare of wet tropical forest around 300 tonnes and a hectare of natural douglas fir forest of NW USA (195 mil. ha), approximately 600 tonnes.

The Forestry Service of the Agriculture Department of USA reports that the 737 mil. acres of forest in USA stock 60 bil. tonnes of carbon (208 tonnes/ha), namely 40 times the national annual carbon emissions.

Due to the forests' capacity to store immense quantities of carbon both in the wood mass and in the organic fraction of the forest soil, they can really become again a source of carbon lock-in and not a carbon source. In this sense, the Forest Research Institute in New Zeeland presented to the Government, in its plea for the increase of the forested area, a report showing that the nation ought to afforest about 100.000 ha/year during the period 2008-2026 for the forests to be able to absorb more carbon than emitted by burning fossil fuels. Actually, the Intergovernmental Commission for climate changes estimated that during the next 50 years, the world forests will be able to absorb around 12-15% of the carbon emitted by burning fossil fuels at that moment, if no action is taken to establish carbon storage as a basic function of the forests.

The ways the forest could be helped to resume its carbon storage functions are in man's power and mean:

- Stopping deforestations
- Afforestation of degraded lands
- Reconsolidating affected forests
- Improving exploitation techniques
- Using wood to create long-term goods, to prolong storage duration
- It is obvious, for instance, that wood used for furniture or houses keeps carbon locked in incomparably longer than wood turned into paper or fuel

The same commission estimates that tropical forests regeneration and conservation has the greatest carbon-locking potential in the future, at least for two reasons:

- These forests have a very fast growth and implicitly wood mass accumulation rhythm
- Deforestations in the tropical area represent the most important carbon-emitting source for the atmosphere

Numerous ways of payment have begun to appear from the great emitters of carbon in the atmosphere, such as: support for afforestations or subventions to preserve the forests. Economists themselves estimate that the value of the carbon-locking function for a hectare of forest amounts to several thousands of dollars/year, and it is increasing exponentially, since deforestations continue at the present rhythm.

Robert Constanza of Maryland University, coordinator of a world research group, putting together the results of 1000 studies thanks to special computerized programmes, managed to estimate the value of most of the services that the forest ecosystems can provide. The result was shocking, as his conclusion was that the present economic value of the services of the world's forest ecosystems is at least between $ 16-54 thousand billion /year, going even over the world GDP, which was for instance of $ 28 thousand billion, in 1995. We consider that if every service, of each type of ecosystem, were measured, and if not just one service, for its main protection function, but several of them, were attributed to it, the final value would be much greater.

The setting, certainly following careful analyses, of a price as precise as possible for the benefits brought by forests is essential, yet just as essential is also the recognition that not everything has a price. Most functions and implicitly services provided by forest ecosystems are actually invaluable. The costs of losing the forest services can illustrate how valuable these "free" services really are.

Atmospheric pollution is also increasingly responsible for the forests' quality. Exposure to pollution weakens the trees, making them more vulnerable to viruses, diseases, draught and nutrition problems. Over ¼ of the trees of Europe suffer from coloring and defoliations triggered by industrial pollution, according to regular reports drafted by the Ecological Commission for Europe of the U.N., the most affected being the forests of Poland, the Czech Republic and Germany.

It is admitted, today, that acid rains, in the industrialized countries, are menacing the forests' vitality, diminishing, at the same time, the functions of: soil protection against erosion, water flow regulation and biodiversity conservation.

The forests' decline was very strong in the Federal Republic of Germany, where, during the period 1980-1984, for instance, the proportion of threes affected grew from 8% to 50%, whereas abnormal defoliation affected 15% of the trees in the EU countries (WRI).

Polluters commonly claim that many of the unfavorable effects on the forests and on the environment in general are reversible and predictable as evolutions and consequences although, due to the complexity of the factors involved, it is increasingly difficult to demonstrate this, both by modern simulation methods and especially practically. Without the deregulations produced by men, forests would be able to lock in more carbon than they free.

The most recent FAO reports show that in the years 1985-1995, more carbon has been freed in the atmosphere from the world forests, mostly due to deforestations from the tropics. At the same time, it has been estimated that deforestations produce 25% of all man-made carbon, while 75% come from burning fossil fuels in domestic and industrial activities.

Worrying as the statistics related to deforestations and the decreasing quality of the forest ecosystem may be, at least equally worrying appears the global image of the world's forests, which, despite all efforts, is very hard to depict, involving a huge work volume, the only source a bit more comprehensive being the FAO Report of the UN. Often, the data are published late and do not reflect the pressures and dangers of certain moments and areas. And, since FAO relies mostly on governmental reports, and most States do not have the capacity of realizing a systematic evaluation of the forests, it results that the data are not uniform first of all as accuracy. At present, there is no independent global monitoring system, and, during this period, FAO anticipates, for the evaluation of forest resources, the use of satellite images that will have to be deciphered and checked on the land.

LOCAL COMMUNITIES' PRESSURE

The local communities dependent on forests become, themselves, a pressure factor, when affected by:

- Uncertainty of ownership right
- Their isolation by lack of interest of the political factor
- Material and educational gap
- Lack of homogeneity and unity

Forest industries and other groups with trading interests have opposed the legitimization of forest management on the level of the local communities. Governmental authorities, media and academic institutions have also questioned the local people's ability to manage their resources rationally, showing that:

1. Local forest users are not able to face the change in socio-demographic and economic conditions, or the new demands of Local Forest Management (LFM)
2. LFM does not represent a guarantee for resource conservation
3. Local forest users cannot face external degradation factors and do not manage to restore degraded forest land

4. Local communities primarily focus on economic and social inequalities and institutional weaknesses (with impact on the rural environment), which represents an obstacle to a sustainable Forest Management

Although one cannot generalize regarding the local population's commitment and capability of maintaining both forest and biodiversity, given the hundreds of millions of people living in the rural area in a close interdependence with the forest, a large part maintains a non-agricultural and non-merchandise relation to the forest. Many of these people face both uncertainty regarding land ownership and lack of political influence.

Forests offer fodder, proteins, medicines, wood for fire, mushrooms, vegetables, building materials and other products. Many peasants (even those whose main activity is agriculture) have an extended experience in the use of forest products and in the regulation of the access to forest resources. However, everywhere, the local communities depending on the forests are little by little dispossessed of their only source of existence.

In India, the hunter-gatherers called Durva (whose tradition consists in transmitting to the future generations a pristine environment) manage their resources rationally to maintain a sustainable exploitation level.

In Romania, in Dâmboviţa County the fact that the basketry workshops of the area Glod-Moroieni were closed has been a wrong action because, beside the fact that the local tradition in this domain has been lost, the communities have been deprived of one of their few sources of revenues.

ISOLATION BY LACK OF INTEREST OF THE POLITICAL FACTOR

There is a great diversity of ownership agreements within which management rules are applied, stimuli determining co-owners to respect the agreements concluded between institutions and the tasks meant to assure compliance with the rules established.

It has to be mentioned, however, that the local management, insufficiently supervised by the State, manipulates the forest in order to meet local needs, affecting therefore the initial state of the forest's ecology.

It is clear that the great cause generating social conflicts is that people deforesting large areas doubtlessly want to maximize their profit in the short run by "wholesale", meaning to meet the needs of remote markets, as they are people who do not know the respective land and have no commitment to it in the long run.

Case studies have shown that ecological decline of the forest area inhabited or situated next to local communities appears when local social institutions and the environment are simultaneously under great external pressures.

And yet, in numerous areas, "overpopulation" is a concept that can be misleading if we consider the distribution of the lands. Zones considered as "overpopulated" are often marginal areas that peasants have been forced to occupy, being chased away from lands dedicated to export-oriented, intensive agriculture, mining exploitations etc.

As case studies on most of the areas under analysis have shown, the tax system, the need to "meet" governmental officials with bribe and tips, the technologies economizing labor force, the new fashion and consumerism have generated a call for cash without a corresponding growth of the market of traditional products. In other words, in situations in which governments leave the people "empty-handed" – from a legal, technical, financial and political perspective – we can expect that, sooner or later, they will surrender to some exterior forces that are not under their control.

Leaving aside these general functions, certain services are specific of certain types of forests. Mangrove forests of the coastal areas protect the shores from storms and erosion and recirculate nutrients, being real fisheries for coastal and marine fish and offering vital resources to the local communities. It ought to be highlighted that coastal protection will become very important, given that the modification of the climate generates increasingly violent storms and their forecast is increasingly difficult (for example, the peat swamps of Malaysia and Indonesia, without the shield of the forests, would leave millions of people with no potable and irrigations water).

With no alternatives, the local population will surrender to the pressures of forest exploitation firms and other trading interests and will lose resources or will sell them for very little revenue, quickly, which has also happened to the forests of Romania, returned to their owners according to Law 18/1991. It is precisely because their own survival and cultural values are at stake, that local communities depending on the forest have the strongest motivation to control the flow of illegal forest and mine exploitations, poachers and colonists. Such is the case of the *Moţi* of Romania, a civilization almost exclusively depending on the forest, who ought to be taken into account at any attempt (legislative initiative) of modification of the structure of the forest ownership in the respective area (Giurgiu, 2004, p 420).

Studies also show that official efforts to restore and manage the forest environment are often absent or both costly and inefficient.

Although the argument of "incapacity of the local communities" is used to take over and maintain the control over forested lands, LFM needs to be regarded with caution. Local communities depending on the forests for subsistence are far from homogeneous.

Common management systems are rarely devoid of internal inequalities (gender, ethnic or religious inequalities), social injustice or practices destroying the environment. However, it has to be admitted by authorities at all levels that communal grazing fields, forests and irrigation systems or fishing areas are daily realities for the great majority of the rural population.

Local people also witness the forests' transformation, by forestry departments, firms or colonizers, in monoculture plantations of various tree species sought on the market. This intervention, along with other cultural, economic and political ones, undermines the local authority, norms and values, and exploits inequalities, generating conflicts.

Many communities are faced with the challenge of reaffirming their values and elaborating new administration methods for the forested lands, an impediment that can be overcome with support from the State interested in a good management of the situation.

MATERIAL AND EDUCATIONAL GAP

Transnational companies play a significant role in forest destruction and, consequently, in local populations impoverishment, because:

- They operate on a much larger scale than local companies, having the technological capacity and capital resources needed to open exploitations in isolated, until recently unreachable forests. This extension of the exploitations triggers further forest destruction by development of other uses.
- The impact of transnational companies is intensified by globalization, which allows the world demand of wood and paper products and other raw matters to prevail over the local population's needs and the need to preserve the forests, in this way determining their fate.
- Foreign companies "draw" profits from forest exploitations in host countries (these profits no longer get to benefit the local population or the economy of the respective country).
- Most transnational companies show no interest in the forest's future, and the infrastructure used for exploitation (including the roads, the plants, etc.) is left behind to deteriorate as soon as wood or mineral resources have been exhausted. The company moves to other regions, letting the local population do what they can with the devastated environment. (Iacob, 2015)

Poverty, population growth and the subsequent increase of food-related and basic needs have led, in many regions, to increasing pressures on the local forest environment.

The inhabitants of these zones—unlike the teams of governmental departments, international agencies or transnational corporations—have an immediate, but also a long-term interest in defending and applying practices preserving a certain biodiversity and self-safety level. Most case studies describe the local communities' role of "watch dog" in answer to the external pressures on the forests belonging to them.

Often, local forest users are closely connected to one another by mutual dependence and shared values, in point of dealing with the forest and access to the forest products and other common resources. Such common ownership systems are administered durably as long as the group members have the power/ right to defend or reacquire their own resources (according to the National Strategy for the Sustainable Development of Romania *New Horizons* 2013-2020-2030).

One can conclude that where communities have a long and still viable managerial tradition, the need of a fast reestablishment of their control over the forest lands is clear. At the same time, where such traditions have been lost long ago by deculturization and destruction of the traditional institutions, a simple return to a management carried out on the level of the local communities could prove destabilizing and destructive.

Many communities are faced with the challenge of reaffirming old values and elaborating new methods of administration of the forested land; this impediment can be overcome with support from the State interested in the good management of these matters. However, rarely do studies mention that governmental authorities are aware of the local communities' importance in the control of the use, towards the exterior, of the forest (yet, there are countries whose governments understood this role: for example, the Columbian government attributed 20 million hectares of forest to the local Amazonian communities).

Lack of Homogeneity and Unity Among Forest Users

Often, local forest users are closely connected to one another by mutual trust and shared values in point of treatment of and access to forest products and other common resources. Such common ownership systems are managed sustainably as long as the group members maintain the power to manage their own resources.

However, these communities often deal with "hit and run" interventions from outsiders – such as wood traders, poachers and corrupt governmental officials – looking for fast profit and speculating easily and cheaply the lack of homogeneity of the forest communities. More often than not, the reasons of deforestation lie outside the boundaries of the forest and outside the community area, county or even nation-state.

One can notice that globalization of economies and the emerging strong transnational corporations sector determine significant changes in the geographic location, type and intensity of forests uses.

Most studies show how local people and NGOs ought to face the interventions of transnational companies which their own governments did nothing to prevent.

Thus, a limited number of transnational companies control an increasingly large part of the forest exploitation, processing and trading operations. In the year 1996, only 10 companies produced 27% of the world production of paper and cardboard.

World Resources Institute (WRI) states that commercial exploitation is the greatest threat for the last large areas of virgin forests (especially in Canada, Brazil and Russia). The same researchers mention that developing mining and power production are a greater threat for these forests than expanding agriculture.

A major force behind the large-scale exploitation of the forests following the development of the infrastructure are the large forest exploitation corporations trading wood, very influential and well-anchored in the power spheres of both great resource producers and importers.

One can appreciate that at present the companies enriched through the exploitation of national wood are using their capital to extend their business in other regions, including to temperate and boreal forests, where most of the wood is exploited and traded by local companies (Iacob, 2015)

People's attitude to forests has changed in time, given the demographic growth and the increase in people's needs.

For millennia, mankind has left its mark on the world's forests, though largely unnoticed and unquantified. At this beginning of century and millennium the dimensions and especially the impact of this "mark" have grown, and the forests, which we have always imagined as endless, are rapidly disappearing, so that today one can appreciate that more than half of the forests covering the planet at the beginning of the second millennium have disappeared.

To conclude, we can say that forests have an essential contribution to the economic growth and the improvement of the standard of living. Well-managed forests are lungs for balanced and healthy natural environments and ecosystems. Multiple political objectives coexist in the EU forest sector. On the one hand, forests and forest industries offer millions of jobs and contribute to our prosperity, especially in the rural areas, and, on the other hand, they are essential for attaining our environmental objectives and respecting the international commitments associated to them, especially in point of biodiversity conservation, reduced climate change, water resource conservation and fight against soil erosion and desertification (Iacob, 2015).

FOREST RESOURCES/ECOSYSTEMS' ROLE IN RURAL AREAS' SOCIO-ECONOMIC DEVELOPMENT

The topic of sustainable forest exploitations occupies an important place in the debates on the future of the Common Agricultural Policy, and in the future the support offered in the long run to the forests in the European Union ought to focus more on the adoption of sustainable production methods keeping a balance between economic, social and environmental interests. The European Commission estimates that efficient and sustainable forest exploitation approaches have the potential of generating more environmental, economic and social advantages than any other soil use (Iacob, 2015).

EAFRD dedicates considerable funds to the sustainable management of the forests and this support is largely cofunded by the measure of Axis 2.

Table 1 offers a general perspective on the main measures and funds available for cofunding by the European Union.

FRD can co-fund different types of sustainable forestry activities by EAFRD tools (Axis 1), for example it can offer cofunding permitting to increase the competitiveness of sustainable forests and improve cooperation between stakeholders. Training and consulting services for sustainable forest exploitation can also be funded within this axis.

The measures (of axis 3) can be used by beneficiaries wanting to make the most of the socio-economic potential of the European Union forests by associated measures, for example, for economic diversification in forest tourism or power supplies

Table 1. Planned sustainable land management EU expenses for the forests during the period 2007-2013 (EAFRD contributions to EU-27)

EAFRD measures	EAFRD funds (in million euros)		
	EU-15	EU-12	EU-27
First reforestations of agricultural lands	908	1012	2390
Other forest measures	2099	414	2758
Aid paid by Natura 2000 sites	22	73	102
Payments for forest environments	160	108	268
Total	3189	1607	5518

Source: European Union Report (2010), Agriculture in the European Union – Statistical and economic information

coming from timber. The cultural and community aspects of the forests can also be developed using the measures (of axis 3), while the sustainable forest exploitation priorities set in the local development strategies LEADER can encourage the use of funds (of axis 4) to facilitate cooperation between the rural regions and other local development factors in this domain. See Table 2.

For Romania, the European Union is an institutional partner from which she should try to learn how to appropriate a possible competitive advantage in her relations with the other member countries and with other countries. Yet, from recent signals, one cannot say that the hopes of most of the Romanians have been fully confirmed. Certainly, not all our expectations can be met only based on intercommunity relations.

At present, in Romania, the agricultural economy represents over 60% of the rural economy, the latter being made up of the social-economic activities provided by the active rural population. On the other hand, only half of the agricultural activities are exerted by land owners, the rest being carried out by service providers (mechanical services and others). The actual and sustainable solution to such a problem consists in stimulating the investments in the rural environment to develop non-agricultural activities in the rural economy. It should be remembered that in the EU, in the rural area, agricultural economy holds just 60- 65%, the rest of about 35% being held by the non-agricultural rural economy. The diminution of the weight of the agricultural economy in the rural economy from 60% at present to 35- 40%, in an average time horizon is really a particularly important strategic goal.

Table 2. Sustainable forest exploitation matters coverable from consulting or training services funded by the National Rural Development Plan

Restrained foreign/invasive tree planting; Correct use and control of chemicals; Integrated pest management; Waste management and minimization; Global and holistic approaches of development planning based on inventory and adequate growth and production data; Result-oriented control system, for monitoring performance and respect of rules; Sustainable culture planning to maintain long-term production capacity; Inclusive forest management, avoiding the dominance of "unique interest" approaches; Fight against fires, diseases and pests; Sustainable biomass production for fuel; Maximizing forests' carbon lock-in potential.	Conserving and restoring natural ecosystems and habitats; Improving landscape functions and features; Conserving cultural goods; Understanding, maintaining and respecting local communities' access rights to the forests; Applying litigation solving mechanisms for forest use, forest access and work conditions/rights for forest workers; Fight against discrimination in employment practices; Forest workers' health and security; Measures limiting unauthorized activities, such as illegal forest exploitation and illicit mining activities.

Source: http://ec.europa.eu/agriculture/fore/publi/communication-strategy_en.pdf

According to the Europe 2020 Strategy, sustainable growth is "[...] promoting a more resource-efficient, greener and more competitive EU." For this reason, this priority has been defined around the concepts of competitiveness, fight against climate change and local and efficient energy. The concept of sustainable growth in the rural area, although old, has rarely been considered as needing combined ecological, economic and social actions. This priority could be pursued by a series of policies wanting to promote the following objectives:

- Competitiveness in agro-food and forest systems
- Food quality and safety
- Fight against climate changes
- Improved natural resources management (biodiversity, water resources and soil protection) (according to Europe 2020 Strategy)

In the future rural development policies, competitiveness plays a central role. However, we need to underline that to attain competitiveness in agriculture, industry, and forestry and agro-food sector, a radical change of strategy is needed. Competitiveness must be determined by adequate criteria: "green technologies", innovation, training human resources, and sustainable growth.

According to the guidelines of the Europe 2020 Strategy, it is necessary to avoid environmental degradation, biodiversity decrease, unsustainable resource use and the adoption of high-power-consuming technologies. This means that support for investments needs to rely on very exacting selection criteria. (Allan, 1994)

The fight against climate change and for an improved natural resources management deserves special attention. This priority, related to rural area-and-environment management, is focused now on Axis 2 of the Rural Development Plan, yet it is no longer enough to reflect the greate future challenges. The climate change challenge has acquired higher generality and importance than all the other priorities (water resources management, development of alternative power and saving power, bio-diversity conservation). Consequently, it seems more adequate to select the environmental priorities taking into account the Member States' needs. The choice of the most adequate measures should go to each State in turn, which leads to the abandonment of the logic of putting together homogeneous measures per type of axis. The actions related to the conservation and profitable use of the environment should not be limited to a sub-group of measures (for example, agro-environmental payments, Nature 2000, etc), but need to be extended to all the measures of the future environment. A sustainable resource management should not be limited to Axis 2. The future Rural Development Plan ought to take into account the new environmental priorities.

To conclude, we consider that it is extremely important to keep the rural development policy in the future, the principle permitting the adoption of common European piorities in each Member State. This principle ought to be considered not just for European funds but also for national funds, in a sort of "complementariness". In other words, if Member States/regions pursue the realization of sustainable development priorities by national / regional funds, this ought to be considered when setting minimal thresholds as a guide (Iacob, 2015).

Rural development priorities (extracted from different studies) are:

- Encourage knowledge transfer and innovation in agriculture, forestry and rural areas
- Improve viability and competitiveness for all types of agriculture in all the regions and promote technological innovation and sustainable management
- Promote food chain organization, including processing and sales of agricultural products, animal welfare and risk management in agriculture
- Keep, restore and consolidate agricultural and forest ecosystems
- Promote an efficient resource use in the sectors: agriculture, food and forestry
- Transition to an economy with low CO2 emissions and resilient to climate changes in the sectors: agriculture, food and forestry
- Promote social responsibility, reduce poverty and develop the economy of the rural areas. (Rural Development Strategy of Romania 2014-2020)

Thus, developing countries are faced with an extremely important problem related to finding the answer to the question: is economic growth (increasing GDP per capita) possible without damaging the environment?

A SUSTAINABLE MANAGEMENT OF THE FORESTS AS ECOSYSTEM

The United Nations admits that a sustainable forest management can contribute significantly to sustainable development and declared the year 2011 the "International Year of Forests". The European Union is trying to balance these multiple goals in the EU Forest Action Plan (FAP), for the years 2007-2011. This is a step forward towards the assurance of a better forest policy coordination and towards activities related to the European Union.

The European Agricultural Fund for Rural Development (EAFRD) is the main financial tool supporting the implementation of the EU Forest Action Plan. The rural development policy has been the main tool of implementation of forest measures during the last few years. The estimation of the costs associated to these measures, coming from one EAFRD, during the rural development programming period of 2007-2013, was around 8 billion euros. There are different studies taking a closer look at the way the EU agriculture and rural development policy contributes to promoting sustainability and competitiveness in the European forest sector. We have focused on the progress recorded in this domain, to explore the contributions of the national rural development programmes (NRDP) of the Member States and examine the influence of the forests on the Common Agricultural Policy (CAP).

The rural zones of Europe benefit of financial support from the European Agricultural Fund for Rural Development (EAFRD). In the context of their responsibilities in relation to EAFRD, the Member States ought to assure coherence and compatibility with other funds practiced by the European Union and used in the rural areas. There is a large array of rural development projects using other EU funding sources. Along with the EAFRD projects, this combination of support of the EU for the Member States' rural areas led to significant progress in matters of development and responsibility related to the main socio-economic and environmental aspects.

The European forests offer a multitude of development possibilities for the rural areas and EAFRD has an acknowledged experience in matters of support for forest projects (EC, 2012). Other EU funding sources equally contribute, helping the forest sector to maximize its resources. These sources include operational programmes of the European Agricultural Fund for Rural Development (EAFRD). In this sector, strong synergic connections can be established between the Operational Programmes (OP) of EAFRD and EAFRD. Hubert de Schorlemer, a member of the Private Forest Owners' Association of Luxemburg, played an important role in the LEADER and EAFRD projects. He explained that the aim of the Regiowood Project, applied in four countries, namely: France, Belgium, Luxemburg and Germany, is to improve the management of the forest they inherit or administrate on behalf of the State, to help local people take advantage more of their forests. Considering the number of countries involved in supporting transnational cooperation of EAFRD, a project has been adopted, based on the development of a common approach concerning the improvement of the potential of underused forest resources. Elisabeth Freymann worked on the Regiowood Project and noticed that this project was joined by owners of small private forests who hold 1, 2 or maximum 3 hectares of forest and do not really manage it correctly. With all the owners reunited, 600 ha were concerned, and, as a conclusion, the LEADER programme was much more useful because they were able to use funding packages from the Rural Development Programme, which consisted in preparing and organizing training courses for forest owners on the use and management of their forests (LEADER, 2010).

Specialized studies have focused on four domains, highlighting the connections between rural development policies and forests, namely:

- Sustainable management (related to competitiveness) of forest practices
- Importance of very valuable natural forests
- Contribution to the fight against climate changes
- Social dimension of the EU forest policy

The International Year of Forests, declared by the UN General Assembly would like to draw attention to the disadvantage of the populations of the whole world and the need to consolidate the sustainable management of the forests and guarantee the conservation and sustainable development of all types of forests for the benefit of the present and future generations. Forests are an essential part of sustainable development and over 1.6 billion people depend on them for an average standard of living. According to the UN estimates for food and agriculture (FAO), the afforested area has been decreasing every year by 130,000 km^2 after forest exploitation operations. The European Union has the role to do better than other parts of the world, especially as in reality instead of decreasing, its total forest area increased. To conclude, less wood is exported than it should be, especially as the annual wood crops represent two thirds of the annual growth of the forests on the EU level, yet this proportion differs in some EU member states (some hold 20%, others over 90%).

The EU forests having been providing raw matters and environmental services for centuries, yet it is essential to assure the health condition of our forests, to apply an active management, considering especially the growth risks associated to climate changes, including degradation by fires, pests, diseases and storms. 21 March - being the International Day of the Forest - has been marked by the publication of the brochure "LIFE and European Forests", which explains the forests' benefits for mankind and takes a look at the future up to 2020 (EC, Agriculture and rural development, 2011)

In the year 2005, a revision of the strategy underlined that, despite the progress recorded in the sustainable management of the European Union forests, new questions emerged following the effect of the political context evolution. This determined the adoption, in the year 2006, of the 2007-2011 action plan of the European Union for the forests, containing 18 key actions to be implemented along with the Member States to reach the following goals:

- Improving competitiveness in the long run
- Improving and protecting the environment
- Contributing to a better life quality

- Encouraging coordination and communication.(Sustainable Development Strategy EU – Romania)

A study carried out in the year 2009 noticed that during the first two years, the action plan of the European Union in favor of the forests contributed to the promotion of a more coordinated approach of the actions related to the forests of the European Union. The fruits of this plan touched the main decision factors and actors, but if the information were shared on a larger scale, the contribution of the international forestry processes to the forest administration and the sensitization of the public regarding the forest could be consolidated. This study suggests that there is both among the public and among the political decision-makers a very great gap between the understanding of the forests problems in Europe and the reality we need to face. Thus, most Europeans are impressed by the total afforested area of the European Union which according to them is dwindling, although in reality it has increased during the last 20 years. (Constantza, 1996)

Most of the European Union citizens are in favor of a more active forest management, yet at the same time they consider that wood gathering and the management measures are a serious threat to our forests.

To remedy this lack of knowledge, the Commission launched a communication strategy concerning the forests of the European Union, as measure of implementation of the action plan for forestry, in order to fill the gap between public perception and forest exploitation acts and promote more informed decisions in the problems affecting the forests (CE, 2010).

According to Axis 2, “Improving the Environment and the Countryside,” the Member States have the possibility to choose from seven measures of the rural development programme, specifically aimed at the forests. The forestry sector is also supported by other measures of Axis 1, “Improving the competitiveness of the agricultural and forestry sector” and Axis 3 “Improving the quality of life in the rural areas and encouraging the diversification of economic activity”, and also by LEADER axis measures. Many beneficiaries are owners of small forests, playing an important role in the sustainable management of the forests and the improvement of the wood supply from pristine forests.

An important goal of the present support offered by the Rural Development Plan is to help protect the EU forests against degradation by fire, pollution and natural disasters on an area of over 2 million hectares. Under the climate change effect, the menace of fire risks increasing during the drought period, particularly in the south of Europe. (CE, 2011)

The European Forest Data Centre exploits an information system elaborating forecasts consisting in forest fire risks and making an evaluation of the damages.

The National Rural Network (NRN) is an essential component of the rural development policy (the second pillar of the Common Agricultural Policy). For example, France has chosen to regionalize most of the implementation of this policy by Article 78 of the Law of 27.01.2014 regarding the modernization of the territorial public action, and NRN (National Rural Networks) has been established within a specific national programme. The Specific National Rural Network Programme (SNRNP) was approved by the decision of the European Commission of 13 February 2015. The development of this programme will be assured by three copilots, namely: the Ministry of Agriculture, Food and Forests, the Association of the French Regions and the General Commission for Territorial Equality. The aim of the creation of NRN is to contribute to discussions, exchanges and debates on the rural areas and on political domains relevant for the development of these territories. The objectives and the content of the programme must be coordinated with the regional rural networks that exist in the regional rural development programmes where the regions are the management autorities. The French National Rural Network Programme concerns about 23 million euros EAFRD credit for the period 2014-2020.

These credits shall be used to assure the functioning of the programme, including the training in actor networks. Moreover, during the first part of the year 2015, a call for proposals was launched to selet the thematic networks of the multi-parties concerned. These networks need to be part of the thematic orientations retained when this programme was launched, namely:

- Agroecology
- The relation urban-rural
- Local food governance
- Social, solidary and cultural economy

The European Commission launched an initiative in this sense, under the form of an inventory of the greenhouse effect gas emissions covering the anthropic modifications triggered in the terrestrial carbon stocks, the living biomass above and under the ground, the dead wood and the litter and the organic carbon in the soil for forest lands, pastures, cultivated lands, wetlands and urban areas. In the case of the forests, these things could encourage important management changes. (Popescu, 2004)

In the year 2003, the European programme concerning the climate change established a report presenting the most promising growth measures in point of the improvement of the forests in the European Union and the diminution of climate change. There are several carbon storage possibilties for a longer period, focusing on: long-term wood uses and increasing wood products recycling.

CONCLUSION

The debate on public forest assets and climate change will encourage the discussions that are to be held by the future form of CAP at a moment when the European Union is preparing its new forest strategy.

A new sustainable rural development policy will assume a strong will, based on the support of the villages of the rural areas disadvantaged most as location, accessibility, economic development and services for the population. "The rural world" represents an opportunity for our country in the horizon 2020-2030, when we only need to wish to take advantage of these resources in order to benefit of a more sustainable development.

REFERENCES

Allan. (1994). *Stream Ecology*. Oxford.

Constantza. (1996, October). Gross world product from International Monetary Fund (IMF). *World Economic Outlook*.

Constantza. (1997). *The Development of Ecological Economics*. London: Academic Press.

Iacob, P. (2015a). Forests contribute to a new policy of sustainable rural development. *Annals of Dunărea de Jos*, 108-113.

Iacob, P. (2015b). The role of the forest ressources in the socioeconomic development of the rural area. In *Procedia Economics and Finance*. Science Direct.

Popescu, C. (2014). *Sustainable development in impase*. Internation Multidisciplinary Scientific Geo Conference, Albena, Bulgaria.

Popescu. (2004). *Economia protecţiei mediului*. Editura Bibliotheca.

Popescu. (2008a). *Creşterea rolului ecosistemelor forestiere pentru apărarea componentelor de medius*. Al 32-lea Congres ARA, Boston, MA.

Popescu. (2008b). *Stări conflictuale generate de exploatarea abuziva a pădurilor lumii*. Editura Bibliotheca.

Popescu. (2008c). *Conflicting states generated by the operation abusive forest world.* Editura Bibliotheca.

Popescu. (2008d). *Managementul mediului.* UVT University Press.

Popescu. (2009). Carbon is the key. *Conference Proceedings of the Academy of Romanian Scientist.* Editura Academiei Oamenilor de Ştiinţă din România, Bucureşti.

Chapter 7
Green Investments and Food Security:
Opportunities and Future Directions in the Context of Sustainable Development

Corina Ene
Petroleum and Gas University of Ploiesti, Romania

Marian Cătălin Voica
Petroleum and Gas University of Ploiesti, Romania

Mirela Panait
Petroleum and Gas University of Ploiesti, Romania

ABSTRACT

Green investments are the perfect tool to generate complex self-regenerating systems in order to achieve a sustainable development. Even if the burden of transition from high polluting economy to a green economy is high, the cost should be split among all that have interest in achieving this goal. The switch to green is an international current that will ultimately force the change if it is not made willingly. All parties have an interest to promote change before the change gets them on the wrong foot. In this regard, the chapter aims to emphasizing the potential benefits of the transition to a green economy in terms of reducing poverty, enhancing food security, nutrition and health on a sustainable basis while promoting ecosystem stability. Thus, increased green investments throughout the food system are imperatively needed so that changing the way food is obtained could become a powerful force for sustainable development.

DOI: 10.4018/978-1-5225-2081-8.ch007

GREEN INVESTMENTS IN THE CONTEXT OF SUSTAINABLE DEVELOPMENT

Green economy is a new concept related to sustainable development. At Seventh "Environment for Europe" Ministerial Conference held in Astana, 21–23 September 2011, the participants agreed that green economy is a "tool to help achieve sustainable development and eradicate poverty" (UNECE, 2011). Although United Nations member states have not established an agreement on the definition of the green economy, UNEP defines it as "one that results in improved human well-being and social equity, while significantly reducing environmental and ecological scarcities" (UNEP, 2011). As an associated concept, green growth refers to growth that "emphasizes environmentally sustainable economic progress to foster low-carbon, socially inclusive development" (UN DESA 2012).

The greening of the economy is complex process and different from country to country because the particularities of each state must be taken in account. The differences are made by factors like: level of development, natural resource endowments, strength of institutions and laws, nature and size of market failures, public awareness on the green economy (stakeholders like consumers, businessmen, professors or students have their role in the transition to the green economy). The green economy ensures the growth, protects earth's ecosystems, contributes to the poverty alleviation and offers the right responses to the climate, food and economic crises. So, the green economy is compatible with the older concept of sustainable development (UN DESA, UNEP & UNCTAD, 2012).

Green investments have benefits on many fields: environmental protection, social inclusiveness and economic development. The main consequences of these investments are presented in the Table 1.

Table 1. The benefits of green investments

Environmental Protection	Social Inclusiveness	Economic Development
• decreased air pollution • decreased water pollution • decreased soil pollution • decreased ghg emissions • decreased biodiversity loss • decreased natural resources depletion • increased energy efficiency • increased water efficiency	• improved access to goods and services • improved affordability of goods and services • improved work safety • increased green jobs • strengthened effective public participation in environmental matters • improved health protection • improved equity	• increased innovation • increased technology transfer • improved infrastructure • removed barriers • improved competition

Source: https://www.unece.org/sustainable-development/green-economy

Taking into account the complexity of the phenomenon, the transition to green economy must be supported by public authorities, private sector and civil society. The first step is the identification of the main priorities in each country (Table 2). At the level of European Union, the main priorities have been detected and now, the major challenge is the establishment of the proper measures that must be taken.

The public authorities have the major role in this transition process because they must establish a robust framework available for public and private entities from real economy and civil society. For example, instruments like environmental taxes, charges and fees, carbon pricing and subsidies must be imposed in order to shape the behavior of the business. In addition, the companies must be encouraged to have a social responsible attitude through different tools like voluntary guidelines and information-based instruments. In order to raise public awareness on the green economy, stakeholders like consumers, students and educators are important players. The consumers must to be encouraged to give up to unsustainable consumption patterns and to become more conscious about their role in the transition to green economy. The universities have the mission to offer education for sustainable development. According with Nelson Mandela, "Education is the most powerful weapon you can use to change the world." Taking in account this, a new concept has appeared: education for sustainable development. The promoters of this concept are international political and economic forums like United Nations, OECD, ministries like environment or health minister. Research and innovation are also important in order to create environmentally sustainable technologies that reduce waste and increase resource efficiency. In this context, the integrated collaboration between government, industry, academia and civil participants are essential if we consider the Quadruple Helix Model (Carayannis & Campbell, 2009). In order to make the progress, it is also important to established targets and to measure the results. So, the indicators are essential to evaluate the efforts made by different entities.

Table 2. The main priorities for the green economy

Job creation	**GREEN ECONOMY**	Industry
Financing		Agriculture
Education for sustainable development		Water
Sustainable Consumption and Production.		Sustainable and climate-resilient cities
Energy		Green Public Procurement

Source: https://www.unece.org/fileadmin/DAM/env/documents/2011/ece/e.ece.rpm.2011.4.e.pdf

INTERNATIONAL INITIATIVES TO MEASURE AND ACHIEVE GREEN AND SUSTAINABLE DEVELOPMENT

Initiatives to measure the achievement of a sustainable development spawn different benchmarks composed by sets of indicators that indicate the completion of different goals of sustainable development. We will present some of the most important of them which had a great influence on sustainable development and sustainable food systems.

Millennium Development Goals and its Follower: Sustainable Development Goals

Millennium Development Goals is one of the most important initiatives to achieve a sustainable development by setting a set of eight goals in the year 2000 at the Millennium Summit which needs to be accomplished by the end of 2015. The base year for these goals is the year 1990. The United Nations Millennium Declaration was signed by the world leaders, committing their nations to reach the next goals (UN, 2000):

1. Eradicate extreme poverty and hunger
2. Achieve universal primary education
3. Promote gender equality and empower women
4. Reduce child mortality
5. Improve maternal health
6. Combat HIV/AIDS, malaria and other diseases
7. Ensure environmental sustainability
8. Develop a global partnership for development

In order to accomplish these goals, 12 targets had been put in place and 60 indicators have been used to follow the progress for each goal. The most relevant goals for our topic are goals 1 and 7.

To eradicate extreme poverty and hunger many developments have to be made in the food production and supply systems to reduce the number of people that suffer from hunger and are undernourished.

As we can see from Figure 1, the share of people leaving on less than 1.25 USD/day registered an important decrease with 68% in the world and 69% in developing regions. In Sub-Saharan Africa the rate of decrease is slow with only 28% in the analyzed period. As a result of this evolution an excess of 1 billion people left the extreme poverty zone since 1990. Work still needs to continue as a number of 836 million live with less than 1.25 USD/day and the sad fact is that 80% of them live

Figure 1. Proportion of people living on less than $1.25 a day, 1990, 2011 and 2015 (%)
Source: Based on the data available on Millennium Development Goals Report 2015

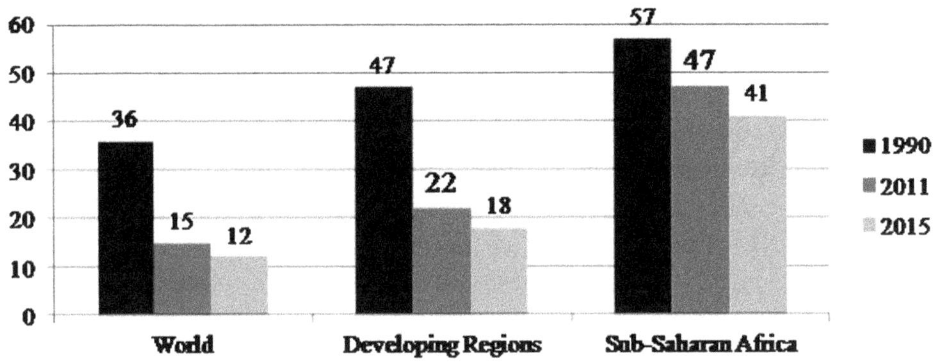

in Southern Asia and Sub-Saharan Africa. As a result, there are 795 million people that are undernourished around the world.

Ensure environmental sustainability is a general desiderate taking into account the influence of climate change on food producing systems. As a result of the acknowledgement of this danger to human kind, the world leaders decided to make the best effort to stop the global warming by reducing the green house gas emissions.

In Figure 2 we can observe that the developed regions registered a decrease of the level of CO_2 emissions, but the developing countries almost tripled their emis-

Figure 2. Emissions of carbon dioxide, 1990, 2000 and 2012(billions of metric tons)
Source: Based on the data available on The Millennium Development Goals Report 2015

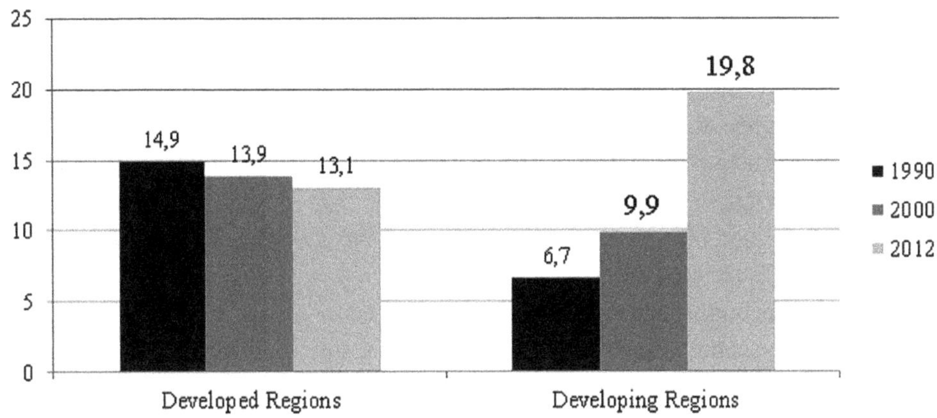

sions in the analyzed period. As a result, the global emissions of CO_2 increased by 50% since 1990. This opposite trend is generated by the need of developing regions to reach a higher level of development and they argue that developed regions already contributed to the global warming problem before its manifestation through climate change. From this point of view the emission problem can only be resolved by the transition to a green economy of both groups of countries and developing countries should receive some kind of assistance because they lack the necessary funds for this transition. Green investments are the only way forward because if the emissions of green house gases continue the planet will get warmer and warmer with long-lasting changes of climate, endangering people lives and ecosystems with irreversible consequences. These consequences will be felt across the globe and will affect the agriculture which may lead to food shortages.

The Millennium Development Goals concentrated the international community towards the accomplishment of eight goals. As a result, the resources were concentrated on these goals and the results showed that fifteen year goals are feasible and eliminates the possibility of being concentrated on too many targets at the same time and miss them. The results were so good that the world leaders decided "to free the human race from the tyranny of poverty" and "to heal and secure our planet" (UN, 2015) and in September, 2015 the General Assembly of United Nations approved the Agenda 2030 as the next level with 17 Sustainable Development Goals and 169 targets as it fallows:

1. End poverty in all its forms everywhere
2. End hunger, achieve food security and improved nutrition, and promote sustainable agriculture
3. Ensure healthy lives and promote well-being for all at all ages
4. Ensure inclusive and equitable quality education and promote life-long learning opportunities for all
5. Achieve gender equality and empower all women and girls
6. Ensure availability and sustainable management of water and sanitation for all
7. Ensure access to affordable, reliable, sustainable, and modern energy for all
8. Promote sustained, inclusive and sustainable economic growth, full and productive employment and decent work for all
9. Build resilient infrastructure, promote inclusive and sustainable industrialization and foster innovation
10. Reduce inequality within and among countries
11. Make cities and human settlements inclusive, safe, resilient and sustainable
12. Ensure sustainable consumption and production patterns
13. Take urgent action to combat climate change and its impacts

14. Conserve and sustainably use the oceans, seas and marine resources for sustainable development
15. Protect, restore and promote sustainable use of terrestrial ecosystems, sustainably manage forests, combat desertification, and halt and reverse land degradation and halt biodiversity loss
16. Promote peaceful and inclusive societies for sustainable development, provide access to justice for all and build effective, accountable and inclusive institutions at all levels
17. Strengthen the means of implementation and revitalize the global partnership for sustainable development

In order to accomplish the Sustainable Development Goals an immense financial effort must be made to develop specific mechanism that allow the efficient way towards the completion of these goals. New legal frameworks must be created in order to implement the Sustainable Development Goals. Also the Global Partnership for Sustainable Development must be strengthened by intensifying the cooperation between governments, private sector and civil society.

The EU Set of Sustainable Development Indicators (SDIs)

Sustainable development is an important objective of the European Union as it is stated in the Article 3 of the Treaty on European Union. The progress towards sustainable development of the EU is measured with the help of Eurostat through the set of sustainable development indicators (EU-SDIs). They are part of the EU Sustainable Development Strategy (EU-SDS) and every two years a report from Eurostat presents the evolution towards sustainable developments.

The first set of EU-SDIs was proposed in 2001 as a result of the EU-SDS adoption and revised in 2006. The EU-SDIs are revised by the Commission under the assistance of a working group formed by statisticians and policy representatives.

The EU-SDIs is composed by ten thematic areas from the economic, social, environmental, global and institutional dimensions (Sustainable development in the European Union — Key messages, 2015): socioeconomic development, sustainable consumption and production, social inclusion, demographic changes, public health, climate change and energy, sustainable transport, natural resources, global partnership, good governance.

Inside each theme there is a three level set of indicators. At the first level we have the headline indicators that are widely used indicators with high communicative power that monitors overall objectives. The second level is composed from indicators related to the operational objectives of the EU-SDS. The third level is composed from indicators that are perfect for progress analysis.

Next we will analyze some indicators with a high impact on the topic of green investments, food security and food systems.

The eco-innovation index is an indicator that wants to depict the eco-innovation performance between EU Member States. It is composed of 16 indicators grouped in five areas: eco-innovation inputs, eco-innovation activities, eco-innovation outputs, resource efficiency and socio-economic outcomes.

As we can see from Figure 3, the highest scores are obtain by the countries from northern Europe, which have a high level of development like Finland, Sweden, Germany, Denmark and United Kingdom with scores of over 120. At the opposite we find former communist countries like, Bulgaria, Poland, Slovakia, Latvia and Croatia with scores of under 60.

The organic farming is promoted and sustained by the European Action Plan for Organic Food and Faming. Between 2007 and 2012 there has been registered an increase of the area cultivated with organic cultures by 42.5%, with an average increase of 7.3% per year, reaching a total of 5.7% of all agricultural area in the EU, generating sales of 22 billion EUR.

In Figure 4 we can see the share of agricultural area used for organic farming in 2012. Austria leads, with a share of 18.5% of its total agricultural area and we cans see that latter members of the EU like Estonia, Latvia, Czech Republic, Slovenia and Slovakia find themselves above the EU average of 5.7%.

In 2014 the European Commission proposed a new regulation on organic farming, the labeling of organic products, and a plan of 18 actions for future of the or-

Figure 3. Eco-innovation index 2013 (EU=100)
Source: Based on the data available on Eurostat

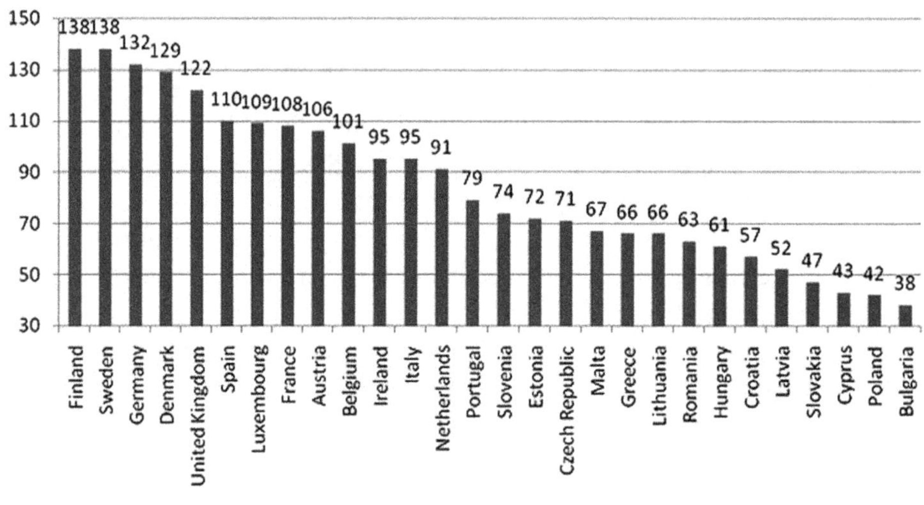

Figure 4. Areas under organic farming 2012 (%)
Source: Based on the data available on Eurostat

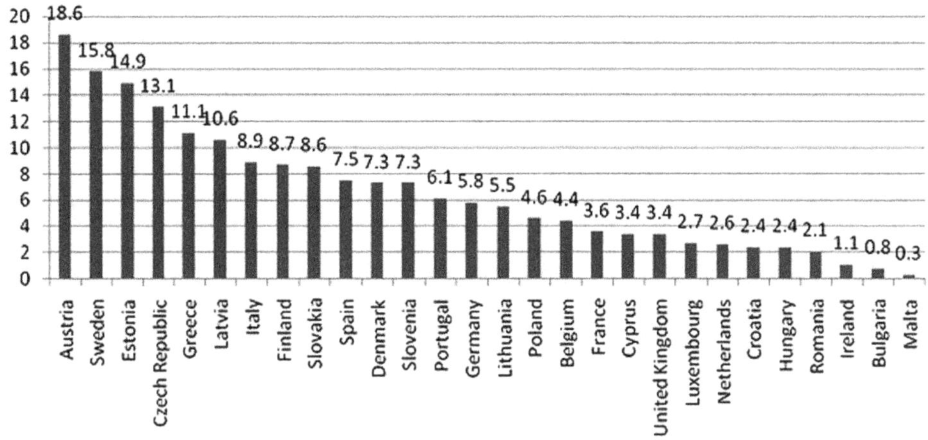

ganic sector up to 2020 (European Commission, 2014). This regulation focuses on two axes, one is to increase the EU organic farmers productivity and the second is to ensure consumer confidence.

The level of annual greenhouse gas emissions is an indicator that includes six gases: carbon dioxide, methane, nitrous oxide, hydrofluorocarbons, perfluorocarbons and sulphur hexafluoride. The emissions of these gases are transformed in CO_2-equivalent using weighting factors according with the global warming potential each gas has.

In Figure 5, we observe that the total CO_2-equivalent emissions have increase over time. This increase is not generalized and we can observe that between 1990 and 2000 all the regions registered increases of greenhouse gas emissions except the EU-28. One aspect that needs to be mentioned here is that in the 1990 – 2000 period, many of the Central and Eastern Europe economies passed through the transition process from communism to capitalism system, which generated a painful restructuration of former industry companies, many of them disappearing and so they stop emitting greenhouse gas emissions. This also influenced the decrease registered by the rest of Europe along with the influence of the Yugoslavian Wars, which produce high economic damage, stopping the activity in former Yugoslavia's countries.

Between 2000 and 2012 we observe that the trend switch for United States, one of the highest generator of greenhouse gas emissions and Americas (excluding USA). EU-28 member states continued their emission reduction mainly due to the European Trading Scheme which is the mechanism used by the EU to implement the Kyoto Protocol stipulations, the success in implementing the national renewable energies promotion in the power sector, creating of building insulation standards, the changes of Common Agriculture Policy etc.

After the transition and the regional conflicts passed, the rest of the Europe group increased their greenhouse gas emissions after revitalizing their industrial and economic activity.

Asia (excluding China) had a steady increase of greenhouse gas emissions along with the rest of the World Group. The development of maritime and aviation sector contributes to the emissions with an important share.

China (including Hong Kong) became in 2012 the largest greenhouse gas emitter in the world surpassing the United States. China based its economic development by ignoring the pollution problem, which now generates important problem for the healthcare system, air and water quality for its citizens.

Green Growth Indicators

OECD Green Growth Indicators aims to measure the evolution towards a greener economy, to prevent climate change and to protect the natural resources and biodiversity. This set of indicators is in concordance with the international initiatives towards measuring the influence of human activities on the environment and the methods used to minimize it.

Green Growth Indicators are composed of four main areas (OECD, 2014):

Figure 5. Greenhouse gas emissions global (million tonnes of CO_2 equivalent)
Source: Based on the data available on Eurostat

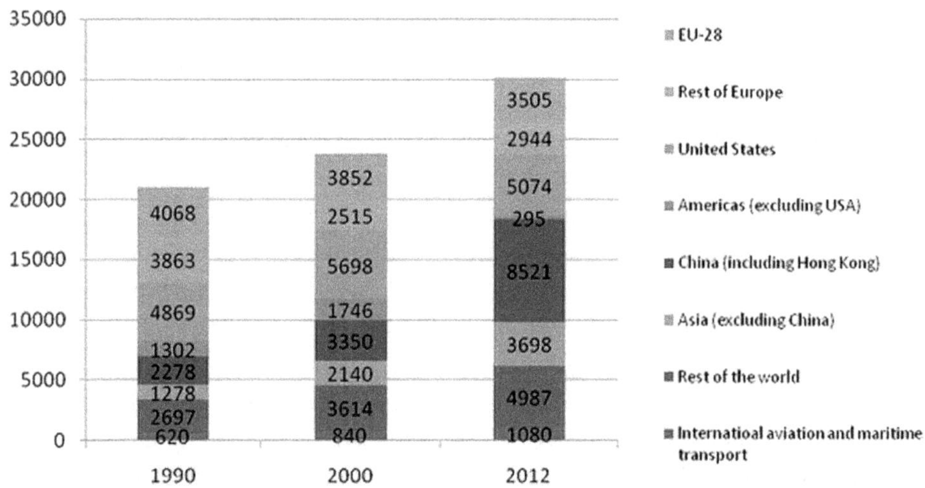

**For a more accurate representation of this figure, please see the electronic version.*

1. **Environmental and Resource Productivity:** To capture the need for efficient use of natural capital and to capture aspects of production which are rarely quantified in economic models and accounting frameworks (1 in Figure 6).
2. **Economic and Environmental Asset:** Because sustained growth requires the asset base to be maintained and because a declining asset base presents risks to future growth. Attention is given to natural assets (2 in Figure 6).
3. **Environmental Quality of Life:** To capture how environment conditions and amenities interact with people's lives (3 in Figure 6).
4. **Economic Opportunities and Policy Responses:** To help discern the effectiveness of policy in delivering green growth (4 in Figure 6).

A fifth group of indicator is represented by the indicators that indicate the socio-economic context and the growth characteristics.

Figure 6. Conceptual measurement framework
Source: OECD (2011), Towards Green Growth Monitoring Progress OECD Indicators

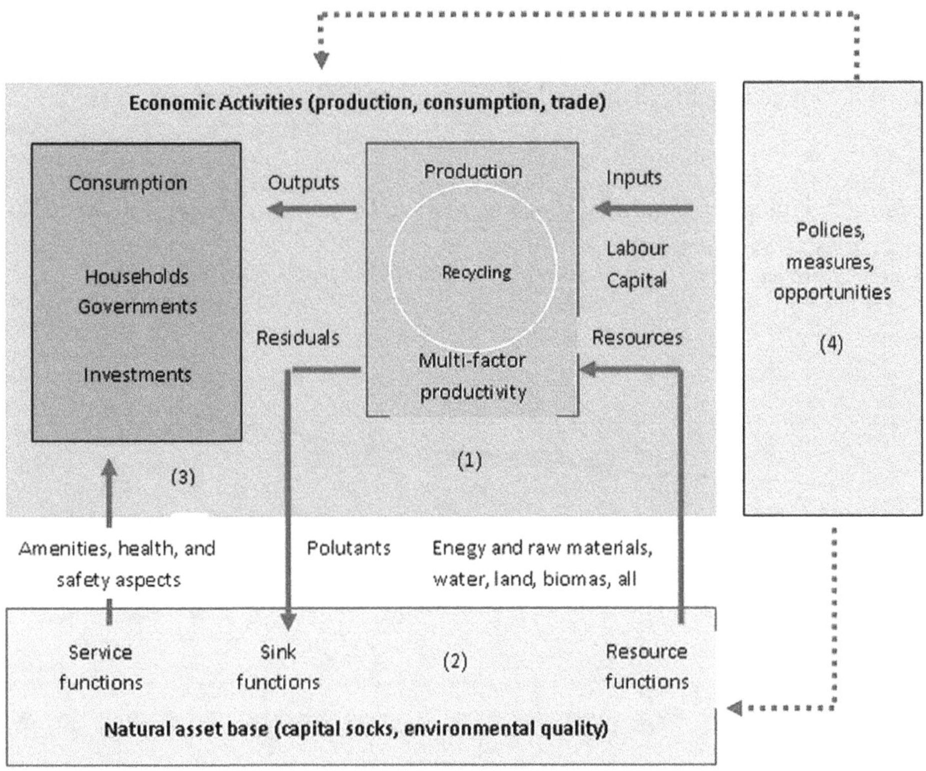

The conceptual framework was presented in Towards Green Growth: Monitoring Progress Report from 2011 which focus on the connection of the principles of green growth, accounting principles and pressure-state-response model for environmental reporting.

Next we will present some of the most relevant indicators to our study.

First indicator that we will explore is the productivity of CO_2 production based. As we can see from Figure 7 the productivity of OECD economies registered a steady growth throughout the entire period. At the same time the emissions of greenhouse gases has increased at a lower rate than the GDP, showing signs of decoupling. The financial crisis had an important effect on the reduction of greenhouse gas emissions due to the reduction of the economic activity. The increase of the production based CO_2 productivity may be the result of a switch towards non-fossil fuel energy, the results of environmental policies, the achievement of energy efficiency and the transition of industry away from energy intensive activities. This productivity is not achieved throughout all the sectors, as almost two thirds of emissions are from transport and electricity/heat generation.

Energy productivity increased in the last decade and this was achieved with the decoupling from environmental effects for some countries as a result of structural changes and the promotion of energy conservation policy. However, these results are not enough to achieve the goal of capping the global warming process.

Figure 7. Production-based CO2 productivity, GDP per unit of energy-related CO2 emissions (US dollars per kilogram)
Source: Based on the data available on OECD, Green Growth Indicators 2014

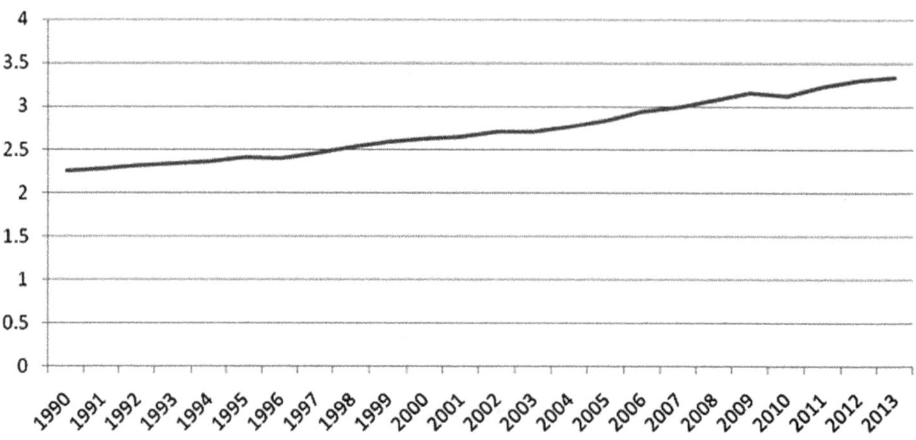

In Figure 8, we can observe the evolution of the share of renewable electricity production from the total produced and we see that the share has increased in the later years. Now, renewable energy accounts for one fifth of the total electric energy generated.

Even though the energy mix changed a lot from 1990, when the oil and coal shares decline in favor of gas and other sources, the OECD countries still rely on fossil fuels in a proportion that exceed 80%. Only a few countries are above the 20% of electricity from renewable sources and the largest share come from biomass and hydropower followed by bioenergy, liquid biofuels, solar and wind.

Freshwater is one of the most important resource for environment and the economy, especially the agriculture. The main problem for this resource is represented by the overexploitation, degradation of environment quality. Its quality is influenced by water abstraction, pollution, climate and weather.

The main concern is to provide an adequate management of water sources so that it can be available and at a suitable quality for the use in human activities and to support aquatic and other ecosystems.

In Figure 9, we see that the level of freshwater abstraction registered a steady descending trend throughout the period. This means that there has been a decoupling effect from GDP growth. This trend has been caused by the efficient use of freshwater in different sectors and the use of alternative water sources like water reuse and desalinization. The agriculture water use increased in many OECD countries, as the irrigated land increased, but the production showed a higher increase.

Figure 8. Renewable electricity, % total electricity generation
Source: Based on the data available on OECD, Green Growth Indicators 2014

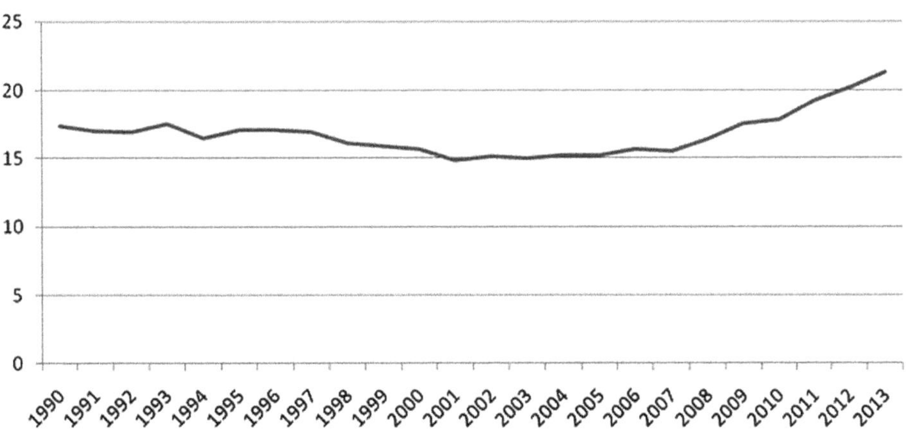

Figure 9. Total freshwater abstraction per capita (Cubic metres per capita)
Source: Based on the data available on OECD, Green Growth Indicators 2014

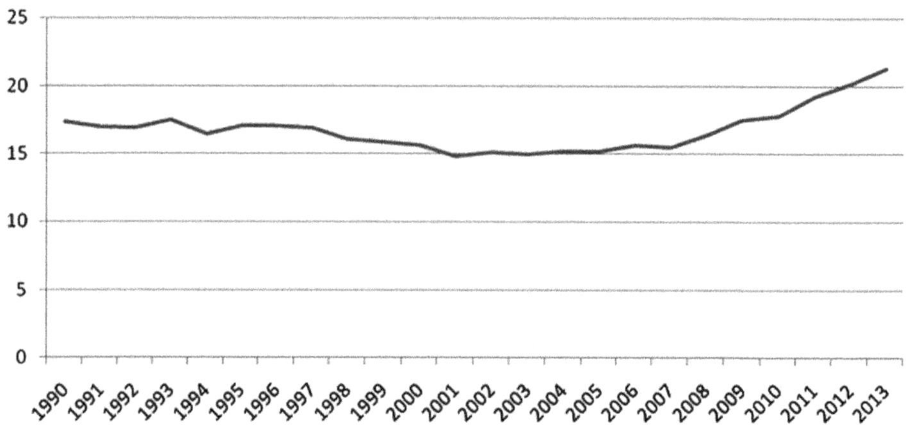

Another important natural asset base resource is represented by the land and soil. They are critical for the production of food and other biomass, the productivity of ecosystems and preservation of wildlife and plants. In order to ensure a sustainable management, we have to reconcile competing demands for land and soil resources, while keeping its essential ecosystem functions. In order to accomplish this we need territorial planning, appropriate governance and coherence with sectoral policies.

In Figure 10, we see the distribution of land use on the next domains: arable and cropland, forest, pastures and meadows and other land use. The arable and cropland registered a descending trend throughout the period from 13.55% in 1992 to 12.07% in 2013 as the pastures and meadows which decreased from 25.1% in 1992 to 23.22% in 2013.

Forest area registered an increase from 30.88% in 1992 to 31.24% in 2013. The highest increase was registered by the other land from 30.47% in 1992 to 33.47% in 2013. Because of these trends, the biodiversity has declined in OECD countries. The fragmentation, degradation of environment and conversions to other types of land is a phenomenon that needs to be closely watched. Pastures have declined as they have been converted to forests. As of 1990, the agricultural land area registered a decrease of around 0.5% per year as the farmland is converted to forestry and urban development.

Agri-Environmental Indicators

In order to promote sustainable development in agriculture, the Food and Agriculture Organization of the United Nations created a set of Agri-environmental indicators

Figure 10. Distribution of land resources (% of total land area)
Source: Based on the data available on OECD, Green Growth Indicators 2014

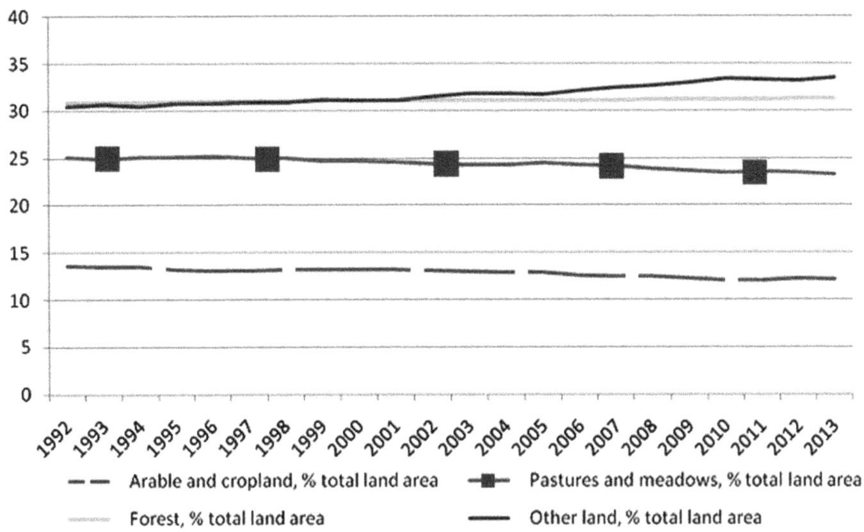

(AEI) with the role to describe and evaluate the evolution of agricultural environmental performance (Table 3). This has the role to supply scientists and policymakers with the suitable data regarding the environment and the effects and efficiency of policies on the environment. This set of indicators needs to be relevant to the targeted public and, that is why, they are organized to five categories in concordance with the Driving force-Pressure-Stat-Impact-Response (DPSIR) model proposed by the European Environment Agency (EEA, 1999) based on the PSR mode (OECD, 1993).

Next, we will analyze some of the representative of agri-environmental indicators. Ammonia emissions are generated by animal farms and they are responsible for acidification. The main sector with the highest ammonia emissions is the agriculture with shares of 80%-99%. Ammonia contributes to soil and water acidification, and the ammonia from atmosphere can combine with other industrial and transport contributing to secondary particle pollution.

In Figure 11, we observe that the share of ammonia emissions from agriculture in the atmosphere had a steady level of around 60% between 1992 and 2006 when the trend changed and became ascending until 2009 when it surpassed 90%

Table 3. Agri-environmental indicators

Domain	Subdomain	Indicator
Air and Climate Change	*Ammonia emissions*	Ammonia (NH_3) emissions from agriculture as a % of total NH_3 emissions
Energy	*Energy use in Agriculture and Forestry*	Agriculture and forestry use as a % of total energy use
	Bioenergy Production	Bioenergy production as a % of total renewable energy production
Fertilizers Consumption	*Nitrogen consumption*	Nitrogen nutrient use on arable and permanent crop area (N tonnes/1000 ha)
	Phosphate consumption	Phosphate nutrient use on arable and permanent crop area (P205 tonnes/1000 ha)
	Nitrogen Phosphate	Nitrogen and Phosphate nutrient use on arable and permanent crop area (N+P205 tonnes/1000 ha)
Land	*Agricultural area*	Agricultural area as a % of land area
	Agricultural area use change	Changes in agricultural area (% per year)
	Area equipped for irrigation	Area equipped for irrigation as a % of agricultural area
	Conservation agriculture	Conservation agriculture area (>30% group cover) as a % of agricultural area
	Cropping patterns	Permanent crops area as a % of agricultural area
	Organic agricultural area	Permanent meadows and pastures area as a % of agricultural area
	Protected land area	Arable land area as a % of agricultural area
Livestock	*Livestock Density*	Livestock total per hectare of agricultural area (livestock total number/ha)
	Cattle and Buffalo	Cattle and Buffalo as a % of total livestock
	Pigs	Pigs as a % of total livestock
	Sheep and goats	Sheep and goats as a % of total livestock
	Poultry birds	Poultry birds as a % of total livestock
Pesticide	*Pesticides Use*	Pesticide use on arable and permanent crop area (tonnes/1000 ha)
Soils	*Soil Erosion - GLASOD*	Average soil erosion expressed in GLASOD erosion degree
	Land degradation - GLASOD	Average land degradation expressed in GLASOD erosion degree
	Carbon in topsoil	Average carbon content in the topsoil as a % in weight
Water	*Water use in agriculture*	Water withdrawal for agricultural use as a % of total water withdrawal

Source: FAO, http://faostat.fao.org/site/674/default.aspx

Figure 11. Ammonia (NH_3) emissions from agriculture as a % of total NH_3 emissions
Source: Based on the data available on FAO http://faostat3.fao.org/browse/E/EC/E

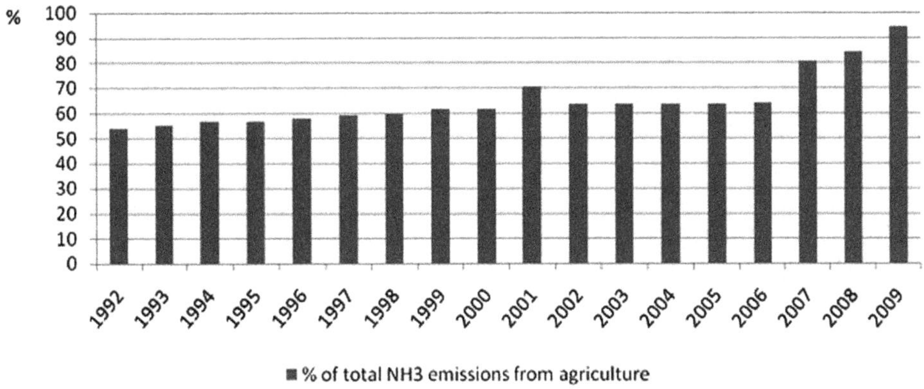

The mineral fertilizers may poison water and pollute the soil with heavy metals and Persistent Organic Pollutants (POP).

In Figure 12, we can observe the distribution of fertilizers by region, and we see that the highest use of fertilizers can be found in Asia which registered an ascending trend from 129.18 tonnes of nutrients per 1000 Ha 2002 to 174.98 tonnes in 2010. The second ranking region is the Americas with 76.97 tonnes in 2010 followed by Africa with 62.79 tonnes, Europe with 58.72 tonnes and Oceania with 16.24 tonnes.

Figure 12. Trend of Nitrogen + Phosphate Fertilizer nutrient use on arable and permanent crop area by continent 2002 – 2010
Source: Based on the data available on FAO, http://faostat3.fao.org/browse/E/EF/E

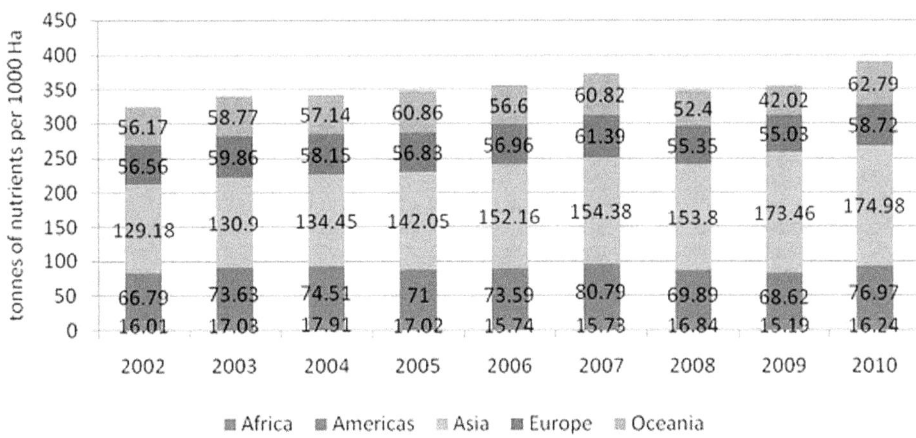

**For a more accurate representation of this figure, please see the electronic version.*

In Figure 13, we can observe the trend of cattle, buffaloes, pigs, sheep, goats, and poultry as a % of total livestock 1991-2011. We observe that the poultry birds increased their share in the analyzed period from 74.97% in 1991 to 83.2% in 2011 based on the reduction of sheep and goats share from 10.89% in 1991 to 7.2% in 2011, cattle and buffaloes from 8.86% in 1991 to 5.99 in 2011 and pigs from 5.29% in 1991 to 3.61 in 2011.

CURRENT DIMENSIONS AND CHALLENGES OF THE WORLD FOOD SECURITY

Humanity is today witnessing startling discrepancies: developed countries have accumulated significant food excess while low income and developing countries face the persistence of malnutrition which cause the death of millions annually, mostly children. In this situation, commendable efforts are made at internationa level, encouraging practical support and long-term involvement of a large number of states in terms of fairness and solidarity.

Figure 13. Trend of cattle, buffaloes, pigs, sheep, goats, poultry as a % of total livestock 1991-2011
Source: Based on the data available on FAO http://faostat3.fao.org/browse/E/EK/E

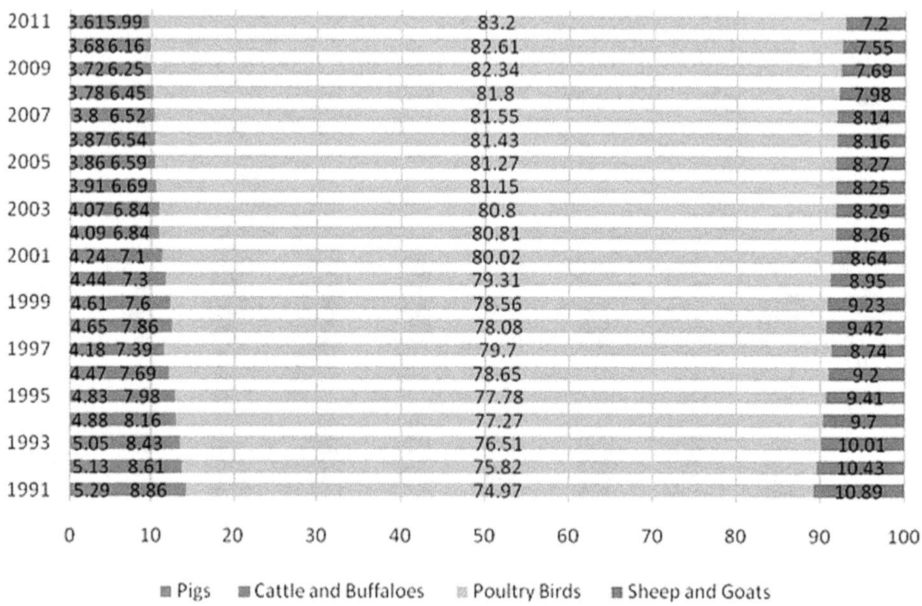

**For a more accurate representation of this figure, please see the electronic version.*

The concept of food security has dynamically evolved over time, expanding its meanings and connections, so that, at present, in the broadest sense, it encompasses all aspects that allow optimal access of population to food. Beyond any socio-economic, political or cultural differences, everyone has a fundamental right - the right to food - whose materialization is not accomplished everywhere in the best conditions.

The internationally dedicated definition – and the most popular - was established at the World Food Summit (WFS) in 1996 and reaffirmed in 2002, affirming that food security exists "when all people at all times have access to sufficient, safe, nutritious food to maintain a healthy and active life"(World Food Summit, 1996).

The concept of food security, as defined above, was approached and developed on multiple levels during many international meetings on food security worldwide, expressing an essential goal of economic and social development. It is built on three pillars which form its foundation and practical reflections (United States Agency for International Development, 1992; World Health Organization, 2015):

- **Food Availability:** Sufficient quantities of food available on a consistent basis;
- **Food Access:** Sufficient resources to procure adequate foods for a nutritious diet;
- **Food Use:** Appropriate use based on knowledge of basic nutrition and care, as well as adequate water and sanitation.

Food security obviously depends on food availability and food access (Gavrilescu & Giurcă, 2001), but it certainly means addressing extended issues simultaneously, including aspects such as food innocuousness and nutritional balance. Individual food consumption behavior also plays a major role within the food use aspect, due to its complex linkages with personal preferences, dietary habits and traditions (Stancu, 2015) and nutrition education level.

These sides can be covered by right correlation between food and nutrition policies. Food policy aims to ensure the necessary quantity and quality of foods for the entire population at affordable prices, while nutrition policy should effectively approach food and nutrition education (Jukes, McGuire, Method, & Sternberg, 2002).

All these meanings and correlations involve, firstly, ensuring adequate foods obtained either from domestic production, imports or food aid. As a specific type of measure, the motivation of international agricultural interventions assumes that generating income at family level is an effective means to reduce poverty and ensure food security (Bonnard, 1999). Thus, achieving food security is synonymous with dealing with many facets of the food problem - globally, regionally and nationally (Gavrilescu & Giurcă, 2001).

At the moment, the world food situation is not reassuring, since widening disparities between rich and poor countries continuously add new dimensions to the food problem. Inequality and inequity in foods distribution lead to absurd situations that are hardly conceivable for the contemporary civilization.

In this context, international cooperation is becoming more geared towards tackling the food issue and its related aspects - of systemic nature - that humanity is facing today.

Being an essential starting point at global level, the WFS in 1996 set the target of halving the number of undernourished people by 2015 compared to the period 1990-1992. Four years later, the same objective was reaffirmed by the Millennium Development Goals (MDG) proposing two related goals: halving both the proportion of people suffering from hunger and the proportion of those living on less than $ 1.25/day (United Nations, 2000; United Nations Development Programme, 2002). On this theme, the Food and Agriculture Organization of the United Nations (FAO) report entitled "The State of Food Insecurity in the World" (SOFI) is drafted each year as a result of the continuous efforts of FAO and other international partners to monitor nutritional status and to analyze the vulnerability of worldwide population facing the food problem. All editions of SOFI report provide the latest estimates of the number of chronically undernourished people at global level as well as reports on global and national efforts made to achieve the WFS and MDG goals.

A common element of SOFI reports of recent years until 2010 was the indication that, globally, the pace of reduction in population suffering from hunger was so slow that, if it persisted, it would not allow the accomplishments of WFS and MDG commitments. Yet, each successive report starting 2011 pointed out that in several countries and regions significant progress have been made in reducing the number of undernourished people. In this regard, the SOFI 2014 report outlines essential estimates and accomplishments, as follows(Food and Agriculture Organization of the United Nations [FAO], International Fund for Agricultural Development [IFAD] & United Nations World Food Programme [WFP], 2014):

- Even if global hunger reduction continued, in the period 2012–2014 about 805 million people were still chronically undernourished, while the prevalence of undernourishment has fallen from 18.7% to 11.3% globally and from 23.4% to 13.5% for developing countries;
- Regarding the comparison with WFS and MDG goals, since 1990-1992, 63 countries have reached the hunger target of MDG and 25 countries have achieved the WFS target, while undernourishment level fell below 5% for 11 of the 63 developing countries, proving that the hunger target of the MDG still was within reach;

- Even though overall progress in increasing food security was obvious, significant differences persist across regions: while Latin America and the Caribbean have made the most visible overall progress – by strengthening political commitment to food security and nutrition, modest progress were reported for sub-Saharan Africa and Western Asia - afflicted by conflict and natural disasters;
- Hunger eradication should rely on sustained political commitment at the highest level, considering food security and nutrition as top priorities, as it requires an integrated approach including: investments for enhancing agricultural productivity; access to inputs and markets; measures for rural development; social protection; specific nutrition programmes.

Marking the moment of final balance from the perspective of the MDG monitoring period, the SOFI 2015 report highlights a series of facts revealing global and regional dates and facts (FAO, IFAD & WFP 2015):

- Over the last ten years, global hunger has continued to gradually decline, with a reduction of 167 million hungry people, to an estimated 795 million undernourished people (especially in developing countries);
- The MDG hunger target was missed by a small margin, considering the developing regions, while some regions (Latin America, the eastern and south-eastern regions of Asia, the Caucasus and Central Asia, and the northern and western regions of Africa) have reached the target due to their fast progress in reducing undernourishment;
- Out of 129 developing countries, 72 have reached the MDG hunger target due to economic growth, stable political conditions and adequate social protection policies;
- Inclusive economic growth is a key factor of success in reducing undernourishment, providing real opportunities for the poor to improve their livelihoods: raising the productivity of family farmers, strengthening social protection mechanisms, well-functioning markets and equitable governance;
- Protracted crises caused by conflict, political instability or natural disasters had a heavy impact on vulnerability and food insecurity, imposing the need for strong political commitment, and the integration of humanitarian and development.

Yet, despite the progress made by some countries and regions, the food global problem is far from being resolved in a definitive and durable manner.

Every edition of SOFI report reveals several factors hindering the growth of food production in some parts of the world, the most common being:

- Reducing the areas of agricultural land due to desertification, erosion, floods, waste deposit, use for various construction;
- Lack of irrigation water during the crops growing season;
- Application of primitive technologies;
- Poor availability of permanent pastures for the whole livestock;
- Low level of agricultural yields;
- Insufficient financial resources allocated for agricultural production and food industry compared to other branches of the economy;
- Population growing faster than agricultural production.

Also, most SOFI reports insist that a healthy agricultural sector could be the way out of the crisis, especially in low-income countries, and a possible decline in investment in the sector should be avoided (FAO, 2009), so that agriculture plays its role as an engine of resuming growth, poverty reduction – being a long-term pillar in the fight against hunger.

COULD GREEN AGRICULTURAL PRACTICES BECOME THE KEY TO FOOD SECURITY?

In order to analyze the food issue as a global problem of humanity and to identify possible eradication ways it is necessary to start with a systematic approach to economic phenomena and processes. Currently, this complex array includes a number of trends, contradictions and paradoxes, of particular concern being the danger of environmental degradation, with serious implications for the future of humanity.

The Key Role of Agriculture in Ensuring Food Security

As a primary field of activity, agriculture has known over time stages that have strengthened its economic and strategic importance, its results being closely linked with the very existence and development of mankind. Agriculture has always been and remains the main source of food for a growing population, especially considering the demographic explosion in low-income countries.

For these reasons, it is clear that agriculture plays a decisive role for the rapid economic progress, the industry development and raising living standards depend on it; for that matter, agriculture ultimately enables access to food security.

World's experience shows that before reaching their actual level, industrialized countries went through an agriculture-based development, and that, at present, a modern economy is inconceivable without an advanced agriculture. Everywhere in the civilized world, food production is considered of high priority, agriculture representing a main branch of economy, while food security is considered to be a key element in any project for agricultural development.

This approach involves prioritizing and according facilities to increase the capacity of agriculture to feed the population, based on the rational use of natural resources and on specific opportunities that support the development of numerous upstream and downstream activities, revitalizing and improving the attractiveness of rural areas (Zahiu, 1999), using a complex set of instruments (Figure 14).

Specifically, a number of national and sectoral policies and measures could support the role of agriculture in solving the food problem (Bulgaru, 1996; Chivu, 2002; Gavrilescu &Giurcă, 2001):

- **Fiscal Policy:** It aims to create fiscal incentives for farmers to enhance their ability to be profitable and to obtain loans for investment. This policy accompanies and guides the transformation dynamics of farmers from households scale farms (created for subsistence) to investment-oriented commercial farms, implying a gradual adjustment of fiscal policies;
- **Agriculture Support Policies:** These aim to create the necessary support structures so that farming becomes a profitable branch: investments in rural infrastructure (electrification, road maintenance, irrigation); support for agricultural research and development – focusing on family farms; support for the development of agriculture extension and advisory services;
- **Food Production Development Support Policies:** Measures to facilitate investment in research etc.

Figure 14. Instruments for agri-food policies

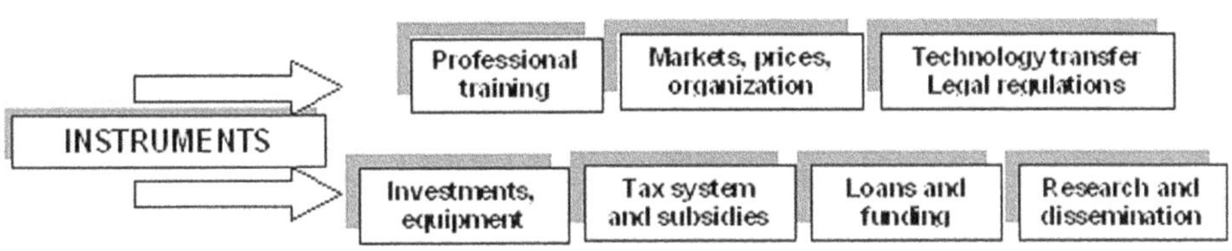

- **Support Measures for the Development and Operation of Agriculture:** Input/output market, market transparency, exports support
- **Support Policies for Quality:** Their objective is to ensure that foodstuffs (local or imported) comply with accepted international standards. This involves defining standards for quality and safety, establishment and operation of control bodies which operate according to internationally accepted standards.

Another aspect of food security lies in the adequacy of food intake, which implies a permanent balance between body's physiological needs and the amount of nutrients consumed. An important fact is that not all agricultural projects that have a potential nutritional impact aim to explicit nutritional purposes. Often, the nutritional impact appears as an unplanned, indirect effect. In this case, it is not monitored within the projects, even if it exists (Bonnard, 1999).

At present, there is a strong orientation trend towards sustainable agriculture based on organic fertilizers and pest control measures derived from nature, which could constitute the key to environmental protection and to solving food problem in the same time.

The Need for Green Agriculture: Present and Perspectives

In many countries, global economic and environmental developments lie in the core of growing concerns, intensified by prolonged global crises (including energy, financial and food crises) and underscored by scientists warning about the effects of exceeding environmental limits.

In these conditions, green economy (in its various forms) has been proposed as a means of supporting sustainable development by catalyzing national policy development and international cooperation (United Nations Department of Economic and Social Affairs [UN DESA], 2012).

During the last years, these preoccupations continuously amplified, but a series of setbacks have slowed the development in this field: confusion or lack of consensus on terminology; a lack of clarity regarding specific policy measures and their integration within national priorities and objectives, a lack of experience in designing, implementing and reviewing the costs and benefits of green economy policies (UN DESA, 2012).

A series of recent publications regarding green economy or green growth show the growing interest in this approach which is regarded as a possible solution, a necessary way to go and as an integrated manner of addressing current and future local and global stringent issues. the most important contributions in the field belong to the following organizations: UNEP, UN DESA, the United Nations Conference on Trade and Development (UNCTAD), the International Labour Organisation (ILO), the World Bank, the Organisation for Economic Cooperation and Development (OECD), the Global Green Growth Institute (GGGI), the Green Economy Coalition, Stakeholder Forum, the Green Growth Leaders etc. (UN DESA, 2012).

A decisive set of discussions on the green economy held place within the United Nations Conference on Sustainable Development at Rio de Janeiro in June 2012 (also referred to as Rio+20), which covered two themes: (a) a green economy in the context of sustainable development and poverty eradication; and (b) the institutional framework for sustainable development. FAO's contribution to the Rio+20 agenda included an initiative aiming to shaping the definition and implementation of the green economy, named The Greening the Economy with Agriculture (GEA), with a particular emphasis on food security (FAO, 2012).

The "Green Economy" approach of UNEP to sustainable development is based on the need to catalyze sustained economic development through the regeneration of life-sustaining natural resources by re-focusing the global economy towards investments and expenditures in specific economic sectors, including agriculture.

Food security and nutrition as a global issue is also a major preoccupation of the Group of Twenty (G20) agenda, which turns to an integrated and sustainable "food systems" approach. In this direction, G20 actual Food Security and Nutrition Framework drafted in 2014 sets out three integrated priority objectives, as follows (G20, 2014):

1. Increase responsible investment in food systems
2. Increase incomes and quality employment in food systems
3. Increase productivity sustainably to expand the food supply

Unfortunately, agriculture itself is a part of the range of human activities that generate pollution effects of air, water and soil (Iacovoiu, 2009) due both to massive deforestation and to the use of pesticides, fertilizers and genetically modified organisms. Because of unsuitable management practices, agriculture is a significant contributor to climate change; crop and livestock production is responsible for 13.5% of global greenhouse gas emissions. Its considerable ecological impact stimulates increasing global concern.

The perspective of increasing environment degradation gradually acquired new dimensions since, in the context of increased globalization, the setting of permissive environment countries in developing countries facilitated the transfer of highly polluting activities through foreign direct investment made by developed countries (Iacovoiu, 2009).

While the Green Revolution was the right solution for the food crisis fifty years ago, FAO appreciates that today the world needs an innovative way forward that responds to actual needs, as challenges are different (FAO, 2014).

In the context of global concern for food security of recent years, the concept of sustainable agri-food development was formulated - inextricably linked to the global development process. Within this frame, food availability is derived from domestic agricultural output resulting from the use of sustainable natural resources (Webb & Rogers, 2003).

In the same line, The Committee on World Food Security (CFS) which acts as an intergovernmental body for review food security policies approved in October 2014, during its Committee on World Food Security 41st Session, the Principles for Responsible Investment in Agriculture and Food Systems, applicable to all types and sizes of agricultural investments. These principles promote sustainable and inclusive economic development, supporting the conservation and sustainable management of natural resources, diversity, innovation for safe and healthy agriculture and food systems (CFS, 2014).

The global problem of future food security rises from the challenge of feeding a population of 9 billion by 2050 (FAO, 2009; UN DESA 2011), which decisively depends on higher agricultural output.

UNEP's 2011 report, Towards a Green Economy, drafted by Green Economy Initiative in collaboration with economists and experts worldwide contains essential clarifications about greening the global economy, and consistently assist policy makers on reforms needed in order to fructify the full potential of a green economy.

The report contains relevant key messages regarding the role of sustainable agriculture in this context (UNEP, 2011), showing that actual concerns regarding the growing population, poverty, undernourishment, climate change, depletion of natural capital (deforestation, loss of biodiversity, excessive quantities of pollutants), waste and losses could be addressed by investments and policy reforms aimed at greening agriculture, which could ensure food security on a sustainable basis by providing better employment and higher nutritional levels.

In this context, in 2011, FAO also recognized that agriculture based on the intensive use of inputs for the past fifty years led to increased global food production and average per capita food consumption but also created the premises of jeopardizing future productivity by depleting natural resources of agro-ecosystems, and adding to many factors responsible for climate change. As a result, FAO proposed a new paradigm – named "Save and grow" (FAO, 2014) based on sustainable food management for obtaining of intensive crop production that is both highly productive and environmentally sustainable.

This ecosystem-based approach, suitable for small-scale producers is assimilated to a "greening of the Green Revolution" and combines traditional knowledge with modern technologies. It encourages the use of conservation agriculture, soil organic matter, water flow regulation, pollination, biocontrol of insect pests and diseases, judicious use of mineral fertilizer etc (FAO, 2014). Though, its success depends on tangible advantages for farmers – who should be compensated for generating environmental benefits – such as higher incomes, reduced costs and sustainable livelihoods.

The need for innovation in family farming is highlighted in SOFA 2014 report, which shows that over 500 million family farms manage the majority of the world's agricultural land and produce most of the world's food – thus playing a key role in ensuring global food security. The need to feed a growing global population requires solutions adapted to local conditions, providing productivity growth only through sustainable intensification (FAO, 2014), by protecting and enhancing natural resources and ecosystems.

Despite difficulties and crisis, significant achievements were made in the agricultural sector regarding the increased global crop production, opportunities for employment and livelihoods and the shift to organic farming, which proved to be economically profitable (UNEP, 2009). Research show that this new approach in the agricultural sector brought various benefits (UNEP 2009, UNEP 2011) in terms of:

- **Environmental Protection:** Sustainable farm management results in: higher soil fertility, equivalent or higher yields than conventional farming, energy efficiency, lower greenhouse gas emissions than conventional farms, higher carbon sequestration efficiency, higher levels of biodiversity as, as a long-term soil fertility and therefore healthy ecosystems;
- **Food Security:** Increased yields and productivity, sustainable jobs creation – thus supporting community development.

In order to benefit from the economic, social and environmental advantages associated to greener and sustainable agriculture, governments and businesses should follow existing investment opportunities in this field, including: storage and transport infrastructure, green processing, production, marketing and trade of green inputs (e.g. organic fertilizers, biological/ integrated pest control methods), irrigation infrastructure; loans programmes for farmers (UNEP, 2009).

This commitment towards greening agriculture requires national and international policy reforms, innovation and technology transfer (G20, 2014), backed by investment, research and capacity building (UNEP, 2011).

On the same note, in order to minimize adverse impacts of biofuels production on global food security, there is a need to intensify efforts for the development of technologies for second-generation biofuels produced from non-food biomass feedstock (UNEP, 2011).

The transition to green and more sustainable farming practices is expected to enhance agricultural production and improve the quality and quantity of food supplies (Herren, Bassi, Tan, & Binns, 2012). In terms of job creation, transitioning to a green economy is expected to create more employment – over 200 million fulltime jobs by 2050 (FAO 2012; Herren at el., 2012) – and many more over the long term across the entire food production and related systems. (Herren et al., 2012; Fan, Ringler, Nkonya, & Stein, 2012).

This shift towards more sustainable practices will require substantial changes in policy interventions:

- Fiscal measures (such as subsidies, taxes, public R&D);
- Regulatory actions (such as standards, mandates and certification procedures);
- Public and international funding, especially for interventions in developing countries, due to their limited access to financial capital and foreign exchange;
- Public information and awareness campaigns.

This shift towards green agriculture should be sustained by governments and stakeholders focus efforts in creating and maintaining the appropriate framework involving subsidies, fiscal and monetary instruments, trade measures, agricultural research, personnel training, building partnership, waste reduction, sustainable choices, health and environment requirements, institutions and entrepreneurial skills (UNEP, 2009).

Large corporations in the field will play a major role in supporting the transition to greener agriculture (UNEP, 2011), as they have the capacity to develop specific strategies and support sustainably oriented investments.

Investments in Agriculture: Under the Sign of Sustainability

The agricultural sector has an important role in the transition process to the green economy. This transition must have an ecosystem approach because the agriculture has the role:

- To ensure the right to adequate food, food and nutrition security (food availability, access, stability and utilization)

- To meliorate the quality of rural livelihoods
- To manage efficiently natural resources
- To improve resilience and equity throughout the food supply chain

At international level, there are many initiatives that focused on o sustainable agriculture and are interesting for many stakeholders implicated in this field (like states, inter-governmental and regional organizations, financing institutions, donors, foundations, research organizations, universities, smallholders, business enterprises, including farmers, civil society organizations, workers and their organizations, communities, consumer organizations):

- UNCTAD, FAO, IFAD and World Bank promote the Principles for Responsible Agricultural Investment
- The Committee on World Food Security (CFS) endorsed the Principles for Responsible Investment in Agriculture and Food Systems

In addition, FAO launched The Greening the Economy with Agriculture (GEA) Initiative. The main objective of this initiative is to increase the stability and resilience of food systems. Factors like extreme weather events, energy scarcity, economic and social disruption, malfunctioning of global markets are threats to the stability of food systems. (FAO, 2012).

The process of transition to green agriculture must take in account:

- The importance of agriculture in the national economies and the numerous stakeholders implicated
- The negative impact of agriculture on environment (loss of biodiversity and degradation of ecosystem services, depletion and erosion of top soil nutrients, an increasing scarcity of freshwater, aggravated water pollution)
- The existence of two types of agriculture:
    - Conventional/industrial agriculture that are energy-intensive, highly mechanized, has high productivity relies on the extensive use of chemical fertilizers, herbicides, pesticides, fuel, water, determined the shrinking the agricultural labor force and request continuous new investments in different types equipment and seeds
    - Traditional (subsistence) smallholder agriculture based on older farming practices and characterized by low productivity

In fact, the specialists proposed a mix of the farming practices and technologies used for the greening of agriculture inspired by these types of agriculture. The purposes of the green investments in agriculture are the increase of farm productivity, the assurance of provision of food, the generation of positive externalities, the reconstruction of ecological resources, the more efficient use of natural resources and reduction of pollution.

The transition to green agriculture (Table 4) is a complex process that implicates public and private efforts. The activity of international organizations is essential in this process because they have the role to support the national authorities and to endorse guidelines or principles that are voluntary used by private actors.

FUTURE RESEARCH DIRECTIONS

In order to ensure good nutrition, in addition to the policy of ensuring the food availability (through production, distribution, international trade) to cover the consumption needs of the whole population, there is a strong need for a policy regarding the responsible resources utilization. The more so as, in the food chain of industrialized countries, the amount of energy consumed for processing, preparation, packaging, transport, distribution and storage of food is much higher than for agricultural production itself, further research is needed in order to design and promote both new concepts on the cost and value of food consumption and calculations for determining its effectiveness.

Table 4. Potential indicators for measuring progress towards green agriculture (UNEP 2011)

Action Indicators	Outcome Indicators
number of enacted and implemented policy measures and officially approved plans that promote sustainable agriculture	percentage and amount of land under different forms of green agriculture
level of governmental support to encourage farmers to invest in conversion to green agriculture and get the farm and the product certified	decline in use of agro-chemicals as a result of conversion to green agriculture; and the number and percentage of farmers converting to green agriculture
percentage of agricultural budget that is earmarked for environmental objectives	increasing proportion of payments for environmental services as a percentage of total farm income
proportion of available producer support used for environmental objectives as a percentage of total agricultural producer support	number of agriculture extension officers trained in green agriculture practices
approved measures that reduce or eliminate barriers to trade in technologies and services needed for a transition to a green agriculture	number of enterprises set up in rural areas, especially those that produce local natural agricultural inputs, to offer off-farm employment opportunities.

As a result, the objective of food security - to ensure for all, at any time, effective access to the food they need at a reasonable cost - must be doubled by optimizing the energy and nutritious cost of food up to the final consumption stage.

Other possible direction for research aims to establish a set of indicators of food security regulation, which include eco-investment in agriculture as an administrative tool to harmonize supply and demand of agricultural products, to increase employment level and to fulfill the requirements of sustainable development at the same time.

CONCLUSION

During the last decade, several concurrent crises – including food crisis – have unfolded, putting the livelihoods of billions at risk, affecting food security and consequently human health. Current economic approach based on sustainable development requirements are closely related to the recent orientation towards green economy, which could be a new engine of growth and a strategy for the elimination of persistent poverty and food insecurity. The efforts to achieve the goals of sustainable development are huge and suppose private initiative and public actions. The stakeholders like the private companies and individuals, governments, foundations, civil society organizations, development banks, governments, research and academic institutions response individually to the challenges of greening, but collective efforts are better and synergetic.

Sustainability is a desiderate that must be achieved in agriculture field too. Taking in account the importance of this sector in some national economies, the process of greening the economy is lead by agriculture. Even in the developed countries, the promotion of green agriculture is essential because the agriculture has many negative impacts on environment like land conversion and habitat loss, wasteful water consumption, soil erosion and degradation, pollution.

Agricultural sector is the focus of national and international efforts to ensure food security, remaining the engine of development of most low-income countries. Food security is an inalienable human right, an essential component of life safety, national security, and a supreme obligation of governments. The categories facing difficulties in terms of food security can fit in a wide variety of situations or typologies:

- Countries having significant agricultural potential in terms of natural and human resources (e.g. Asia, Latin America)
- Countries with low natural potential in terms of soil quality, climate, infrastructure, institutions (e.g. Africa)

- Countries with imbalances between forms of habitat, improper nutritional status of the population in rural areas, seasonal malnutrition, harvest instability due to climate and weather conditions (e.g. drought, floods)
- Conflict and political instability as major obstacles to development;
- Outdated agrarian structures
- Inadequate agricultural policies

Solving the food security issue should be addressed in a systematic and differentiated manner, both globally and nationally by:

- Reducing malnutrition
- Demographic growth regulation
- Ensuring food availability by developing agricultural production as a matter of priority, in accordance with the natural resources available in each country, avoiding depletion of nonrenewable natural resources
- Redesigning and improving food production in developing countries by industrialization, changing agricultural structures and introduction of green technologies and techniques that would simultaneously solve the problem of unemployment, increasing population incomes and purchasing power
- Obtaining clean and safe food, reducing food overconsumption and excess and malnutrition in industrialized countries, as it calls forth severe health implications of some categories of population
- Saving food resources, reducing costs and wastage, better utilization of resources in the food chain from the farm to the final consumer, in order to get affordable products with high nutritional value

Food access and use directly depends on the purchasing power of the population – which can be increased by creating jobs through investment policies that help reducing unemployment, increase income, thus enabling effective acquiring of necessary livelihood.

Emergency aid or imports do not provide a reliable basis for reducing the frequency and scale of food crises, so this doesn't provide a solution for sustainable agricultural development in poor countries to improve food consumption for the starving population.

Thus, the goal to ensure food security requires the reconsideration of the importance of agriculture by promoting its strategic role of utmost importance to the overall success of food policies. In this respect, it is necessary to establish several strategies to foster green investments directed towards specific areas like:

- Small farms production or farms that use extensive workforce
- Raising agricultural productivity
- Encouraging local processing of raw materials
- Enriching food resources by reconsidering certain plant and animal species

Addressing the food-population equation cannot occur by chance but by economic and social restructuring measures of agriculture in developing countries and by the systematic support of the international community, particularly through the facilities of green investment and technology transfer.

To ensure food security in the decades ahead, the focus will be on developing specific food security programs in each country, which will include orientation towards green agriculture and attracting the necessary investments in this area.

At present, agriculture stands as a key sector for greening economies, having a high potential to generate trade opportunities while contributing to the transition to a green economy. Food security and sustainable agriculture are placed at the center of the green economy and represent top priorities for many international meetings (e.g. Rio 20+).

In agriculture field, a new challenge is the production of the biofuels. The problem is that the land, the water and other resources are not used to produce foods. So, the food security could be affected. Because of that, the public authorities must have correlate the food security policy and biofuel policy and the main priority should be food security and the right to food. Taking in account the efforts made at international level to promote social responsibility in agriculture sector, the Principles for Responsible Investment in Agriculture and Food Systems should be implemented and monitored in the case of investments for biofuel production. The implications of foreign investors in the land acquisitions in developing countries raise an additional problem. The purchases of lands, often characterized as "land grabs", have implications on the local agricultural production and on the availability of foods for the local population.

REFERENCES

Andrei, J. V. (2013). Multifunctional Agriculture and the Green Economy. In I. Subic & D. Dusmanescu (Eds.), *Sustainable Technologies, Policies, and Constraints in the Green Economy*. doi:0.4018/978-1-4666-4098-6

Bonnard, P. (1999). *Increasing the Nutritional Impact of Agricultural Interventions*. Presented in The Greater Horn of Africa Regional Workshop: Agricultural Policy, Resource Access and Human Nutrition, Ethiopia. Retrieved from http://www.eldis.org/vfile/upload/1/document/0708/DOC7724.pdf

Bulgaru, M. (1996). *Dreptul de a mânca- Disparităţi mondiale si realităti româneşti*. Bucharest: Economic Publishing House.

Carayannis, E. G., & Campbell, D. F. (2009). Mode 3andQuadruple Helix: Toward a 21st century fractal innovation ecosystem. *International Journal of Technology Management*, *46*(3-4), 201–234. doi:10.1504/IJTM.2009.023374

Chivu, L. (2002). *Competitivitatea în agricultură – analize şi comparaţii europene*. Bucharest: Expert Publishing House.

Committee on World Food Security. (2014). *Global Strategic Framework for Food Security & Nutrition* (3rd ed.). Retrieved from http://www.fao.org/cfs/cfs-home/global-strategic-framework/en/

Committee on World Food Security. (2014). *Principles for Responsible Investment in Agriculture and Food Systems*. International Agreement on Responsible Investment in Agriculture and Food Systems. Retrieved from http://www.fao.org/cfs/cfs-home-old/resaginv/en/

European Commission. (2014). *Action Plan for the future of Organic Production in the European Union*. COM(2014) 179 final. Author.

Eurostat. (2015). *Sustainable development in the European Union – 2015 monitoring report of the EU Sustainable Development Strategy*. Luxembourg: Publications Office of the European Union.

Fan, S., Ringler, C., Nkonya, E., & Stein, A. J. (2012). *Ensuring Food and Nutrition Security in a Green Economy*. IFPRI Policy Brief 21. Retrieved from http://www.ifpri.org/publication/ensuring-food-and-nutrition-security-green-economy

FAO Statistical Pocketbook. (2015). *Food and Agriculture Organization of the United Nations, Rome*. Retrieved from www.fao.org/3/a-i4691e.pdf

Food and Agriculture Organization of the United Nations. (2009). *Investing in food security*. Rome: FAO. Retrieved from https://www.responsibleagroinvestment.org/sites/responsibleagroinvestment.org/files/FAO_Investing%20in%20FS_2009.pdf

Food and Agriculture Organization of the United Nations. (2012). *Greening the Economy with Agriculture*. Swiss Confederation, FAO. Retrieved from www.fao.org/docrep/015/i2745e/i2745e00.pdf

Food and Agriculture Organization of the United Nations, International Fund for Agricultural Development, & United Nations World Food Programme. (2014). *The State of Food Insecurity in the World 2014. Strengthening the enabling environment for food security and nutrition.* Rome: FAO. Retrieved from http://www.fao.org/3/a-i4030e.pdf

Food and Agriculture Organization of the United Nations. (2014). *The State of Food and Agriculture 2014*. Rome: FAO. Retrieved from http://www.fao.org/3/a-i4036e.pdf

Food and Agriculture Organization of the United Nations, International Fund for Agricultural Development, & United Nations World Food Programme. (2015). *The State of Food Insecurity in the World 2015. Meeting the 2015 international hunger targets: taking stock of uneven progress.* Rome: FAO. Retrieved from http://www.fao.org/3/a-i4646e.pdf

Food and Agriculture Organization of the United Nations & United Nations World Food Programme. (2009). *The State of Food Insecurity in the World 2009, Econmic crises – impacts and lessons lerned.* Rome: FAO. Retrieved from http://www.fao.org/docrep/012/i0876e/i0876e00.htm

Gavrilescu, D., & Giurcă, D. (Eds.). (2001). Economie agroalimentară. Expert Publishing House.

Group of Twenty (G20). (2014). *Food Security and Nutrition Framework*. Retrieved from https://g20.org/wp-content/uploads/2014/12/g20_food_security_nutrition_framework.pdf

Herren, H. R., Bassi, A. M., Tan, Z., & Binns, W. P. (2012). *Green Jobs for a Revitalized Food and Agriculture Sector*. Natural Resources Management and Environment Department, FAO. Retrieved from http://www.fao.org/fileadmin/user_upload/suistainability/pdf/FAO_green_jobs_paper_March_31.pdf. http://ec.europa.eu/eurostathttp://faostat3.fao.org/

Iacovoiu, V. (2009). *Investiţiile străine directe între teorie şi practică economică. Analize comparative*. Bucharest: ASE Publishing House.

Jukes, M., McGuire, J., Method, F., & Sternberg, R. (2002). Nutrition and Education. In *Nutrition: A Foundation for Development*. Geneva: ACC/SCN. Retrieved from http://www.unscn.org/layout/modules/resources/files/Brief1-12EN.pdf

Organisation for Economic Co-operation and Development. (2011). *Towards Green Growth, OECD Green Growth Studies*. Paris: OECD Publishing; doi:10.1787/9789264111318-en

Organisation for Economic Co-operation and Development. (2014). *Green Growth Indicators 2014, OECD Green Growth Studies*. OECD Publishing.

Stancu, A. (2015). An Analysis of the Relation Between Wine Consumption and Cultural Models. *Economics of Agriculture*, *62*(1), 207-227. Retrieved from http://www.ea.bg.ac.rs/index.php/home/2-uncategorised/39-archive-2015-1

United Nations. (2000). *Millennium Development Declaration, Resolution No. 55/2*. Retrieved from http://www.un.org/millennium/declaration/ares552e.htm

United Nations. (2015). *The Millennium Development Goals Report*. Retrieved from http://www.un.org/millenniumgoals/reports.shtml

United Nations Department of Economic and Social Affairs. (2011). *World Population Prospects: The 2010 Revision*. Retrieved from https://dl.vecnet.org/files/xs55mc11m

United Nations Department of Economic and Social Affairs. (2012). *A guidebook to the Green Economy*. Retrieved from www.uncsd2012.org

United Nations Department of Economic and Social Affairs, United Nations Development Programme, United Nations Conference on Trade and Development. (2012). *The Transition to a Green Economy: Benefits, Challenges and Risks from a Sustainable Development Perspective*. Retrieved from http://www.unep.org/greeneconomy/Portals/88/documents/research_products/UN-DESA,%20UNCTAD%20Transition%20GE.pdf

United Nations Development Programme. (2002). *Millennium Development Goals: Goals and Indicators*. UNDP. Retrieved from http://mdgs.un.org/unsd/mdg/host.aspx?Content=indicators/officiallist.htm

United Nations Economic and Social Council, Economic Commission for Europe (UNECE). (2011). *A green economy in the context of sustainable development and poverty eradication*. Retrieved from http://www.unece.org/fileadmin/DAM/env/documents/2011/ece/e.ece.rpm.2011.4.e.pdf

United Nations Environment Programme. (2009). *Agriculture: A Catalyst for Transitioning to a Green Economy: A UNEP Brief*. Retrieved from www. unep.org/greeneconomy

United Nations Environment Programme. (2011). *Green Economy. Agriculture. Investing in natural capital.* Retrieved from http://www.unep.org/greeneconomy/Portals/88/documents/ger/2.0_Agriculture.pdf

United Nations Environment Programme. (2011). *Towards a Green Economy: Pathways to Sustainable Development and Poverty Eradication.* Retrieved from www.unep.org/greeneconomy

United Nations Environment Programme. (2013). *Green Economy and Trade. Agriculture.* Retrieved from http://www.unep.org/greeneconomy/portals/88/getreport/pdf/chapitre%202%20agriculture.pdf

United States Agency for International Development. (1992). *Policy Determination, Definition of food security.* USAID. Retrieved from http://pdf.usaid.gov/pdf_docs/Pnaav468.pdf

Webb, P., & Rogers, B. (2003). *Adressing the "in" in Food Security.* USAID Office of Food for Peace, Occasional Paper no.1. Retrieved from http://www.fantaproject.org/focus-areas/food-security/addressing-in-food-insecurity-ffp-op1

World Food Summit. (1996). *Declaration on World Food Security.* Retrieved from http://www.fao.org/docrep/003/w3613e/w3613e00.htm

World Health Organization. (2015). *Food Security.* Retrieved from http://www.who.int/trade/glossary/story028/en/

ADDITIONAL READING

Constantini, A. M., Cannella, C., & Tomassi, G. (1999). *Fondamenti di Nutrizione Umana.* Roma: Il Pensiero Scientifico.

Federal Ministry of Food and Agriculture (BMEL). (2015), *Global Forum for Food and Agriculture, Summary of Results.* Retrieved from http://www.bmel.de/EN/Agriculture/Global-Food-Situation-FAO/_Texte/GFFA-2015.html

Fidanza, F. (Coord.). (1996). Alimentazione e Nutrizione Umana: Alimente: caratteristiche nutrizionali, analisi, controllo, Napoli: Idelson.

Fidanza, F., & Liguori, G. (1995). *Nutrizione Umana.* Napoli: Idelson.

Food and Agriculture Organization of the United Nations. (2015). *The State of Food and Agriculture 2015*, Rome, FAO. Retrieved from http://www.fao.org/3/a-i4953e.pdf

Lipper, L. (2014). *Stability of food security in a green economy environment*, presentation at FAO/OECD Expert Meeting on Greening the Economy with Agriculture, Paris, 5 – 7 September 2011. Retrieved from http://www.fao.org/fileadmin/user_upload/suistainability/Presentations/Stability.pdf

Naqvi, A. (2011). *Informal seminar for FAO permanent representations*, UNEP - Green Economy Team, Green Economy and Agriculture, Rome, 4 November. Retrieved from http://www.fao.org/fileadmin/user_upload/suistainability/Presentations/Naqvi.pdf

Sirbu, R. M., Draghici, A., Lobont, O. R., & Sirbu, A. (2015). *Debate on the decision making process for green investments in sustainable development context*, MakeLearn & TIIM 2015, Bari, Italy; 05/2015, pp. 1187-1194. Retrieved from http://www.toknowpress.net/ISBN/978-961-6914-13-0/MakeLearn2015.pdf

Zahiu, L. (1999). Funcţia alimentară a agriculturii, in Tribuna Economică, n0. 12/24 Mar.

KEY TERMS AND DEFINITIONS

Carbon Sequestration: Capturing anthropogenic or atmosphere carbon dioxide (CO2) before it is released to the atmosphere.

Food Insecurity: Lack of secure access to sufficient amounts of safe and nutritious food for a normal and healthy life.

Food Intake: An amount of food taken into the body as nourishment.

Greenhouse Gas: Gases whose absorption of solar radiation is responsible for the greenhouse effect.

Undernourishment: A state of inability to acquire enough food resulting in insufficient food intake to meet dietary energy requirements.

Chapter 8
Sustainable Development in Manufacturing Systems

Farnaz Ghazi Nezami
Kettering University, USA

Ali Ghazinezami
Wichita State University, USA

Krishna K. Krishnan
Wichita State University, USA

ABSTRACT

This chapter discusses sustainable development (SD) planning in manufacturing facilities. The industrial sector uses half of the world's energy, and manufacturing, as the core of this sector, contributes significantly to energy consumption and environmental footprints. In this chapter, in the first step, energy consumption, as one of the main factors influencing SD in manufacturing, is analyzed from different perspectives, and its impact on SD is studied. Thereafter, several energy-aware operations management approaches are proposed. These approaches integrate energy consumption into classic production planning and scheduling decisions. In the second step, a generic sustainability-based decision-making framework is proposed for maintenance strategy selection problem, considering three pillars of sustainability. For this purpose, various indicators are proposed for each sustainability factor that has an impact on maintenance planning decisions. The maintenance strategy alternatives are evaluated for each indicator and the best alternative is selected using a decision-making method.

DOI: 10.4018/978-1-5225-2081-8.ch008

INTRODUCTION

This chapter studies sustainable development planning in manufacturing systems from different perspectives. Brundtland et al. (1987) defines a sustainable development (SD) plan as one that satisfies the needs of the current generation without compromising the needs of future. Today, human/corporation activities have an extensive impact on the environment, and these influences are mostly long term. Sustainable development planning places more responsibility on corporations for the effects of their activities on the society and environment. A general misconception occurs when sustainability is considered solely as a set of environmental factors. However, environmental issues constitute one dimension of the sustainability framework. A sustainable development plan is based on three "P"s of People, Planet, and Profit, and a balance must be attained among them. Efforts to preserve the environment must yield benefits from economic and societal perspectives as well to ensure the achievement of sustainability goals (Jayal et al., 2010).

Manufacturing can contribute to SD by designing products and establishing processes which are more environmentally-friendly and are accompanied by social interest and support (Jasiulewicz-Kaczmarek & Drozyner, 2011). Energy as a catalyst of development (Mohamed & Lee, 2006) is an indispensable factor in sustainable development of societies and manufacturing facilities. In addition, energy consumption is one of the key criteria in life-cycle assessment (LCA) studies. Usually, there is not enough information about energy usage during the manufacturing phase in the LCA studies, and various assumptions must be made (Seow & Rahimifard, 2011). This fact, along with the scarcity of natural non-renewable resources, environmental concerns, new restrictive regulations, the increasing price of energy and the growth of society's awareness about environmentally friendly products, persuade manufacturing facilities to monitor their material and energy consumption and seek sustainable solutions. Financial savings and societal benefits associated with green policies are the other motivations for sustainability-based efforts in most organizations.

In spite of technological advancement, the global need for energy will grow by 37% in 2040 (International Energy Agency a), in line with the growth of the population. Therefore, analyzing energy consumption, and integrating sustainability criteria into various level decision-making problems for sustainable development purposes is critical. This chapter studies these concerns in manufacturing systems.

BACKGROUND: SUSTAINABIE MANUFACTURING SYSTEMS

The industrial sector, consuming approximately half of the world's energy, is the largest consumer of energy (U.S. Energy Information Administartion). Energy consumption in this sector will increase by 0.7% per year through 2040 (U.S. Energy Information Administartion). Meanwhile, the energy usage mix in this sector will remain stable, with coal and oil being the dominant sources of fuel. Over the same period, the worldwide demand for coal is expected to increase by 15% (International Energy Agency a). Consequently, given the energy mix and the growth in demand, especially in developing countries, more energy will need to be generated, which in turn, will lead to more CO_2 emissions and other environmental pollution, as well as resource depletion. Manufacturing is the core of the industrial sector, and a significant number of studies have been conducted to address different aspects of environmentally conscious manufacturing systems, aimed at minimizing energy and material usage. Nonetheless, there is no unique definition for sustainable manufacturing. Among the proposed definitions, the most comprehensive one is proposed by the U.S. Department of Commerce:

Sustainable manufacturing is defined as the creation of manufactured products that use processes that minimize negative environmental impacts, conserve energy and natural resources, are safe for employees, communities, and consumers and are economically sound.

This definition suggests that environment is a key factor in sustainable manufacturing systems, but not the only criterion to consider while pursuing a sustainable development plan.

In sustainable corporations, a conservative environmental mindset should be integrated into business strategies as well as the political, social and economic decisions. It also incorporates people's participation and support in planning and executing activities (Elkington, 1994). Generally, in corporations the decisions are made at three levels: strategic, tactical and operational (Bryson, 2011; Griffin, 2013; Lussier, 2011): Strategic decisions are leadership and managerial resolutions that define long-range plans which the organization needs to deploy in order to achieve the predetermined missions. On the contrary, operational decisions are short-term plans that address the details of activities on a daily basis. Tactical decisions are medium-term decisions that support strategic decisions by translating them into functional plans in each specific domain for the lower levels. In a company pursuing SD, sustainability-based goals and general directions first need to be determined at a strategic level in order to be integrated into the lower-level daily operations.

Achieving sustainable development does not necessarily require significant investments. This fact is of great importance because SD planning costs are a major concern for small to medium corporations (Isaksson & Garvare, 2003). As stated above, regardless of the size of the company, sustainability is a mindset which can be built into the management system of the corporation (Isaksson & Garvare, 2003) in order to yield sustainable solutions. However, measuring the level of achievement of these goals is challenging for most corporations.

Sustainable development plans usually lead to significant savings in manufacturing facilities. The savings are obtained by deploying technological advancements (technological solution), and/or non-technical remedies, such as controlling and updating the existing processes (Seow & Rahimifard, 2011). This chapter analyses SD in the manufacturing setting via deploying the non-technological approach. The first (technological) approach mostly requires significant initial investments and has a longer payback period. Using new more energy efficient equipment is an example of the technological approach. The second (non-technological) approach, however, is usually more desirable for corporations due to lower implementation costs. Acquiring detailed information about energy profiles of individual machineries during different operating modes and developing energy efficient operating schedules are the foundation of the second approach. As a result of both practices, not only do the material and energy requirements and negative environmental footprints decrease, but also the operating expenses are reduced.

MAIN FOCUS OF THE CHAPTER

This chapter proposes business strategies and solutions to assist manufacturing systems in sustainable development planning. These non-technological ideas must be incorporated while modelling energy-aware manufacturing systems. The following constitutes two main contributions of this chapter:

1. In the first research direction, the manufacturing machine's energy consumption profile, as a key enabler in SD, is analyzed, and then the energy-aware operations management policies are proposed. This approach is concerned about the environmental and economic pillar of sustainability and examines the integration of energy management efforts into operational- and tactical-level decisions. For this purpose, initially the manufacturing energy consumption is studied from different perspectives. Then several sub-scenarios are designed in an energy-aware production system where the integration of energy consumption concept can influence production planning (medium term) and scheduling (short term) decisions. Examples of these decisions include a production plan, machine operating schedule, and efficient batch-size determination. Energy consumption and waste costs are usually ignored in most of the classic production planning and scheduling problems (Nezami et al., 2012; Yildirim &

Nezami, 2014). In this chapter, the significance of this inclusion for designing an effective sustainable system will be discussed. The consequences of this approach on a company's operational plans, profits and savings, and progress toward SD will also be described.

2. The second contribution introduces a sustainability-based decision-making framework. In this research direction, a sustainability-based framework is presented to select the best maintenance strategy. Selecting the most appropriate maintenance strategy for a manufacturing facility pursuing SD is a complex strategic/tactical multiple-criteria decision-making problem because this process requires simultaneous consideration of economic and technical, environmental and societal criteria, along with the decision makers' input. In this setting, the alternatives are the possible maintenance policies, and the decision criteria are various sustainability-based criteria. For this purpose, initially a list of indicators (criteria) is proposed to measure each sustainability factor. In the next step, the role of each criterion in comparative analyses of the alternatives is discussed. In the last step, any multiple-criteria decision making technique can be utilized to select the best maintenance policy with respect to the decision makers' input.

Because of the two presented scenarios in this chapter, the mutual relationship between sustainability criteria in each of the three categories of economy, society and environment, and operational and tactical planning decisions will be investigated. Decreased operating cost, reduced material and energy consumption, lower negative environmental impacts, and improved system efficiency and work satisfaction level are examples of the expected benefits, which are measurable and can be used to assess the level of achievement of sustainable development. Environmental, societal and financial metrics empower the corporations to measure their growth in each area and assess the effectiveness of their efforts towards sustainability. This growth impacts the corporation's opportunities in competitive markets.

ENERGY-AWARE MANUFACTURING SYSTEMS

Energy consumption in manufacturing facilities can be analyzed at upper or lower levels. Figure 1 presents the energy analysis breakdown:

At the upper level (plant level), the entire enterprise is being evaluated to quantify material and energy consumption and identify sources of waste for manufacturing and non-manufacturing supporting activities. This type of industrial assessment

Figure 1. Energy consumption in manufacturing is analyzed at different levels

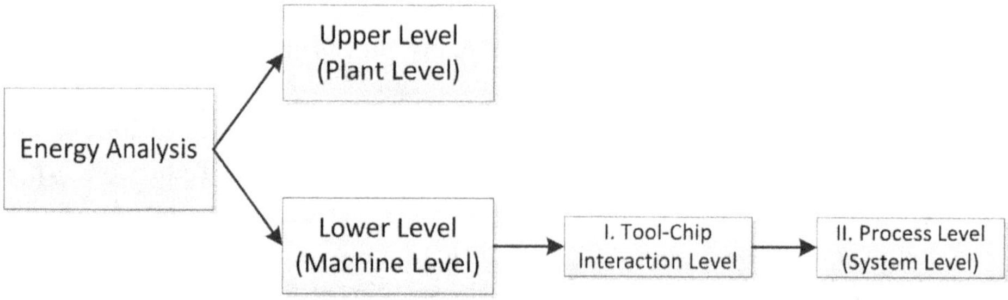

utilizes energy management systems (EMS) to monitor the manufacturing and supporting activities, and can help manufacturing facilities reduce their material and energy consumption and waste. When the sources of waste are identified, the companies seek corrective recommendations which can help them save money and be environmentally and economically sustainable. The cost of the corrective proposals varies: sometimes the recommendations might be costly to be implemented and in some situations are very cheap, or even free of cost. Increasing the insulations of walls, roofs and windows, exchanging the HVAC units with new more efficient systems, or upgrading the lighting systems (light bulbs and blasts) with more energy-efficient ones, and establishing waste heat-recovery systems are examples of high-cost recommendations with large payback periods. Decreasing the pressure of air compressors to the minimum required level, night setback during non-working hours, changing the workload model or developing standard work to perform a process, or turning off the machines during idle periods are examples of almost free-of-charge recommendations with immediate payback duration. Meanwhile, there are other corrective actions for which the cost of implementation and payback period are medium. Installing occupancy sensors or variable frequency drives are instances of medium-cost recommendations. It is worth mentioning that the implementation cost of any of the corrective actions depends significantly on the size of the facility and the availability of their resources. Once the recommendations are implemented, the corporations can measure the amount of energy and material they could save. Considering the savings and the implementations costs help the corporations determine their returns on the investments and assess their environmental and economic growth.

At lower-level (machine level) energy analysis, the tool-chip interaction and manufacturing processes are studied. The tool-tip interaction addresses energy consumption from an individual machine/operation standpoint (Vijayaraghavan & Dornfeld, 2010), whereas the processing energy analysis considers power consumption from a product perspective for a sequence of operations on one or several machines with respect to a production schedule. In other words, the processing approach is more systematic, while the tool-tip interaction is following an individual approach.

Energy Consumption at Tool-Chip Interaction Level

As described above, the tool-chip interaction targets an individual manufacturing operation on a single machine. There are several studies that address energy consumption at this level, showing that not all the amount of the consumed power on a machine during manufacturing operations goes to actual manufacturing activities. For example, Gutowski et al. (2005, 2006) showed that in a machining process, 15% of the total amount of energy is devoted to actual machining process and the rest is consumed for running background processes, even during the idle period.

At the single-machine level of energy consumption characterization, typically it is observed that 43% of the machine energy consumption is due to the base load consumption (Abele et al., 2012), and the rest occurs because of the actual manufacturing process on the machine. The base load (i.e., tare power) is the sum of constant and variable power, where the constant load occurs because of running auxiliary components, and variable power refers to power consumption by the components that require a constant load but may not be used for all manufacturing operations on the machine (Helu et al., 2011). Seow and Rahimifard (2011) provided a similar energy breakdown to control and calculate the energy usage per unit of product more accurately. In their study, initially energy consumption in manufacturing activities is categorized into "direct" and "indirect energy" (DE and IE). The direct energy covers manufacturing activities and indirect energy addresses the physical environment in which the production occurs. They also divided "direct" energy into "theoretical" and "auxiliary" categories. "Theoretical energy" (TE) is the amount of energy used for the actual manufacturing processes and "auxiliary" energy (AE) is more like the tare power consumption described earlier and might be used even when machine is running idle.

Once manufacturing facilities determine whether their dominant power demand is due to auxiliary or theoretical energy for running actual manufacturing process, they can propose appropriate strategies to minimize their energy consumption and waste. At this level (tool-chip interaction), operation time-reduction techniques and the incorporation of new technologies into an existing machine, such as retrofitting a current machine or replacing it with new efficient machinery, are some of the methods being used to reduce the machine's energy consumption (Duflou et al., 2012; Apostolos et al., 2013).

The energy profile characterization of a machine can help the experts determine a more efficient maintenance plan with respect to historical power usage data. In other words, the energy consumption profile can be utilized as an indicator of the need for performing preventive maintenance (Yildirim & Nezami, 2014); any increase in power draw in comparison to similar processing conditions notifies the experts about the necessity of preventive maintenance implementation, as the machine is not working as expected.

From an economic perspective, energy analysis at the machine level allows the managers to calculate the energy consumption amount and measure the environmental footprints to produce one unit of throughput on each individual machine more accurately. In order to determine the energy usage per unit of production, total IE used in the production area is divided by the total number of parts produced in that area and will be added to the TE and AE values. The AE consumption can be calculated using equipment manufacturer specifications, or it can be measured separately, and TE is monitored and recorded while performing actual manufacturing processes such as casting or machining.

Using the above energy categories, various measures might be obtained for energy efficiency ratios. At the plant level, energy efficiency might be obtained by

$$\sum \frac{DE + AE}{Total\, Throughput}.$$

At the machine level, different ratios such as $\frac{TE}{AE}$ or $\frac{DE}{IE}$ can also be used to identify the machines which are more energy efficient.

Investigating machineries individually from a detached perspective is a necessary step in order to propose a green manufacturing system, as the combinations of these pieces of equipment and machines collectively define the manufacturing system.

Energy Consumption at Process Level

Energy analysis at tool-chip level ignores the interaction of the machine with the rest of the system and the production plan. The production plan and demand arrival schedule have an impact on the working condition and parameter settings of the machine. Therefore, there is a significant need to expand the focus of energy consumption analysis in manufacturing from an individual machine perspective (tip-tool interaction) to a systematic scale. The knowledge obtained in the tool-chip level is utilized as a key input into the process level. At process level, using machine energy profile data, the processing order of the jobs (products) and machine working modes, such as "idle," "switching," or "processing," can be optimized via a new energy-aware production schedule. The energy-aware scheduling system influences total energy consumption, including energy waste, as well as the production planning and scheduling performance measures (Nezami et al., 2012; Yildirim & Mouzon, 2012).

Determining the product processing sequence and machine operating schedule are short-term operational-level decisions. The individual- and system-level energy analyses have reciprocal impacts: the individual machine power usage characterization provides the required information to come up with an energy-efficient production schedule at the system level. On the other hand, the environmentally benign production schedule has an impact on the operating condition of individual machines and the associated energy consumption at the tool-chip level.

Defining energy productivity as the ratio of total input energy/total throughput enhances the attention on the total energy consumption including energy waste. In a production system, a significant amount of energy is used when a machine is in idle mode, which means the machine is running with no value-added activity being performed. It implies the need for an effective energy-efficient production schedule in order to minimize machine idle time and energy waste. Another concern which most of the manufacturing facilities with high energy requirements are dealing with is energy demand, which is of significant importance from a financial perspective. In a parallel machine setting, when several machines are running simultaneously, there will be a peak in power demand, which imposes extra costs to the companies. The energy-aware production schedule plays a key role in managing the energy demand and reducing the associated charges.

ENERGY-AWARE OPERATIONS MANAGEMENT

This section provides examples of incorporating energy-aware approaches into classic production planning and scheduling problems and investigates the potential benefits of each case.

Energy-Aware Production Scheduling

In classic production scheduling systems, the jobs processing sequences are being optimized in order to minimize common performance criteria such as makespan, total completion time, or tardiness. These studies simply do not consider various machine operating modes and their impact on sustainability. However, learning about the energy consumption profile and other machine characteristics, such as reliability parameters during different running modes, can influence the jobs (products) processing order and machine operating schedule. Significant energy is being consumed during machine idle time and in switch mode (when the machine is switching between different operating modes), whereas common job-scheduling problems ignore energy consumption during these modes. Turning off the machine or switching to low-energy consumption mode during the idle period has been considered as an energy-saving method in several studies (Chen et al., 2013; Yildirim & Mouzon, 2012), as well as the industrial assessment database reports (IAC). However, when the machine is switching between modes, there will be a spike in power draw which can have an impact on energy consumption, energy demand, and system reliability (Kim, 2007; Seow & Rahimifard, 2011).

Failure probability in most of the machines during the switch is higher than the processing duration, which, in turn, is larger than the value in the idle mode. Figure 2 illustrates three potential operational planning decisions for a sample two-job problem such that job 1 is ready at time 0 with 5 units of time for processing, and job 2 will be ready at time 7 with 8 time units to be processed: Scenario 1 postpones job1 processing to prevent any idle time, but it increases total completion time (22 units). In the last two scenarios, job 1 is started on time to ensure that the minimum total completion time is achieved (20 units in both cases), but in scenario 2, the machine is running idle during the interarrival period to prevent undesirable power spikes and reliability issues, at the cost of waste in energy. In the last scenario, the machine is turned off to save the idle energy; however, it imposes more risk to

Figure 2. Energy consumption can have an impact on operational decisions

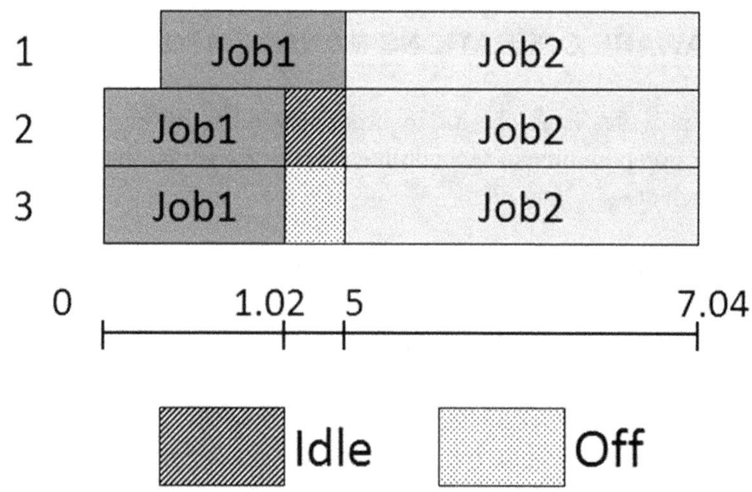

machine reliability in comparison to the previous scenarios. As a result, a trade-off should be achieved between energy, reliability, and total completion time. To combat this problem, an appropriate breakeven duration should be determined as explained in the next section.

Breakeven Duration Concept

One of the intermediate concepts introduced in the literature to link energy characterization at the machine level to the process/system level is the "breakeven duration" (Mouzon et al., 2007; Nezami et al., 2012; Yildirim & Mouzon, 2012). Breakeven duration determines the minimum allowable time for which the machine can be turned off or switched to a low-energy-consumption mode. This concept is a function of machine specifications, such as power consumption data and reliability parameters during the idle, switch, and processing modes, as well as the switch and warm-up duration of the machine. The breakeven period is the output of the "tool-chip-level energy analysis" phase, and is an input into the system-level analysis phase. Once the breakeven duration is calculated for a machine, it is compared with the interarrival time between two consecutive products' arrival for processing. If the interarrival period is greater than the breakeven duration, the machine can be turned off (or switched to low-energy consuming mode) instead of running idle when there is no production.

If inter-arrival time ≥ breakeven duration
Then Turn off (switch to energy saving mode)
Else Run the machine idle

This practice results in some energy savings and preserves machine's reliability which leads to more financial savings as well.

Peak Power Management in Sustainable Production Systems

Electricity is the second dominant type of energy and the industrial sector constitutes 42.3% of the total amount of electricity in the world (International Energy Agency b). Based on the Energy Information Administration, the price of electricity is expected to increase by 27% from 2011 to 2035, from the average of 8.6 cents per kilo-watt hour (kWh) to 10.9 cents per kWh. The increasing price provides an additional motivation for implementing energy management approaches. Time-of-Use (TOU) pricing is one of the energy management methods deployed by utility companies and is aiming at shifting the demand from the expensive peak periods to less-expensive non-peak hours to flatten the load curve and decrease the deficit risks in energy supply.

The electricity consumption data are monitored by distribution companies based on the real time data, and industrial facilities are charged for their electricity demand as well as the actual amount of energy consumed. While many contractual agreements exist between manufacturing companies and electricity distribution facilities for pricing, electricity charges generally can be categorized as two types: consumption charge and demand charge. Consumption charges are calculated according to the total electrical energy consumed by a company during a given period based on Kilowatt-hour. These charges, which include energy production expenses, may vary throughout a day to motivate shift of consumption away from peak hours. Demand charges address the overhead expenses that utility companies bear to provide the service. Energy demand charges are based on the highest energy level demanded over a given period of time during the billing period and are usually calculated as the highest "average fifteen-minute demand" for a month. Energy demand is measured in kilowatts (kW) and often represents a significant percentage of charges on utility bills for industrial users. Adjusting the production schedule with respect to energy prices, determining the number of energy-intensive equipment which can be running in parallel, and deciding on the simultaneous switches to bring the machines to processing mode are all examples of decisions that can be affected by energy demand charges considerations. The integration of TOU polices into operations management can also have a significant impact on job-machine assignments and job-processing orders, and affects energy consumption at the system level.

Therefore, it can be concluded that the integration of energy demand and consumption charges can impact operational planning decisions in manufacturing extensively.

Integrated Production-Maintenance Planning Problem

Maintenance and production are conflicting objectives, and simultaneous planning of these activities requires significant efforts. Frequent maintenance reduces machine availability for production, and lack of enough maintenance increases the risk of machine breakdown. Frequent machine failure leads to significant repair costs and production loss costs.

For integrating maintenance into production planning, a critical piece of information is the products' processing duration, which is mostly assumed to be fixed and independent of machine-health status. In this integrated problem, the objective is to minimize the overall costs of the system, including the costs of production, inventory, setup, energy, maintenance, and repair.

Maintenance has a tight connection with sustainability because when a machine degrades, it may result in safety and environmental issues, production loss, and non-conforming products, all of which contribute to reduction in profit. In some cases, like cutting tools, machine or fixture degradation may prolong processing time. Defining energy as "power consumption x duration of the activity", it can be concluded that in these scenarios, by prolonging the process duration, more energy is being consumed to obtain the same throughput. Therefore, monitoring energy consumption, as discussed earlier, can be used as an indirect indicator of maintenance planning. To bridge the gap between maintenance and production planning, a helpful assumption is to define process duration as a function of maintenance and machine-health status as explained by (Yildirim & Nezami, 2014) such that:

$$l_{jt} = u_j \, y_{t-1} + (1 - y_{t-1})(1 + \theta) l_{jt-1} \qquad \forall t = 2, ..., T, \forall j = 1, ..., n, \tag{1}$$

where *j* and *t* represent product and period simultaneously. Products processing times in the first period, when the machine is working in normal condition, u_j, are known, and y_t is the maintenance indicator at the end of period *t*. Based on this equation, if preventive maintenance is not performed at the end of the previous period ($y_{t-1} = 0$), then the time to process products increases by a constant percentage (θ), and total energy consumption and its associated costs increase accordingly. However, if maintenance is performed ($y_{t-1} = 1$), the processing times will be the same as that of the first period. Once the process duration is determined, the problem will be a classic production planning model that includes maintenance cost and time.

As a result, in this approach, it can also be concluded that maintenance and sustainability are interrelated concepts, such that maintenance impacts energy consumption and overall cost of the system and energy requirement analysis data can be used as an indicator of a maintenance activity.

SUSTAINABLE MAINTENANCE STRATEGY SELECTION PROBLEM

A sustainable development plan consolidates economic, environmental, and social criteria and has an impact on the decisions made at different levels within hierarchies. Defining appropriate metrics for each factor provides a basis for corporations to evaluate the effectiveness of their decisions. This section provides an example of integrating sustainability factors into maintenance strategy selection problem (MSSP), which is a medium- to long-term decision-making problem in manufacturing facilities. Note that, in this section, maintenance is about the inspection of manufacturing machinery and equipment and does not include buildings or supporting structure.

Maintenance constitutes 15-60% of total cost of the production systems depending on the type of industry (Mobley, 2002). Jasiulewicz-Kaczmarek and Drozyner (2011) and Nezami and Yildirim (2013) discussed the impact of maintenance actions on SD. Maintenance influences the health status of the machine and has an impact on TE and AE (direct energy) consumption. As a machine degrades over time, its energy consumption increases (Yan & Hua, 2010). Therefore, implementing an effective maintenance technique to retrieve it to its normal operating condition may result in significant savings in energy and material. There are different maintenance techniques, and determining the best policy with respect to different criteria will be a challenging task. There are many studies that address maintenance strategy selection in different settings (Mechefske & Wang, 2003; Al-Najjar & Alsyouf, 2003; Bertolini & Bevilacqua, 2006; Wang, et al., 2007; Jafari et al., 2008; Mousavi et al., 2009; Vahdani et al., 2010; Zaim et al., 2012). These studies consider various maintenance techniques and comparison criteria, but the common selection criteria in most of these studies are based on the technical and financial principles of maintenance implementations, with only a few considering environmental and societal concerns. The majority of studies provide an incomplete set of comparison criteria, and this section is aimed at proposing a comprehensive list of criteria for each sustainability pillar to be regarded in MSSP.

The advent of the sustainability concept has had an impact on this selection process by bringing new criteria into the decision-making domain. Emphasizing the role of environmental and societal factors along with economic and technical factors can alter previously made decisions about maintenance strategies. In this decision-making structure, environmental, societal, and business/technical factors are the general comparison measures, and various key criteria will be proposed for each factor. The maintenance techniques are positioned at the very bottom of this decision-making structure. Therefore, it is concluded that MSSP is a multiple-criteria decision-making (MCDM) problem, where one best alternative should be selected in the presence of several decision criteria which might be conflicting.

Maintenance Strategy Alternatives

There are different maintenance strategy alternatives of which the most common categories are briefly introduced below:

1. **Alternative I. Failure-Based (corrective) Maintenance:** In this strategy, no maintenance is planned until a failure occurs. Usually this policy is applied when the machines are low in cost and the mean time to repair is small.

2. **Alternative II. Preventive Maintenance:** In this strategy, the machine is inspected based on a predetermined schedule, cumulative production amount since last maintenance or number of operating hours to sustain the machine's health status, and detect any potential source of failure.
3. **Alternative III. Total Productive Maintenance Strategy:** This alternative utilizes the quality circles method to integrate maintenance and production and reduce their existing conflict. It requires a high level of trained-employee involvement and is aimed at minimizing various types of waste.
4. **Alternative IV. Condition-Based (predictive) Maintenance:** This strategy, which is costly to implement, utilizes sensor data such as vibration, energy usage, and ultrasonic sound level to predict the risk of machine breakdown.
5. **Alternative V. Reliability-Centered Maintenance:** The main goal of this strategy is to sustain the reliability and health state of the machine, rather than restoring it to an ideal situation, in order to minimize total cost of maintenance.

Sustainability-Based Criteria

This section introduces various criteria (indicators) for each sustainability factor, such that the effectiveness of each maintenance alternative should be assessed in satisfying the objective of each criterion. A similar framework is proposed by Nezami & Yildirim (2013); however, the framework described here is more generic.

Environmental indicators (EI):

- Eliminating toxic/undesirable emissions into air, water, and soil
- Reducing energy consumption
- Reducing non-renewable resource depletion
- Reducing solid waste production
- Reducing material waste
- Satisfying environmental standards and governmental regulations
- Adopting effective waste recapturing and recovering systems

In order to achieve environmental sustainability and measure the progress of the corporation toward this target, the corporation should plan for eliminating any toxic or undesirable pollutants to air, water, and soil. The Environmental Protection Agency (EPA) has released a list of 187 hazardous air pollutants. These emissions not only harm the environment, but also have a significant impact on people's health. Furthermore, considering energy consumption level as the key metric in SD, the ability to reduce energy requirements and substitute renewable sources for power generation is critical in being environmentally sustainable. Incorporating systems to assist in reducing solid waste, landfilling, and waste of raw material are other important criteria to consider while evaluating environmental SD. Note that a machine or equipment working in a sub-standard working state leads to more material waste or low-quality products that might be discarded. Additionally, this condition might result in higher energy consumption than expected due to several reasons: some energy might be wasted in the form of heat due to degradation, or the processing durations might take longer, and, as a result, more energy would be consumed to achieve the same level of output. Curing the composite in the furnace, one of the most important steps in composites fabrication, is one example for this scenario. The quality of the final products highly depends on how well the curing process is performed. Inappropriate vacuum sealing or any heat loss in the furnace requires the furnace to work for a longer period to maintain as constant a temperature as possible. Therefore, lack of maintenance on the furnace can lead to energy loss and low product quality, as well as waste of material.

The capability to satisfy environmental regulations set by the EPA or local governmental policies is also crucial for surviving in competitive markets, and for maintaining the company's reputation and its relationship with suppliers or customers. Integrating cost-effective creative methodologies to reduce the environmental footprints, such as CO_2 emissions recapturing systems, can also be used as another metric to assess environmental sustainability achievements. Each maintenance alternative should be judged for its effectiveness in helping the corporation accomplish any of the above environmentally-oriented goals.

Societal indicators (SI):

- Stakeholders' support and participation.
- Personnel acceptance, involvement, and communication
- Employee education and training
- Fair wage system
- Safety and health standards within and outside of the company

Success in implementing any strategy in an organization is affected by the stakeholders and the support and involvement of employees. In order to achieve this, the objectives and processes must be communicated clearly across the facility. For a successful adoption, the system needs to satisfy the technical requirements provided by the technicians and experts within the organization. In other words, one may need to ensure that there is enough training and expertise for the personnel while implementing a new maintenance strategy. Furthermore, the workload and required expertise associated with the designated strategy should be proportional to the wage/payments to the involved employees. This has a mutual impact on the corporation's attainment of SD goals, since a fair wage system can encourage the employees to work more committedly. It is apparent that maintenance polices, influencing machine degradation and operating conditions, plays a key role in determining health and safety standards. As explained earlier, a machine that is not working in a normal operating state might result in more energy consumption, more pollutant emissions, and material waste, as well as safety risks to the workers

Business indicators (BI):

- Profitability
- High-quality products
- Short lead time
- Satisfying customer expectations
- High system reliability (High system availability and uptime)
- Satisfying production schedule performance criteria
- Feasibility appraisal for proposed solutions
- System flexibility
- Innovation and creativity
- Effective risk management
- Competitive advantage
- Production variety
- Effective inventory management system

The above criteria are key metrics in defining business and economic sustainability as proposed in the literature. Being profitable is the first measure used to assess the economic status of a corporation. In this context, implementing a feasible maintenance strategy which is cost effective and has acceptable return on investment, and decreases the overall cost of repair and maintenance in the system is of prerequisites of being economically sustainable. Before adopting a maintenance strategy, a feasibility analysis should be performed thoroughly to ensure that the selected alternative is suitable from both technical and economic perspectives. In addition, an inappropriate maintenance plan decreases system reliability and the availability for production (uptime) and may lead to production-loss cost, which in turn has an impact on competitive opportunities in the business market. Moreover, unavailability for production prolongs the lead time. This fact, as well as poor product quality resulting from machine working status, can have a significant impact on the customers' satisfaction, the company's reputation, and profit. Suboptimal maintenance policy selection may also lead to significant deviations from scheduling performance measures such as makespan, tardiness, or total completion time minimization, by affecting the system uptime. Deploying an effective maintenance plan affects system flexibility and its ability to produce a variety of products, which are key performance metrics in evaluating system innovation status. The maintenance strategy dictates the level of inventory to carry for spare parts and the investment designated for spare inventory. Additionally, maintenance policy determines the system readiness to tackle expected and unexpected risks and variability.

Considering all of the above criteria in MSSP seems a critical and challenging task, especially since sometimes these criteria might be in conflict. In this MCDM problem, different maintenance alternatives should be evaluated for all 25 criteria (7 environmental, 5 social and 13 business/economic indicators) by decision makers. Figure 3 represents a sample decision-making tree based on the original sustainability criteria and five maintenance alternatives.

The decision makers can be the managers, technical staff, and stakeholders. Making decision with respect to 25 criteria is complex for human being. Therefore, one can utilize different statistical data analysis techniques, such as Factor Analysis (FA), to use the correlation between the indicators and reduce the number of involved criteria. The goal of this process is to propose a reduced decision-making tree and facilitate the decision-making process for the decision makers. Once the reduced decision-making tree is obtained, the decision maker(s) can evaluate the effectiveness of each maintenance alternative relating to the goals of each sustainability criterion. Nezami & Yildirim (2013) proposed a modified fuzzy VIKOR method for choosing the best sustainable maintenance alternative using the inputs of a group of decision makers. Other methodologies, such as the Analytical Hierarchy Process (AHP), Analytic Network Process (ANP), or TOPSIS can also be utilized for the group decision-making procedure and determining the final rankings of the alternatives.

Figure 3. Sustainability criteria impact maintenance selection process

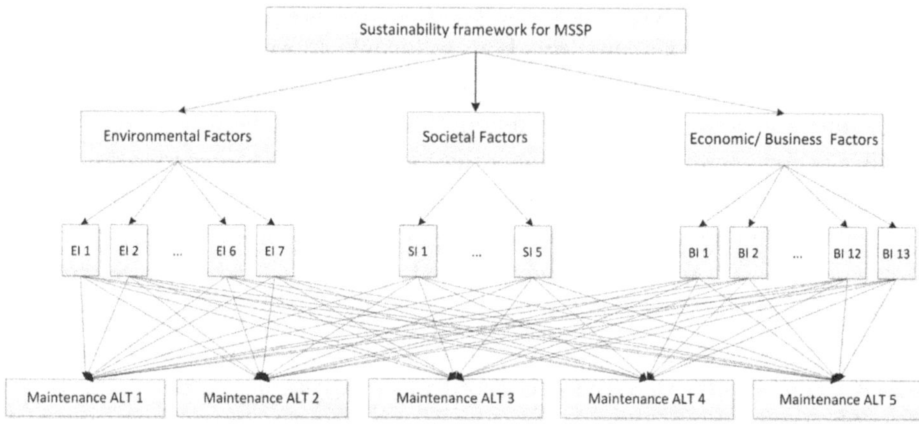

FUTURE RESEARCH DIRECTIONS

In this chapter, several approaches are proposed to enhance the operational planning and modeling of sustainable manufacturing systems. A literature survey shows a recent trend in research studies to include energy consumption and associated costs in production planning and scheduling decisions. Most of these research studies address a very narrow area by concentrating on cost minimization, including some of the energy and recycling costs. Inclusion of societal and other environmental factors rather than only energy costs into planning and scheduling decisions is not well investigated in the literature. Also, defining relevant measurable indicators for each sustainability criterion, especially for the societal factor, and integrating them into different decision-making problems in manufacturing systems is the other area of research which is not well studied.

In manufacturing, conducting experimental studies to assess the relation between green policies and the lifetime of the system might be of great benefit, as some energy-saving policies might have an adverse impact on the life of the manufacturing system components. Manufacturing and production constitute the core of the physical products supply chains. However, focusing on manufacturing will not be enough to achieve SD. In order to be sustainable, the sustainability approach should be built into all the steps of the supply chain, from the supplier-selection phase to customer delivery and reverse logistics processes.

CONCLUSION

This study provides a guide for manufacturing facilities pursuing sustainable development plans via:

1. Analyzing energy consumption and integrating energy-aware approaches into classic production planning and scheduling decisions
2. Incorporating a sustainability framework into a medium-long term decision

Increasing the awareness of manufacturing corporations about the energy consumption breakdown helps them promote efficient utilization of equipment/machineries and eliminate non-value-added energy-consuming time intervals by adopting an energy-aware scheduling and planning system. It also assists them in identifying inefficient equipment, and proposing corrective actions to reduce energy and material requirements and waste. Learning about the energy profiles of the machines facilitates designing of a more effective scheduling system for production processes and maintenance plans, which in turn can yield significant financial savings, and reduce energy usage. Utilizing energy-aware approaches is the cheapest and fastest method in meeting global environmental concerns. As a result of energy monitoring and control in manufacturing systems, corporations can reduce their undesirable environmental impacts and energy requirements, save money, and improve their opportunities in competitive markets. Once energy-conscious policies are implemented, in the next step, organizations can think of other sustainability-based solutions to enhance their sustainability achievements. CO_2 recapture and storage systems for the purpose of power generation and/or utilizing renewable sources of energy are examples of these solutions. In order to achieve sustainable development, all the sustainability criteria from environmental, societal and business/economic pillars, should be integrated into various level decision-making problems, rather than only concentrating on the production-based processes. The proposed general sustainability-based framework in this chapter exemplifies how sustainability criteria can contribute to a medium-long term decision such as maintenance strategy selection problem. A similar approach can be followed for other types of decision-making problems in manufacturing.

REFERENCES

Abele, E., Schrems, S., Eisele, C., & Schraml, P. (2012). *Simulation-Based Assessment of the Energy Consumption of Manufacturing Processes. In Leveraging Technology for a Sustainable World* (pp. 375–379). Springer. doi:10.1007/978-3-642-29069-5_64

Al-Najjar, B., & Alsyouf, I. (2003). Selecting the most efficient maintenance approach using fuzzy multiple criteria decision making. *International Journal of Production Economics*, *84*(1), 85–100. doi:10.1016/S0925-5273(02)00380-8

Apostolos, F., Alexios, P., Georgios, P., Panagiotis, S., & George, C. (2013). Energy efficiency of manufacturing processes: A critical review. *Procedia CIRP*, *7*, 628–633. doi:10.1016/j.procir.2013.06.044

Bertolini, M., & Bevilacqua, M. (2006). A combined goal programming-AHP approach to maintenance selection problem. *Reliability Engineering & System Safety*, *91*(7), 839–848. doi:10.1016/j.ress.2005.08.006

Brundtland, G., Khalid, M., Agnelli, S., Al-Athel, S., Chidzero, B., Fadika, L., & Okita, S. (1987). *Our Common Future, Brundtland Report*. Oxford, UK: Oxford University Press.

Bryson, J. M. (2011). *Strategic planning for public and nonprofit organizations: A guide to strengthening and sustaining organizational achievement* (Vol. 1). John Wiley & Sons.

Chen, G., Zhang, L., Arinez, J., & Biller, S. (2013). Energy-efficient production systems through schedule-based operations. *IEEE Transactions on Automation Science and Engineering*, *10*(1), 27–37. doi:10.1109/TASE.2012.2202226

Duflou, J. R., Sutherland, J. W., Dornfeld, D., Herrmann, C., Jeswiet, J., Kara, S., & Kellens, K. et al. (2012). Towards energy and resource efficient manufacturing: A processes and systems approach. *CIRP Annals-Manufacturing Technology*, *61*(2), 587–609. doi:10.1016/j.cirp.2012.05.002

Elkington, J. (1994). Towards the sustainable corporation: Win-win-win business strategies for sustainable development. *California Management Review*, *36*(2), 90–100. doi:10.2307/41165746

Environmental Protection Agency. (n.d.). Retrieved December 9, 2015, from http://www3.epa.gov/ttn/atw/188polls.html

Ghazi Nezami, F., Yildirim, B., & Wang, P. (2012, May). *Sustainable Single-machine Scheduling Problem with Reliability and Energy Consumption.* Paper presented at the 2012 Industrial and Systems Engineering Research Conference proceeding, Orlando, FL.

Griffin, R. W. (2013). *Fundamentals of management*. Cengage Learning.

Gutowski, T., Dahmus, J., & Thiriez, A. (2006, May). *Electrical energy requirements for manufacturing processes.* Paper presented at the 13th CIRP international conference on life cycle engineering, Lueven.

Gutowski, T., Murphy, C., Allen, D., Bauer, D., Bras, B., Piwonka, T., & Wolff, E. et al. (2005). Environmentally benign manufacturing: Observations from Japan, Europe and the United States. *Journal of Cleaner Production*, *13*(1), 1–17. doi:10.1016/j.jclepro.2003.10.004

Helu, M., Rühl, J., Dornfeld, D., Werner, P., & Lanza, G. (2011). Evaluating Trade-Offs Between Sustainability, Performance, and Cost of Green Machining Technologies. In *Glocalized Solutions for Sustainability in Manufacturing* (pp. 195-200). Springer.

International Energy Agency. (2014a). *World Energy Outlook 2014*. Retrieved December 9, 2015, from http://www.iea.org/textbase/npsum/weo2014sum.pdf

International Energy Agency. (2014b). *Key World Energy Statistics 2014*. Retrieved December 9, 2015, from http://www.iea.org/publications/freepublications/publication/keyworld2014.pdf

Isaksson, R., & Garvare, R. (2003). Measuring sustainable development using process models. *Managerial Auditing Journal, 18*(8), 649–656. doi:10.1108/02686900310495142

Jafari, A., Jafarian, M., Zareei, A., & Zaerpour, F. (2008). Using Fuzzy Delphi Method in Maintenance Strategy Selection Problem. *Journal of Uncertain Systems, 2*(4), 289–298.

Jasiulewicz-Kaczmarek, M., & Drozyner, P. (2011). *Maintenance management initiatives towards achieving sustainable development. In Information Technologies in Environmental Engineering* (pp. 707–721). Springer.

Jayal, A., Badurdeen, F., Dillon, O. Jr, & Jawahir, I. (2010). Sustainable manufacturing: Modeling and optimization challenges at the product, process and system levels. *CIRP Journal of Manufacturing Science and Technology, 2*(3), 144–152. doi:10.1016/j.cirpj.2010.03.006

Kim, J.-H., Park, D.-H., Kim, J.-B., & Kwon, B.-H. (2007, October). *An active gate drive circuit for high power inverter system to reduce turn-off spike voltage of IGBT.* Paper presented at the 7th Internatonal Conference on Power Electronics, Daegu. doi:10.1109/ICPE.2007.4692362

Lussier, R. (2011). *Management fundamentals: Concepts, applications, skill development.* Cengage Learning.

Mechefske, C., & Wang, Z. (2003). Using fuzzy linguistics to select optimum maintenance and condition monitoring strategies. *Mechanical Systems and Signal Processing, 17*(2), 305–316. doi:10.1006/mssp.2001.1395

Mobley, R. (2002). *An introduction to predictive maintenance.* Butterworth-Heinemann.

Mohamed, A. R., & Lee, K. T. (2006). Energy for sustainable development in Malaysia: Energy policy and alternative energy. *Energy Policy, 34*(15), 2388–2397. doi:10.1016/j.enpol.2005.04.003

Mousavi, S., Nezami, F., Heydar, M., & Aryanejad, M. (2009, July). *A hybrid fuzzy group decision making and factor analysis for selecting maintenance strategy.* Paper presented in the International Conference on Computers & Industrial Engineering, Troyes. doi:10.1109/ICCIE.2009.5223824

Mouzon, G., Yildirim, M. B., & Twomey, J. (2007). Operational methods for minimization of energy consumption of manufacturing equipment. *International Journal of Production Research*, *45*(18-19), 4247–4271. doi:10.1080/00207540701450013

Nezami, F. G., & Yildirim, M. B. (2013). A sustainability approach for selecting maintenance strategy. *International Journal of Sustainable Engineering*, *6*(4), 332–343. doi:10.1080/19397038.2013.765928

Seow, Y., & Rahimifard, S. (2011). A framework for modelling energy consumption within manufacturing systems. *CIRP Journal of Manufacturing Science and Technology*, *4*(3), 258–264. doi:10.1016/j.cirpj.2011.03.007

U.S. Energy Information Administration. (n.d.). Retrieved December 9, 2015, from http://www.eia.gov/tools/faqs/faq.cfm?id=447&t=1

Vahdani, B., Hadipour, H., Sadaghiani, J. S., & Amiri, M. (2010). Extension of VIKOR method based on interval-valued fuzzy sets. *International Journal of Advanced Manufacturing Technology*, *47*(9), 1231–1239. doi:10.1007/s00170-009-2241-2

Vijayaraghavan, A., & Dornfeld, D. (2010). Automated energy monitoring of machine tools. *CIRP Annals-Manufacturing Technology*, *59*(1), 21–24. doi:10.1016/j.cirp.2010.03.042

Wang, L., Chu, J., & Wu, J. (2007). Selection of optimum maintenance strategies based on a fuzzy analytic hierarchy process. *International Journal of Production Economics*, *107*(1), 151–163. doi:10.1016/j.ijpe.2006.08.005

Yan, J., & Hua, D. (2010, December). *Energy consumption modeling for machine tools after preventive maintenance.* Paper presented at the IEEE International Conference on Industrial Engineering and Engineering Management (IEEM), Macao. doi:10.1109/IEEM.2010.5674578

Yildirim, M. B., & Mouzon, G. (2012). Single-machine sustainable production planning to minimize total energy consumption and total completion time using a multiple objective genetic algorithm. *IEEE Transactions on Engineering Management*, *59*(4), 585–597. doi:10.1109/TEM.2011.2171055

Yildirim, M. B., & Nezami, F. G. (2014). Integrated maintenance and production planning with energy consumption and minimal repair. *International Journal of Advanced Manufacturing Technology*, *74*(9-12), 1419–1430. doi:10.1007/s00170-014-5834-3

Zaim, S., Turkyilmaz, A., Acar, M. F., Al-Turki, U., & Demirel, O. F. (2012). Maintenance strategy selection using AHP and ANP algorithms: A case study. *Journal of Quality in Maintenance Engineering*, *18*(1), 16–29. doi:10.1108/13552511211226166

KEY TERMS AND DEFINITIONS

Energy Consumption: The actual amount of energy consumed by the company over a specific time period.

Job Scheduling: A practice to determine the optimal processing order of the jobs (products).

Maintenance: A process to sustain the reliability of the machine/equipment and reduce the risk of machine breakdown.

Makespan: A scheduling performance metric that measures the final length of the schedule and is equivalent to the time that the last product (job) leaves the system.

Multi-Criteria Decision Making: A selection process in the presence of various criteria to choose the best option among the available set of alternatives.

Production Planning: Planning the production in manufacturing system with respect to capacity and time constraints. The objective is mostly to minimize total production cost.

Sustainability: A concept that is focused on satisfying the present needs without compromising the needs of future generation and is based on three pillars of environment, society and economy.

Total Completion Time: A scheduling figure performance metric that measures the cumulative time the system is busy with job processing.

Compilation of References

Abele, E., Schrems, S., Eisele, C., & Schraml, P. (2012). *Simulation-Based Assessment of the Energy Consumption of Manufacturing Processes. In Leveraging Technology for a Sustainable World* (pp. 375–379). Springer. doi:10.1007/978-3-642-29069-5_64

Ahmad, F., Zayed, N. M., & Harun, M. A. (2013). Factors behind the adoption of green banking by Bangladeshi commercial banks. *ASA University Review*, *7*(2), 241–255.

Ahmed, S. (2001). *Poverty and microcredit: New realities and strategic issues.* Microcredit Operation Seminar. Bangladesh Bank.

Ahmed, S. (2009). Microfinance institutions in Bangladesh: Achievements and challenges. *Managerial Finance*, *35*(12), 999–1010. doi:10.1108/03074350911000052

Ahmed, S., & Rafi, B. M. (1999). NGOs and evaluation: the BRAC experience. *World Bank Conference on Evaluation and Poverty Reduction*, Washington, DC.

Alamgir, D. A. (2010). *State of Microfinance in Bangladesh.* Dhaka: Institute of Microfinance (InM). Retrieved from http://www.inm.org.bd/publication/state_of_micro/Bangladesh. pdf

Alexander, M. (2013). Management Planning for Nature Conservation, A Theoretical Basis & Practical Guide (2nd ed.). Springer eBooks.

Allan. (1994). *Stream Ecology*. Oxford.

Allan, D. (1994). *Stream Ecology*. Oxford.

Allenby, B. (2006). The ontologies of industrial ecology? *Progress in Industrial Ecology-An International Journal*, *3*(1/2), 28–40. doi:10.1504/PIE.2006.010039

Al-Najjar, B., & Alsyouf, I. (2003). Selecting the most efficient maintenance approach using fuzzy multiple criteria decision making. *International Journal of Production Economics*, *84*(1), 85–100. doi:10.1016/S0925-5273(02)00380-8

Andersen, M. S., & Massa, I. (2000). Ecological modernization — origins, dilemmas and future directions. Journal of Environmental Policy & Planning. *Journal of Environmental Policy and Planning*, *2*(4), 337–345. doi:10.1080/714852820

Andrei, J. V. (2013). Multifunctional Agriculture and the Green Economy. In I. Subic & D. Dusmanescu (Eds.), *Sustainable Technologies, Policies, and Constraints in the Green Economy*. doi:0.4018/978-1-4666-4098-6

Apostolos, F., Alexios, P., Georgios, P., Panagiotis, S., & George, C. (2013). Energy efficiency of manufacturing processes: A critical review. *Procedia CIRP*, *7*, 628–633. doi:10.1016/j.procir.2013.06.044

Armendáriz, B., & Morduch, J. (2010). *The Economics of Microfinance*. MIT Press.

Asadullah, M. N., Savoia, A., & Mahmud, W. (2014). Paths to development: Is there a Bangladesh surprise? *World Development*, *62*, 138–154. doi:10.1016/j.worlddev.2014.05.013

Atuya, G. N. (2014). *Effect of microfinance credit on poverty alleviation at household level in Nakuru county* (Doctoral dissertation). University of Nairobi.

Aziz, M. A. (2012). ASA: Hope for the poor. *ASA University Review*, *6*(2), 248–258.

Banking with the Poor Network. (2013). *Proshika*. Retrieved from <http://www.bwtp.org/arcm/Bangladesh/II_Organisations/Microfinance_Providers/PROSHIKA.html>

Barua, P. (2009). *Targeting the poorest in microfinance: Poverty outreach of BDP ultra poor programme*. esocialsciences.com Working Papers.

Bell, S., McGillivray, D., & Pedersen, O. W. (2013). *Environmental law* (8th ed.). Oxford, UK: Oxford University Press. doi:10.1093/he/9780199583805.001.0001

Bertolini, M., & Bevilacqua, M. (2006). A combined goal programming-AHP approach to maintenance selection problem. *Reliability Engineering & System Safety*, *91*(7), 839–848. doi:10.1016/j.ress.2005.08.006

Bonnard, P. (1999). *Increasing the Nutritional Impact of Agricultural Interventions*. Presented in The Greater Horn of Africa Regional Workshop: Agricultural Policy, Resource Access and Human Nutrition, Ethiopia. Retrieved from http://www.eldis.org/vfile/upload/1/document/0708/DOC7724.pdf

Brown. (1997). State of the World and our Resources. New York: W.W. Norton & Company.

Brundtland, G., Khalid, M., Agnelli, S., Al-Athel, S., Chidzero, B., Fadika, L., & Okita, S. (1987). *Our Common Future, Brundtland Report*. Oxford, UK: Oxford University Press.

Brunori, G. (2013). Biomass, Biovalue and Sustainability: Some Thoughts on the Definition of the Bioeconomy. *EuroChoices*, *12*(1), 48–52. doi:10.1111/1746-692X.12020

Bryman, A., & Bell, E. (2015). *Business Research Methods*. Oxford University Press.

Bryson, J. M. (2011). *Strategic planning for public and nonprofit organizations: A guide to strengthening and sustaining organizational achievement* (Vol. 1). John Wiley & Sons.

Bulgaru, M. (1996). *Dreptul de a mânca- Disparităţi mondiale si realităti româneşti*. Bucharest: Economic Publishing House.

Burkart, K. (2012). *How to define the green economy*. Available at: http://www.mnn.com/green-tech/researchinnovations/blogs/how-do-you-define-the-green-economy

Carayannis, E. G., & Campbell, D. F. (2009). Mode 3andQuadruple Helix: Toward a 21st century fractal innovation ecosystem. *International Journal of Technology Management*, *46*(3-4), 201–234. doi:10.1504/IJTM.2009.023374

Carter, N. (2007). *The politics of the environment: Ideas, activism, policy* (2nd ed.). Cambridge, UK: Cambridge University Press. doi:10.1017/CBO9780511819179

Cato, M. S. (2009). *Green Economics: An Introduction to Theory, Policy and Practice*. London: Earthscan.

Chemin, M. (2008). The benefits and costs of microfinance: Evidence from Bangladesh. *The Journal of Development Studies*, *44*(4), 463–484. doi:10.1080/00220380701846735

Chen, G., Zhang, L., Arinez, J., & Biller, S. (2013). Energy-efficient production systems through schedule-based operations. *IEEE Transactions on Automation Science and Engineering*, *10*(1), 27–37. doi:10.1109/TASE.2012.2202226

Chivu, L. (2002). *Competitivitatea în agricultură – analize şi comparaţii europene*. Bucharest: Expert Publishing House.

Committee on World Food Security. (2014). *Global Strategic Framework for Food Security & Nutrition* (3rd ed.). Retrieved from http://www.fao.org/cfs/cfs-home/global-strategic-framework/en/

Committee on World Food Security. (2014). *Principles for Responsible Investment in Agriculture and Food Systems*. International Agreement on Responsible Investment in Agriculture and Food Systems. Retrieved from http://www.fao.org/cfs/cfs-home-old/resaginv/en/

Constantza, R. (1997). The Development of Ecological Economics. London: Academic Press.

Constantza. (1996, October). Gross world product from International Monetary Fund (IMF). *World Economic Outlook.*

Constantza. (1997). *The Development of Ecological Economics*. London: Academic Press.

Constantza, R. (1996, October). Gross world product from International Monetary Fund (IMF). *World Economic Outlook.*

Croce, R. D., Kaminker, C., & Stewart, F. (2011). *The role of pension funds in financing green growth initiatives.* OECD Working Papers on Finance, Insurance and Private Pensions, No.10, OECD Publishing.

Daley-Harris, S. (2005). *State of the Microcredit Summit Campaign Report 2005.* Retrieved from http://www. microcreditsummit.org/pubs/reports/socr/2005/SOCR05.pdf

Deanna, J. R. (Ed.), *(n.d.). The Industrial Green Game: Implications for Environmental Design and Management.* Washington, DC: The National Academies Press; doi:10.17226/4982

Dobson, A. (2007). Environmental citizenship: Towards sustainable development. *Journal of Sustainable Development, 15*(5), 282–283.

Duflou, J. R., Sutherland, J. W., Dornfeld, D., Herrmann, C., Jeswiet, J., Kara, S., & Kellens, K. et al. (2012). Towards energy and resource efficient manufacturing: A processes and systems approach. *CIRP Annals-Manufacturing Technology, 61*(2), 587–609. doi:10.1016/j.cirp.2012.05.002

Duvendack, M., & Palmer-Jones, R. (2012). High noon for microfinance impact evaluations: Re-investigating the evidence from Bangladesh. *The Journal of Development Studies, 48*(12), 1864–1880. doi:10.1080/00220388.2011.646989

Elkington, J. (1994). Towards the sustainable corporation: Win-win-win business strategies for sustainable development. *California Management Review*, *36*(2), 90–100. doi:10.2307/41165746

Environmental Protection Agency. (n.d.). Retrieved December 9, 2015, from http://www3.epa.gov/ttn/atw/188polls.html

European Commission. (2014). *Action Plan for the future of Organic Production in the European Union*. COM(2014) 179 final. Author.

Eurostat. (2015). *Sustainable development in the European Union – 2015 monitoring report of the EU Sustainable Development Strategy*. Luxembourg: Publications Office of the European Union.

Fan, S., Ringler, C., Nkonya, E., & Stein, A. J. (2012). *Ensuring Food and Nutrition Security in a Green Economy*. IFPRI Policy Brief 21. Retrieved from http://www.ifpri.org/publication/ensuring-food-and-nutrition-security-green-economy

FAO Statistical Pocketbook. (2015). *Food and Agriculture Organization of the United Nations, Rome*. Retrieved from www.fao.org/3/a-i4691e.pdf

Food and Agriculture Organization of the United Nations & United Nations World Food Programme. (2009). *The State of Food Insecurity in the World 2009, Econmic crises – impacts and lessons lerned*. Rome: FAO. Retrieved from http://www.fao.org/docrep/012/i0876e/i0876e00.htm

Food and Agriculture Organization of the United Nations, International Fund for Agricultural Development, & United Nations World Food Programme. (2014). *The State of Food Insecurity in the World 2014. Strengthening the enabling environment for food security and nutrition.* Rome: FAO. Retrieved from http://www.fao.org/3/a-i4030e.pdf

Food and Agriculture Organization of the United Nations, International Fund for Agricultural Development, & United Nations World Food Programme. (2015). *The State of Food Insecurity in the World 2015. Meeting the 2015 international hunger targets: taking stock of uneven progress.* Rome: FAO. Retrieved from http://www.fao.org/3/a-i4646e.pdf

Food and Agriculture Organization of the United Nations. (2009). *Investing in food security*. Rome: FAO. Retrieved from https://www.responsibleagroinvestment.org/sites/responsibleagroinvestment.org/files/FAO_Investing%20in%20FS_2009.pdf

Food and Agriculture Organization of the United Nations. (2012). *Greening the Economy with Agriculture*. Swiss Confederation, FAO. Retrieved from www.fao.org/docrep/015/i2745e/i2745e00.pdf

Food and Agriculture Organization of the United Nations. (2014). *The State of Food and Agriculture 2014*. Rome: FAO. Retrieved from http://www.fao.org/3/a-i4036e.pdf

Fornell, C., & Larcker, D. F. (1981). Evaluating structural equation models with unobservable variables and measurement error. *JMR, Journal of Marketing Research*, *18*(1), 39–50. doi:10.2307/3151312

Fotabong, L.A. (2011). *Comparing microfinance models: MC2 model versus other microfinance model.* Available at SSRN 2007874

Frosch, R. A., & Gallopoulos, N. E. (1989). Strategies for Manufacturing. *Strategies for Manufacturing Scientific American.*, *261*(3), 144–152. doi:10.1038/scientificamerican0989-144

Gani, M. O. (2013, July 29). Green banking: Concept and policy guidelines. *The Financial Express*.

Gavrilescu, D., & Giurcă, D. (Eds.). (2001). Economie agroalimentară. Expert Publishing House.

Georgescu-Roegen, N. (1979). Legea entropiei si procesul economic. Publishing House Politică.

Gerring, J. (2007). *Case Study Research: Principles and Practices*. New York: Cambridge University Press.

Ghazi Nezami, F., Yildirim, B., & Wang, P. (2012, May). *Sustainable Single-machine Scheduling Problem with Reliability and Energy Consumption.* Paper presented at the 2012 Industrial and Systems Engineering Research Conference proceeding, Orlando, FL.

Gheorghe, I. G., & Sima, V. (2014). Transition to Green Economy in Romania. *Annals of the Constantin Brâncuşi, 3*, 32-39. Retrieved from http://eur-lex.europa.eu/legal-content/EN/TXT/PDF/?uri=CELEX:32008L0098&from=ROhttp://www.unep.fr/scp/cp/

Godquin, M. (2004). Microfinance repayment performance in Bangladesh: How to improve the allocation of loans by MFIs. *World Development*, *32*(11), 1909–1926. doi:10.1016/j.worlddev.2004.05.011

Griffin, R. W. (2013). *Fundamentals of management*. Cengage Learning.

Group of Twenty (G20). (2014). *Food Security and Nutrition Framework*. Retrieved from https://g20.org/wp-content/uploads/2014/12/g20_food_security_nutrition_framework.pdf

Gutowski, T., Dahmus, J., & Thiriez, A. (2006, May). *Electrical energy requirements for manufacturing processes*. Paper presented at the 13th CIRP international conference on life cycle engineering, Lueven.

Gutowski, T., Murphy, C., Allen, D., Bauer, D., Bras, B., Piwonka, T., & Wolff, E. et al. (2005). Environmentally benign manufacturing: Observations from Japan, Europe and the United States. *Journal of Cleaner Production*, *13*(1), 1–17. doi:10.1016/j.jclepro.2003.10.004

Hassan, M. K. (2002). The microfinance revolution and the Grameen Bank experience in Bangladesh. *Financial Markets. Institutions & Instruments*, *11*(3), 205–265. doi:10.1111/1468-0416.00051

Helu, M., Rühl, J., Dornfeld, D., Werner, P., & Lanza, G. (2011). Evaluating Trade-Offs Between Sustainability, Performance, and Cost of Green Machining Technologies. In *Glocalized Solutions for Sustainability in Manufacturing* (pp. 195-200). Springer.

Herren, H. R., Bassi, A. M., Tan, Z., & Binns, W. P. (2012). *Green Jobs for a Revitalized Food and Agriculture Sector*. Natural Resources Management and Environment Department, FAO. Retrieved from http://www.fao.org/fileadmin/user_upload/suistainability/pdf/FAO_green_jobs_paper_March_31.pdf. http://ec.europa.eu/eurostathttp://faostat3.fao.org/

Hossain, M. Z., & Ahmed, M. (2015). Green banking in Bangladesh. In Green Banking in Bangladesh and Beyond, (pp. 17-47). Zaman Printing and Packaging.

Hossain, M. Z., Ahmed, M., & Nisha, N. (2015). Consumer attitudes and perception towards green banking in Bangladesh. In Green Banking in Bangladesh and Beyond, (pp. 48-76). Zaman Printing and Packaging.

Hossain, M. Z., Jilani, S. N., & Haque, H. (2015). Islamic finance as a greener alternative. In Green Banking in Bangladesh and Beyond, (pp. 201-217). Zaman Printing and Packaging.

Hossain, M. Z., Rahim, M. A., & Hussain, T. (2015). The future of green banking in Bangladesh. In Green Banking in Bangladesh and Beyond, (pp. 77-88). Zaman Printing and Packaging.

Hulme, D., & Moore, K. (2006). *Why has Microfinance been a policy success in Bangladesh (and beyond)? Economic and Social Research Council (ESRC). Global Poverty Research Group*. GPRG.

Iacob, P. (2015a). Forests contribute to a new policy of sustainable rural development. *Annals of Dunărea de Jos*, 108-113.

Iacob, P. (2015b). The role of the forest ressources in the socioeconomic development of the rural area. In *Procedia Economics and Finance*. Science Direct.

Iacovoiu, V. (2009). *Investiţiile străine directe între teorie şi practică economică. Analize comparative*. Bucharest: ASE Publishing House.

Inderst, G., Kaminker, C., & Stewart, F. (2012). *Defining and measuring green investments: Implications for institutional investors' asset allocations*. OECD Working Papers on Finance, Insurance and Private Pensions, No.24, OECD Publishing.

International Energy Agency. (2014a). *World Energy Outlook 2014*. Retrieved December 9, 2015, from http://www.iea.org/textbase/npsum/weo2014sum.pdf

International Energy Agency. (2014b). *Key World Energy Statistics 2014*. Retrieved December 9, 2015, from http://www.iea.org/publications/freepublications/publication/keyworld2014.pdf

Isaksson, R., & Garvare, R. (2003). Measuring sustainable development using process models. *Managerial Auditing Journal*, *18*(8), 649–656. doi:10.1108/02686900310495142

Islam, M. T. (2015, May 26). Green banking and its present scenario in Bangladesh. *The Daily Observer*.

Islam, M. J., & Khair, R. (2012). Preparation of e-Government in Bangladesh: An exploratory analysis. *JU Journal of Information Technology*, *1*, 19–26.

Jafari, A., Jafarian, M., Zareei, A., & Zaerpour, F. (2008). Using Fuzzy Delphi Method in Maintenance Strategy Selection Problem. *Journal of Uncertain Systems*, *2*(4), 289–298.

Jain, P. S. (2007). *Maturing of microcredit movement: Some Pointers from ASA*. Dhaka: ASA.

Jasiulewicz-Kaczmarek, M., & Drozyner, P. (2011). *Maintenance management initiatives towards achieving sustainable development. In Information Technologies in Environmental Engineering* (pp. 707–721). Springer.

Jayal, A., Badurdeen, F., Dillon, O. Jr, & Jawahir, I. (2010). Sustainable manufacturing: Modeling and optimization challenges at the product, process and system levels. *CIRP Journal of Manufacturing Science and Technology*, *2*(3), 144–152. doi:10.1016/j.cirpj.2010.03.006

Johnson, R. B., Onwuegbuzie, A. J., & Turner, L. A. (2007). Toward a definition of mixed methods research. *Journal of Mixed Methods Research*, *1*(2), 112–133. doi:10.1177/1558689806298224

Jukes, M., McGuire, J., Method, F., & Sternberg, R. (2002). Nutrition and Education. In *Nutrition: A Foundation for Development*. Geneva: ACC/SCN. Retrieved from http://www.unscn.org/layout/modules/resources/files/Brief1-12EN.pdf

Kabeer, N., Mahmud, S., & Isaza Castro, J. G. (2010). NGOs' strategies and the challenge of development and democracy in Bangladesh. *IDS Working Papers*, *343*, 1-71.

Karim, L. (2011). *Microfinance and Its Discontents: Women in Debt in Bangladesh*. U of Minnesota Press. doi:10.5749/minnesota/9780816670949.001.0001

Khalily, M. A. (2004). Quantitative approach to impact analysis of microfinance programmes in Bangladesh - what have we learned? *Journal of International Development*, *16*(3), 331–353. doi:10.1002/jid.1081

Khandker, S. R. (1998). *Fighting Poverty with Microcredit: Experience in Bangladesh*. Oxford University Press.

Khandker, S. R. (2005). Microfinance and poverty: Evidence using panel data from Bangladesh. *The World Bank Economic Review*, *19*(2), 263–286. doi:10.1093/wber/lhi008

Kim, J.-H., Park, D.-H., Kim, J.-B., & Kwon, B.-H. (2007, October). *An active gate drive circuit for high power inverter system to reduce turn-off spike voltage of IGBT*. Paper presented at the 7th Internatonal Conference on Power Electronics, Daegu. doi:10.1109/ICPE.2007.4692362

Kumari, K. (1996, November). Sustinable Forest Management: Myth or Reality? Exploring the Prospects for Malaysia. *Ambio*.

Leikem, K. (2012). *Microfinance: A tool for poverty reduction?*. Senior Honors Projects. Paper 300.

Leopold, A. (1949). A Sound Country Almanac. Oxford.

Loiseau, E., Saikku, L., Antikainen, R., Leskinen, P., & Pitkänen, K. (2015). Conceptual framework and methodological tools used by green economy. In *Implementing the green economy in a European context – lessons learned from theories, concepts and case studies*. PEER Report. Helsinki: Partnership for European Environmental Research, Juvenes Print. Available at http://www.peer.eu/fileadmin/user_upload/publications/PEERreport_ImplementingTheGreenEconomy.pdf

Lussier, R. (2011). *Management fundamentals: Concepts, applications, skill development*. Cengage Learning.

Maanen, G. V. (2004). *Microfinance: Sound of Business or Development Instrument*. Voorburg.

Mallick, D. (2012). Microfinance and moneylender interest rate: Evidence from Bangladesh. *World Development*, *40*(6), 1181–1189. doi:10.1016/j.worlddev.2011.12.011

Masukujjaman, M., & Aktar, S. (2013). Green banking in Bangladesh: A commitment towards the global initiatives. *Journal of Business and Technology*, *8*(1&2), 17–40.

Masum, M. (2015). The need for Green banking in Bangladesh. In Green Banking in Bangladesh and Beyond, (pp. 3-16). Zaman Printing and Packaging.

Matei, M., Stancu, A., & Vukovic, P. (2009). *The interdependence between agriculture and climate change-a European perspective*. Paper presentato al 113th EAAE Seminar, Belgrado.

McDonnell, S. (1999). *The Grameen Bank micro-credit model: Lessons for Australian indigenous economic policy. Discussion paper, Centre for Aboriginal Economic Policy Research no. 178*. Canberra: Australian National University.

McIntosh, C., & Wydick, B. (2005). Competition and microfinance. *Journal of Development Economics*, *78*(2), 271–298. doi:10.1016/j.jdeveco.2004.11.008

Mechefske, C., & Wang, Z. (2003). Using fuzzy linguistics to select optimum maintenance and condition monitoring strategies. *Mechanical Systems and Signal Processing*, *17*(2), 305–316. doi:10.1006/mssp.2001.1395

Meyer, R. L. (2002). The demand for flexible microfinance products: Lessons from Bangladesh. *Journal of International Development*, *14*(3), 351–368. doi:10.1002/jid.884

Mia, M. B., & Ramage, M. (2011). *Overlapping and information systems in microcredit: A Bangladesh perspective*. In *Second European Research Conference on Microfinance*, Groningen, The Netherlands.

Mobley, R. (2002). *An introduction to predictive maintenance*. Butterworth-Heinemann.

Mohamed, A. R., & Lee, K. T. (2006). Energy for sustainable development in Malaysia: Energy policy and alternative energy. *Energy Policy*, *34*(15), 2388–2397. doi:10.1016/j.enpol.2005.04.003

Morduch, J. (1998). *Does Microfinance Really Help the Poor? New Evidence from Flagship Programs in Bangladesh. Research Program in Development Studies.* Woodrow School of Public and International Affairs.

Morduch, J. (1999). The role of subsidies in microfinance: Evidence from the Grameen Bank. *Journal of Development Economics*, *60*(1), 229–248. doi:10.1016/S0304-3878(99)00042-5

Mousavi, S., Nezami, F., Heydar, M., & Aryanejad, M. (2009, July). *A hybrid fuzzy group decision making and factor analysis for selecting maintenance strategy*. Paper presented in the International Conference on Computers & Industrial Engineering, Troyes. doi:10.1109/ICCIE.2009.5223824

Mouzon, G., Yildirim, M. B., & Twomey, J. (2007). Operational methods for minimization of energy consumption of manufacturing equipment. *International Journal of Production Research*, *45*(18-19), 4247–4271. doi:10.1080/00207540701450013

Myers, N. (1993). *The World's Forests: Problems and Potentials*. Corvallis, OR: Pacific Rivers Council.

Nezami, F. G., & Yildirim, M. B. (2013). A sustainability approach for selecting maintenance strategy. *International Journal of Sustainable Engineering*, *6*(4), 332–343. doi:10.1080/19397038.2013.765928

Nisha, N., Idrish, S., & Hossain, M. Z. (2015). Consumer acceptance and use of mobile banking services in Bangladesh. In Green Banking in Bangladesh and Beyond, (pp. 155-182). Zaman Printing and Packaging.

Nunnally, J. C., & Bernstein, I. H. (1994). *Psychometric Theory*. New York: McGraw-Hill.

Odum, E. (1993). *Ecology and our endangered life-support system*. Sunderland.

Organisation for Economic Co-operation and Development. (2011). *Towards Green Growth, OECD Green Growth Studies*. Paris: OECD Publishing; doi:10.1787/9789264111318-en

Organisation for Economic Co-operation and Development. (2014). *Green Growth Indicators 2014, OECD Green Growth Studies*. OECD Publishing.

Pimentel, D. (1997). L'écologie des fôrets. Ed. did. Paris.

Popescu, C. (1999). Protection and integration of the forest heritage of Romania-a problem of national and regional policy. The 24th Congress ARA, Liege.

Popescu, C. (2008). Stări conflictuale generate de exploatarea abuziva a pădurilor lumii. Editura Bibliotheca.

Popescu, C. (2008a). Stări conflictuale generate de exploatarea abuziva a pădurilor lumii. Editura Bibliotheca.

Popescu, C. (2008b). The growth of the forest ecosystems role for the defence of the environmental components. The 32nd Congress ARA, Boston, MA.

Popescu, C. (2011). La durabilité en qualité de nouveau projet civilisateur. 57éme Congrès "Refondation financière, sorties de crise et nouvelles stratégies de croissance économique, Croatia.

Popescu, C. (2011). La durabilité en qualité de nouveau projet civilisateur. 57éme Congrès "Refondation financière, sorties de crise et nouvelles stratégies de croissance économique", Croatia.

Popescu, C. (2012). *The Evaluation of Climate Change Risks*. The XIII th Annual International Conference Risk In Contemporary Economy, Galaţi.

Popescu, C. (2014). *Reconsidering the Relationship Between Socio-Economic System and Natural Environment*. The 2nt International Conference ESPERA 2014 – Economic Scientific Research Theoretical, Empirical and Practical Approaches organizată de National Institute for Economic Research, Bucharest, România

Popescu, C. (2014). *Sustainable development in impase*. Internation Multidisciplinary Scientific Geo Conference, Albena, Bulgaria.

Popescu, C. (2015). *Le développement durable en tant que concept multidimensionnel*. Le 59ème Congrés de l'AIELF Croissance, population, protection sociale. Faits et theories face aux enjeux", Paris, France.

Popescu. (2004). *Economia protecţiei mediului*. Editura Bibliotheca.

Popescu. (2008a). *Creşterea rolului ecosistemelor forestiere pentru apărarea componentelor de medius*. Al 32-lea Congres ARA, Boston, MA.

Popescu. (2008b). *Stări conflictuale generate de exploatarea abuziva a pădurilor lumii.* Editura Bibliotheca.

Popescu. (2008c). *Conflicting states generated by the operation abusive forest world.* Editura Bibliotheca.

Popescu. (2008d). *Managementul mediului.* UVT University Press.

Popescu. (2009). Carbon is the key. *Conference Proceedings of the Academy of Romanian Scientist.* Editura Academiei Oamenilor de Ştiinţă din România, Bucureşti.

Popescu, C. (2003). *Economia protectiei mediului.* Târgovişte: Editura Bibliotheca.

Rahman, M. W., Luo, J., Ahmed, S., & Xiaolin, W. (2012). The synthesis of Grameen Bank, BRAC and ASA microfinance approaches in Bangladesh. *World Applied Sciences Journal, 20*(7), 1055–1062.

Roy, J. K. (2015a, August 1). Green stocks: Green investment, green return. *The Financial Express.*

Roy, J. K. (2015b, July 15). Promoting green businesses in Bangladesh. *The Financial Express.*

Rudrabhatla, R., Roy, S., & Bose, S. K. (2015). Role of microfinance and microfinance institutions model in improving quality of life: A critical review. *International Journal of Engineering, Business and Enterprise Applications, 12*(1), 70–76.

Sarder, M.M.R., & Golzare, N. (2012). *Dynamics of Micro Finance Programs in Poverty Alleviation in Bangladesh: Present Status, Challenges and Policy Actions.* Research Report. Bangladesh Bank.

Saunders, M. N., Saunders, M., Lewis, P., & Thornhill, A. (2011). *Research Methods for Business Students.* Pearson Education India.

Scherhorn, G. (1997). *Discuţiile de la Toblach* [The Discussions of Toblach]. Academic Press.

Schweisfurth, K. L. (2014). *Der Metzger, der kein Fleisch mehr isst Oekom Verlag.* München.

Seow, Y., & Rahimifard, S. (2011). A framework for modelling energy consumption within manufacturing systems. *CIRP Journal of Manufacturing Science and Technology, 4*(3), 258–264. doi:10.1016/j.cirpj.2011.03.007

Shakil, M. H., Azam, M. K. G., & Raju, M. S. H. (2014). An evaluation of green banking practices in Bangladesh. *European Journal of Business and Management, 6*(31), 8–16.

Shil, N. C. (2009). Micro finance for poverty alleviation: A commercialized view. *International Journal of Economics and Finance, 1*(2), 191–205. doi:10.5539/ijef.v1n2p191

Sima, V., & Gheorghe, I. (2009). *Eco-Efficiency – A Romanian Perspective.* The 12th IBIMA Conference, "Creating Global Economies through Innovation and Knowledge Management", Kuala Lumpur, Malaysia.

Sima, V., & Gheorghe, I. G. (2014). Analyze of environmental performance in Romania based on environmental performance index. *Annals of the Constantin Brâncuşi, 3*, 101-104.

Sima, V., & Gheorghe, I. G. (2014). Labour market trends in România in the context of green economy. *Annals of the Constantin Brâncuşi*, 116-123. Retrieved from http://www.utgjiu.ro/revista/ec/pdf/2014-04.Special/22_Sima,%20Gheorghe.pdf

Stahel, W. R. (1997). The Functional Economy: Cultural and Organizational Change. In Cultura civică şi dreptul antreprenorial. Editura Lumina Lex.

Stancu, A. (2015). An Analysis of the Relation Between Wine Consumption and Cultural Models. *Economics of Agriculture, 62*(1), 207-227. Retrieved from http://www.ea.bg.ac.rs/index.php/home/2-uncategorised/39-archive-2015-1

The Financial Express (2015, February 15). BB to create $500m fund for green industries. *The Financial Express.*

U.S. Energy Information Administration. (n.d.). Retrieved December 9, 2015, from http://www.eia.gov/tools/faqs/faq.cfm?id=447&t=1

Ullah, M. M. (2013). Green banking in Bangladesh – A comparative analysis. *World Review of Business Research, 3*(4), 74–83.

United Nations Department of Economic and Social Affairs, United Nations Development Programme, United Nations Conference on Trade and Development. (2012). *The Transition to a Green Economy: Benefits, Challenges and Risks from a Sustainable Development Perspective.* Retrieved from http://www.unep.org/greeneconomy/Portals/88/documents/research_products/UN-DESA,%20UNCTAD%20Transition%20GE.pdf

United Nations Department of Economic and Social Affairs. (2011). *World Population Prospects: The 2010 Revision*. Retrieved from https://dl.vecnet.org/files/xs55mc11m

United Nations Department of Economic and Social Affairs. (2012). *A guidebook to the Green Economy*. Retrieved from www.uncsd2012.org

United Nations Development Programme. (2002). *Millennium Development Goals: Goals and Indicators*. UNDP. Retrieved from http://mdgs.un.org/unsd/mdg/host.aspx?Content=indicators/officiallist.htm

United Nations Economic and Social Council, Economic Commission for Europe (UNECE). (2011). *A green economy in the context of sustainable development and poverty eradication*. Retrieved from http://www.unece.org/fileadmin/DAM/env/documents/2011/ece/e.ece.rpm.2011.4.e.pdf

United Nations Environment Programme. (2009). *Agriculture: A Catalyst for Transitioning to a Green Economy: A UNEP Brief*. Retrieved from www. unep.org/greeneconomy

United Nations Environment Programme. (2011). *Green Economy. Agriculture. Investing in natural capital*. Retrieved from http://www.unep.org/greeneconomy/Portals/88/documents/ger/2.0_Agriculture.pdf

United Nations Environment Programme. (2011). *Towards a Green Economy: Pathways to Sustainable Development and Poverty Eradication*. Retrieved from www.unep.org/greeneconomy

United Nations Environment Programme. (2013). *Green Economy and Trade. Agriculture*. Retrieved from http://www.unep.org/greeneconomy/portals/88/getreport/pdf/chapitre%202%20agriculture.pdf

United Nations. (2000). *Millennium Development Declaration, Resolution No. 55/2*. Retrieved from http://www.un.org/millennium/declaration/ares552e.htm

United Nations. (2015). *The Millennium Development Goals Report*. Retrieved from http://www.un.org/millenniumgoals/reports.shtml

United States Agency for International Development. (1992). *Policy Determination, Definition of food security*. USAID. Retrieved from http://pdf.usaid.gov/pdf_docs/Pnaav468.pdf

Vădineanu, A. (1998). *Sustainable development*. Press University of Bucharest.

Vahdani, B., Hadipour, H., Sadaghiani, J. S., & Amiri, M. (2010). Extension of VIKOR method based on interval-valued fuzzy sets. *International Journal of Advanced Manufacturing Technology*, *47*(9), 1231–1239. doi:10.1007/s00170-009-2241-2

Vijayaraghavan, A., & Dornfeld, D. (2010). Automated energy monitoring of machine tools. *CIRP Annals-Manufacturing Technology*, *59*(1), 21–24. doi:10.1016/j.cirp.2010.03.042

Wahid, A. N. M. (1994). The Grameen Bank and poverty alleviation in Bangladesh: Theory, evidence and limitations. *American Journal of Sociology*, *53*(1), 1–15.

Wang, L., Chu, J., & Wu, J. (2007). Selection of optimum maintenance strategies based on a fuzzy analytic hierarchy process. *International Journal of Production Economics*, *107*(1), 151–163. doi:10.1016/j.ijpe.2006.08.005

Webb, P., & Rogers, B. (2003). *Adressing the "in" in Food Security*. USAID Office of Food for Peace, Occasional Paper no.1. Retrieved from http://www.fantaproject.org/focus-areas/food-security/addressing-in-food-insecurity-ffp-op1

Wind in Power. (2015). *European Statistics: The European Wind Energy Association*. Retrieved May 24 2016 from https://windeurope.org/wp-content/uploads/files/about-wind/statistics/EWEA-Annual-Statistics-2015.pdf

World Food Summit. (1996). *Declaration on World Food Security*. Retrieved from http://www.fao.org/docrep/003/w3613e/w3613e00.htm

World Health Organization. (2015). *Food Security*. Retrieved from http://www.who.int/trade/glossary/story028/en/

Yan, J., & Hua, D. (2010, December). *Energy consumption modeling for machine tools after preventive maintenance*. Paper presented at the IEEE International Conference on Industrial Engineering and Engineering Management (IEEM), Macao. doi:10.1109/IEEM.2010.5674578

Yildirim, M. B., & Mouzon, G. (2012). Single-machine sustainable production planning to minimize total energy consumption and total completion time using a multiple objective genetic algorithm. *IEEE Transactions on Engineering Management*, *59*(4), 585–597. doi:10.1109/TEM.2011.2171055

Yildirim, M. B., & Nezami, F. G. (2014). Integrated maintenance and production planning with energy consumption and minimal repair. *International Journal of Advanced Manufacturing Technology*, *74*(9-12), 1419–1430. doi:10.1007/s00170-014-5834-3

Yin, R. K. (2009). *Case Study Research: Design and Methods*. London: Sage Publications.

Yuge, Y. (2011). *The Current Situation of Microfinance in Bangladesh: A Growing Concern about Overlapping Loan Problems–From a Field Visit to Rajshahi and Comilla. Student Research Series*. The Fletcher School, Tufts University.

Yunus, M. (1998). Poverty alleviation: Is economics any help? Lessons from the Grameen Bank experience. *Journal of International Affairs*, *52*(1), 47–65.

Zaim, S., Turkyilmaz, A., Acar, M. F., Al-Turki, U., & Demirel, O. F. (2012). Maintenance strategy selection using AHP and ANP algorithms: A case study. *Journal of Quality in Maintenance Engineering*, *18*(1), 16–29. doi:10.1108/13552511211226166

Zaman, M. (2013). Achievement and problems of microfinance of two leading MFIs in Bangladesh: A case study of GB and ASA. *ASA University Review*, *7*(2), 183–198.

About the Contributors

Mihai Mieila, PhD, is associate professor at Department of Accounting, Finance and Banks, Faculty of Economic Sciences from "Valahia" University of Targoviste. Regarding his education, he holds a PhD in Investments Management granted by Bucharest Academy of Economic Studies in 2007, is MBA graduated of Conservatoire National des Arts & Métiers Paris in 2004, and MA in Financial and Insurances Management at "Valahia" University of Targoviste (2001). He is member of Editorial Boards of: International Journal of Sustainable Economies Management (USA); Supply Chain Management Journal; Valahian Journal of Economic Studies; and Revue Valaque des Etudes Economiques. He is member of scientific organizations: CEDIMES Institute in Paris, European Association of Agricultural Economists in Hague (2008), and founder member of The Balkan Scientific Association of Agrarian Economists (Serbia, 2007). His area of expertise is investments management and econometrics where he published five books, journal articles (over 20), and conference presentations and deployed teaching missions within the European Program Erasmus.

* * *

Corina Ene currently holds the position of PhD Associate Professor at the Petroleum-Gas University of Ploiesti (Romania), Faculty of Economics, within the Business Administration Department. Her actual occupational field is: Education, Teaching and Research. Corina Ene graduated in 1998 as a Bachelor of Economic Sciences at Petroleum-Gas University of Ploiesti, in the field of Science of Commodities. In 1999 she became a Bachelor of Advanced Studies in Quality Management, at Bucharest University of Economic Studies. In 2006 she obtained the Academic title of Doctor in Economics (Science of Commodities) at Bucharest University of Economic Studies. The doctoral dissertation topic was: "The impact of food security in the elaboration of nutrition and food policies". During the last years, she attended several training courses in different areas of interest. Her work experience derives from and includes: teaching courses and seminaries; co-coordinating students' graduation papers; research activities; participating in scientific conferences; participating as editor of a scientific publication included in relevant international databases; reviewer for several international scientific journals and conferences. Regarding research activities, these are represented by publishing over 30 scientific papers in the field of interest: science of commodities, consumer protection; 4 books – three as co-author; two as single author; and participating in over 10 national and international scientific conferences.

Farnaz Ghazi Nezami is an Assistant Professor in the Industrial and Manufacturing Engineering Department at Kettering University, Flint, MI. She holds a Ph.D. in Industrial and Manufacturing Engineering from Wichita State University, KS. She is a Certified Six Sigma Green Belt (CSSGB) from the American Society for Quality (ASQ) and has received the Industrial Assessment certification from the Department of Energy (DOE). Her research interests include sustainability, applied optimization, operations management, energy efficiency, and engineering education.

Ali Ghazinezami is a PhD student in Mechanical Engineering at Wichita State University. Research interests include Sustainability, Composite/Nanocomposite, Design, manufacturing, testing of composites and nanocomposites, and Numerical and analytical modeling of composites and nanocomposites.

Ileana Georgiana Gheorghe holds the position of Associate Professor in the Department of Business Administration, Faculty of Economics, Petroleum-Gas University of Ploiesti Romania. She obtained a Ph.D. in Economics from Bucharest University of Economic Studies. She has published about 50 international papers in outstanding journals (h-index 8), 3 book chapters in an edited book and 2 authored books, being interested in Human Resources Management, Green Economics, and Social Responsibility. She also participated in research projects in the field Human Resources Development.

Maria-Luiza Hrestic is lecturer at the Faculty of Sciences and Engineering from "Valahia" University of Târgovişte – Romania. She holds a Ph.D in Law, specialized in General Theory of Law, grated by the Institute of Legal Researches "Acad. Andrei Rădulescu" from the Romanian Academy of Bucharest, in 2011. Also she deployed post-doctoral research at the same institution, where she graduated in 2015. During her post-doctoral studies, two of her articles, entitled: "The Value of Interpretation in Law" and "Specific features of the interpretation of law" were awarded by the Romanian Academy in Bucharest. During the Bachelor studies (2004-2005), based on a national copmetition she earned a scholarship granted by the Romanian Government (the National Office of Scholarships for Studies Abroad) at the Lausanne University – Switzerland, where she got a "Diploma of Advanced Studies in European Law and International Economic Law". She is a member of: the Centre for Researches in Social Sciences within "Valahia" University of Târgovişte; the "Romanian Society of European Law"; the "Romanian Association of Penal Sciences"; "Centre d'Etudes du Développement International et des Mouvements Economiques et Sociaux» – CEDIMES – France; the "Dâmboviţa Legal Advisers College". She wrote 3 books (two as single author and one as co-author) and she has 57 articles/studies (as single author and co-author) published in ISI Journals, journals with recognized prestige in legal sciences or journals indexed in recognized international data bases.

Silvia Elena Iacob (born in 22 January 1985 in Targoviste) is Associate Professor at Academy of Economic Studies, Bucharest, Faculty Theoretical and Applied Economics, Chair of Communication and Economic Doctrines. She took her BS in Economy and Economic Communication, Faculty of General Economy, Academy of Economic Studies, Bucharest, in 2007. She also took her BS in Economie, Management juridique, Management financier, Diagnostic economique et financier, Communication, Analyse de gestion (Economy, Juridical management, Financial management, Economic and financial diagnosis, Communication, Administration analysis) at Universite d'Auvergne Clermont Ferrand, Institut Universitaire Professionnalisé, France, where she graduated: Duma 1, Duma 2, Licence, Master I, Master II Specialization: Management and corporate management in 2008. She holds PhD in Economic sciences at Academy of Economic Studies, Bucharest in 2011. Iacob Silvia Elena finished Postdoctoral Studies in Economic Sciences at Academy of Economic Studies, Bucharest in 2015. She is also a member of following professional associations: AIELF (International Association of Economists of Francaises Languages), CEDIMES (Development Centre International and Economic and Social Movements, Franta), ARSR (ROMANIAN ASSOCIATION OF REGIONAL SCIENCE), ERSA (European Regional Science Association) and RSAI (Regional Science Association Inaternational). Her area of expertise is economics, communication and sustainable development where she published books (5), Journal articles (60) and presentations by national and international conferences.

Krishna Krishnan is a professor of the Industrial & Manufacturing Engineering Department at Wichita State University. His research is the area of manufacturing systems. He primarily works in facilities planning, supply chain systems, production planning and integrated manufacturing systems.

Mirela Matei currently holds the position of PhD Associate Professor at the Petroleum-Gas University of Ploiesti (Romania), Faculty of Economics, within the Cybernetics, Computer Science Economy, Finance and Accounting Department. Her actual occupational field is: Education, Teaching and Research. From 2012, she is the vice dean of Faculty of Economics. Mirela Panait graduated in 1996 as a Bachelor of Economic Sciences at Bucharest University of Economic Studies, in field of International Business and Economics. In 2004, she obtained the Academic title of Doctor in Economics at Romanian Academy. The title of doctoral thesis was "The role o foreign investment in Romanian transition economy". In 2013, she completed postdoctoral studies at Romanian Academy. The postdoctoral dissertation topic was: "Social responsibility of corporations and institutions and Romanian sustainable development". Her work experience derives from and includes: teaching courses and seminaries; co-coordinating students' graduation papers; research activities; participating in scientific conferences; reviewer for several international scientific journals and conferences. Regarding research activities, these are represented by publishing seven books and over 90 scientific papers in the field of interest: foreign investment, capital market, social responsibility and sustainable development.

Nabila Nisha is currently teaching as a Senior Lecturer at the Department of Accounting & Finance under School of Business and Economics of North South University. She completed her Bachelor's degree with dual concentration in Accounting & Finance and Marketing from North South University, Bangladesh. She received her Master's degree in Banking & Finance from University of Essex, UK. Besides teaching, she has been part of a research project on Green Banking financed by World Bank and Ministry of Education of Bangladesh. Her research interests include technology acceptance models, banking sector, accounting disclosures, empirical research methods in finance and business case studies. She has a number of international journal publications in USA, UK and India, along with local and international book chapters as part of her research work. She has authored two books as well, which have been published by Lambert Academic Publishing and are available in the international market.

Contanta Popescu graduated in Management and holds a Postgraduate Degree from Bucharest University of Economic Studies. Also, she holds a Executive Diploma in Management at Conservatoire National des Arts et Métiers in Paris and a PhD in Management at Dunarea de Jos University of Galati. Currently she is Full Professor and PhD conductor in Management at the Valahia University of Targoviste. She deployed a remarkable publishing activity, with eighteen books and book chapters in Romania and abroad; more than 140 scientific articles in press; over 120 papers presentations at internal and international scientific events (in: France, Spain, Italy,

Germany, Belgium, Poland, Great Britain, Lithuania, Croatia, Macedonia, Serbia, Slovakia, Egypt, Tunisia, Algeria, USA, and Canada); in 27 research projects (national and international) she has been director, coordinator, expert and research team member. She is a member of: CEDIMES Institute and l'Association Internationale des Economistes de Langue Française (AIELF) in Paris; The Romanain Association of Faculties in Economics; and of the Center of Applied Researches and Studies in Management and Marketing from the "Valahia" University of Târgovişte.

Constantin Popescu graduated in Forestry Engineering from Transylvania University of Brasov – Faculty of Forestry and Forest Engineering. He holds a Ph.D in the field Sylviculture and Forestry Management (Transylvania University of Brasov - 2002). Currently he is Director in Sylviculture Department, and Associate Professor at Valahia University of Targoviste, Romania, having competences such as: Sustainable Development in Forestry, Environment Management, economy of the environmental protection, economy of natural resources, management of protected areas. He published over 50 articles in journals, magazines and volumes resulting from conferences and presented over 45 articles at scientific international conferences in France, Spain, Canada, the U.S.A, Serbia, Poland, Belgium, Croatia and Romania. He is a single-author of three books and co-author of three other. In the same time, he is member in twelve research projects; member of CEDIMES, AIELF and of the Centre for research and expertise of natural resources and environment at "Valahia" University of Targoviste.

Afrin Rifat is a Lecturer of Accounting & Finance at the School of Business of North South University. Since September 2012, Ms. Rifat has been teaching introductory courses of Financial Accounting, Managerial Accounting and Cost Accounting at the undergraduate level. Ms. Rifat earned her Bachelor of Business Administration (BBA) degree with major in finance and accounting and minor in economics from North South University, Bangladesh and Master's Degree in Banking and Finance from University of Essex, UK in 2010 and 2011, respectively. Her current research interests include technology acceptance models, accounting policies, financial statement analysis and decision-making, banking strategies, capital market, and empirical research methods in finance and country specific studies.

Ana-Lucia Ristea graduated from the Academy of Economic Studies, Bucharest, Faculty of Commerce, in 1969. In 1987 she graduated her PhD in Economics at the Academy of Economic Studies, Bucharest. Currently she is full Professor at "Valahia" University of Targoviste, Faculty of Economic Sciences. Her scientific research activity (starting with 1969 to present) consist in 33 books (as a single-author, co-author or coordinator), courses and monographies, over 100 articles published in specialized journals and/or presented at the international and national scientific conferences, and eight national research projects (as a director and coordinator). She is a member of: CEDIMES, AROMAR and the Center for researches and studies in Management and Marketing, from "Valahia" University of Targoviste.

Violeta Sima holds the position of Associate Professor in the Department of Business Administration, Faculty of Economics, Petroleum-Gas University of Ploiesti Romania. She obtained a Ph.D. in Economic Cybernetics and Statistics from Bucharest University of Economic Studies. She has published about 55 international papers in outstanding journals (h-index 10), 3 book chapters in edited books and 4 authored books. Her research and teaching interests encompass Customer Relationship Management, Marketing Research, Business to Business Marketing, Green Marketing, and Social Responsibility. She has participated in research projects in the field of Marketing and Human Resources Development.

Marian Catalin Voica currently holds the position of Professor Assistant at the Petroleum-Gas University of Ploiesti (Romania), Faculty of Economics, within the Cybernetics, Computer Science Economy, Finance and Accounting Department. His actual occupational field is: Education, Teaching and Research. Marian Catalin Voica graduated in 2008 as a Bachelor of Economic Sciences at Petroleum-Gas University of Ploiesti, in the field of Accounting and Management Information Systems. In 2011 he became a Bachelor of Advanced Studies in management and funding of development projects, at the Petroleum-Gas University of Ploiesti. He obtained the Academic title of Doctor in Economics (Finance) at Bucharest University of Economic Studies. The doctoral dissertation topic was: "The impact of foreign investments on production costs". During the last year of his doctoral studies he received a scholarship from the European Social Fund through Sectoral Operational Programme Human Resources Development 2007-2013, project number POSDRU/159/1.5/S/134197 "Performance and excellence in doctoral and postdoctoral research in Romanian economics science domain". His work experience derives from and includes: teaching courses and seminaries; research activities; participating in scientific conferences; reviewer for several international scientific journals. Regarding research activities, these are represented by publishing 11 scientific papers in the field of interest: finance, financial markets, sustainable development, green investments and participating in 5 national and international scientific conferences.

Index

www.ingramcontent.com/pod-product-compliance
Lightning Source LLC
LaVergne TN
LVHW061536290926
849162LV00004B/812
* 9 7 8 1 5 2 2 5 2 0 8 1 8 *